More information about this series at http://www.springer.com/series/7408

Raghunath Nambiar · Meikel Poess (Eds.)

Performance Evaluation and Benchmarking: Traditional to Big Data to Internet of Things

7th TPC Technology Conference, TPCTC 2015
Kohala Coast, HI, USA, August 31 – September 4, 2015
Revised Selected Papers

 Springer

Editors
Raghunath Nambiar
Cisco Systems, Inc.
San Jose, CA
USA

Meikel Poess
Oracle Corporation
Redwood City, CA
USA

ISSN 0302-9743   ISSN 1611-3349   (electronic)
Lecture Notes in Computer Science
ISBN 978-3-319-31408-2   ISBN 978-3-319-31409-9   (eBook)
DOI 10.1007/978-3-319-31409-9

Library of Congress Control Number: 2016934030

LNCS Sublibrary: SL2 – Programming and Software Engineering

Printed on acid-free paper

This Springer imprint is published by Springer Nature
The registered company is Springer International Publishing AG Switzerland

Preface

The Transaction Processing Performance Council (TPC) is a non-profit organization established in August 1988. Over the years, the TPC has had a significant impact on the computing industry's use of industry-standard benchmarks. Vendors use TPC benchmarks to illustrate performance competitiveness for their existing products, and to improve and monitor the performance of their products under development. Many buyers use TPC benchmark results as points of comparison when purchasing new computing systems.

The information technology landscape is evolving at a rapid pace, challenging industry experts and researchers to develop innovative techniques for evaluation, measurement, and characterization of complex systems. The TPC remains committed to developing new benchmark standards to keep pace with these rapid changes in technology. One vehicle for achieving this objective is the TPC's sponsorship of the Technology Conference Series on Performance Evaluation and Benchmarking (TPCTC) established in 2009. With this conference series, the TPC encourages researchers and industry experts to present and debate novel ideas and methodologies in performance evaluation, measurement, and characterization.

This book contains the proceedings of the 7th TPC Technology Conference on Performance Evaluation and Benchmarking (TPCTC 2015), held in conjunction with the 40th International Conference on Very Large Data Bases (VLDB 2015) in Kohala Coast, Hawaii, USA, from August 31 to September 4, 2014, including eight selected peer-reviewed papers, a keynote, and a vision paper.

The hard work and close cooperation of a number of people contributed to the success of this conference. We would like to thank the members of the TPC and the organizers of VLDB 2015 for their sponsorship; the members of the Program Committee and Publicity Committee for their support; and the authors and the participants who are the primary reason for the success of this conference.

February 2016   Raghunath Nambiar
                                                                    Meikel Poess

TPCTC 2015 Organization

General Chairs

Raghunath Nambiar   Cisco, USA
Meikel Poess   Oracle, USA

Program Committee

Chaitanya Baru	SDSC, USA
Daniel Bowers	Gartner, USA
Michael Brey	Oracle, USA
Paul Cao	HP, USA
Alain Crolotte	Teradata, USA
Akon Dey	University of Sydney, Australia
Harumi Kuno	HP Labs, USA
Dhabaleswar Panda	The Ohio State University, USA
Tilmann Rabl	University of Toronto, Canada
Reza Taheri	VMWare, USA
Marco Vieira	University of Coimbra, Portugal
Francois Raab	Infosizing, USA
Yanpei Chen	Cloudera, USA
Berni Schiefer	IBM, Canada

Publicity Committee

Raghunath Nambiar	Cisco, USA
Andrew Bond	Red Hat, USA
Andrew Masland	NEC, USA
Meikel Poess	Oracle, USA
Reza Taheri	VMware, USA
Michael Majdalany	L&M Management Group, USA
Forrest Carman	Owen Media, USA
Andreas Hotea	Hotea Solutions, USA

About the TPC

Introduction to the TPC

The Transaction Processing Performance Council (TPC) is a non-profit organization that defines transaction processing and database benchmarks and distributes vendor-neutral performance data to the industry. Additional information is available at http://www.tpc.org/.

TPC Memberships

Full Members

Full Members of the TPC participate in all aspects of the TPC's work, including development of benchmark standards and setting strategic directions. The full-member application can be found at http://www.tpc.org/information/about/app-member.asp.

Associate Members

Certain organizations may join the TPC as associate members. Associate members may attend TPC meetings, but are not eligible to vote or hold office. Associate membership is available to non-profit organizations, educational institutions, market researchers, publishers, consultants, governments, and businesses that do not create, market, or sell computer products or services. The associate member application can be found at http://www.tpc.org/information/about/app-assoc.asp.

Academic and Government Institutions

Academic and government institutions are invited join the TPC and a special invitation can be found at http://www.tpc.org/information/specialinvitation.asp.

Contact the TPC

TPC
Presidio of San Francisco
Building 572B (surface)
P.O. Box 29920 (mail)
San Francisco, CA 94129-0920
Voice: 415-561-6272
Fax: 415-561-6120
E-mail: info@tpc.org

How to Order TPC Materials

All of our materials are now posted free of charge on our website. If you have any questions, please feel free to contact our office directly or by e-mail at info@tpc.org.

Benchmark Status Report

The TPC Benchmark Status Report is a digest of the activities of the TPC and its technical subcommittees. Sign-up information can be found at the following URL: http://www.tpc.org/information/about/email.asp.

TPC 2015 Organization

Full Members

Actian	MapR
Cisco	Microsoft
Cloudera	NEC
Dell	Oracle
Fujitsu	Pivotal
HP Enterprise	Red Hat
Hitachi	SAP
Huawei	Teradata
IBM	Unisys
Inspur	VMware
Intel	

Associate Members

IDEAS International
ITOM International Co.
San Diego Super Computing Center
Telecommunications Technology Association
University of Coimbra, Portugal

Steering Committee

Michael Brey (Oracle)
Matthew Emmerton (HP)
Raghunath Nambiar (Cisco)
Jamie Reding (Microsoft)
Wayne Smith (Intel), Chair

Public Relations Committee

Andrew Bond (Red Hat)
Raghunath Nambiar (Cisco), Chair
Andrew Masland (NEC)
Meikel Poess (Oracle)
Reza Taheri (VMware)

Technical Advisory Board

Andrew Bond (Red Hat)
Paul Cao (HP)
Matthew Emmerton (IBM)
John Fowler (Oracle)
Andrew Masland (NEC)
Jamie Reding (Microsoft), Chair
Wayne Smith (Intel)

Contents

Reinventing the TPC: From Traditional to Big Data to Internet of Things

Raghunath Nambiar[1([X])] and Meikel Poess[2]

[1] Cisco Systems, Inc., 275 East Tasman Drive, San Jose, CA 95134, USA
rnambiar@cisco.com
[2] Oracle Corporation, 500 Oracle Parkway, Redwood Shores, CA 94065, USA
meikel.poess@oracle.com

Abstract. The Transaction Processing Performance Council (TPC) has made significant contributions to the industry and research with standards that encourage fair competition to accelerate product development and enhancements. Technology disruptions are changing the industry landscape faster than ever. This paper provides a high level summary of the history of the TPC and recent initiatives to make sure that it is a relevant organization in the age of digital transformation fueled by Big Data and the Internet of Things.

Keywords: Database benchmarks · Big data · Internet of things

1 Reinventing the TPC

The Transaction Processing Performance Council (TPC) was formed in 1988, as a non-profit corporation focused on defining database processing benchmarks and disseminating objective, verifiable performance data to the IT industry. Over the years the TPC has gained the reputation of providing the most credible performance results to the industry often referenced in a role of consumer reports for the computing industry. The most critical contribution of the TPC has been providing the industry with a solid foundation for complete, system-level performance and methodologies for calculating the total price and price for performance.

Over the years the TPC has changed its mission – to define transaction-processing benchmarks (when founded in 1988), to defining transaction processing benchmarks and database benchmarks (1999) and to defining data-centric benchmarks (2015) inline with industry trends.

The first set of benchmark standards were focused on transaction processing. Later standards were developed for decision support systems addressing industry demands until the late 1990s, but the TPC was unable to address the rapidly changing industry landscape in the early part of the last decade with the emergence of virtualization, cloud, energy efficiency, etc. The main challenges were very long benchmark development cycles, unable to reach consensus on standards, failed benchmark standards due to lack of traction from the industry and industry consolidation of member companies [1, 2].

© Springer International Publishing Switzerland 2016
R. Nambiar and M. Poess (Eds.): TPCTC 2015, LNCS 9508, pp. 1–7, 2016.
DOI: 10.1007/978-3-319-31409-9_1

In 2009, the TPC initiated a set of initiatives to reinvent itself. The first major initiative was the International Technology Conference Series on Performance Evaluation and Benchmarking to bring industry experts and researcher to accelerate benchmark developments [3–8]. The second major initiative was the TPC Express benchmark initiative where benchmarks based on predefined, executable kits can be rapidly deployed and measured [8, 9]. The third major initiative is developing a set of benchmarks for emerging areas such as big data, analytics and Internet of Things [8, 22].

2 TPC Benchmark Timelines

To date, the TPC has approved a total of thirteen independent benchmarks. Of these benchmarks, TPC-C, TPC-H, TPC-E, TPC-DS, TPC-VMS, TPC-DI and TPCx-HS are currently active. TPC-VMC, TPCx-V, TPC-DS 2.0. TPCx-BB and TPC-IoTare under development. The timelines are shown in Fig. 1.

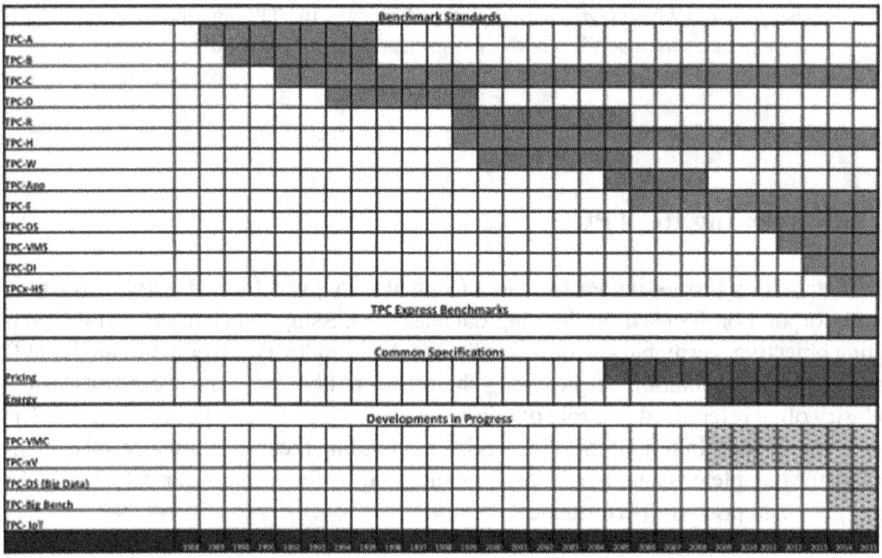

Fig. 1. TPC Benchmark Timelines

A high level summary of current active standards are listed below:

- TPC-C: An On-Line Transaction Processing (OLTP). It has been TPC's foundational and flagship benchmark with several hundreds of result publications across a variety of hardware and software systems. Historical analysis shows that the performance and price performance trend of TPC-C results has followed Moore's Law [10, 11].
- TPC-H: An ad-hoc, decision support benchmark widely popular in the industry and academia. Vendors continue to publish results on single node configurations as well as large scale-out configurations [12].

- TPC-E: An On-line Transaction Processing (OLTP) workload simulates the workload of a brokerage firm. It has been a popular benchmark but odate all publications have been on one database platform and on single node configurations [13].
- TPC-DS: A complex decision support benchmark representative of modern decision support systems. TPC took several years to develop this benchmark and reach consensus approving it as a standard. No official publications as of date. TPC-DS 2.0 is under development, one major change is loosening the relational database properties to support emerging platforms like Hadoop [14–16].
- TPC-VMS: A Single system virtualization benchmark leveraging TPC-C, TPC-E, TPC-H and TPC-DS benchmarks by adding the methodology and requirements for running and reporting performance metrics for virtualized databases [17].
- TPC-DI: Data Integration (also known as ETL) benchmark combines and transforms data extracted from a brokerage firm's OLTP system along with other sources of data, and loads it into a data warehouse. No official publications as of date [18].
- TPCx-HS: Industry's first big data benchmark standard, also TPC's first benchmark in the TPC Express benchmark category. Modeled on a simple application, the standard is highly relevant to hardware and software dealing with Big Data systems in general. There have been over a dozen results publications till date [19, 20].

A high level summary of standards under development are listed below:

- TPC-VMC: A complex virtualization benchmarkfor database workloads [21].
- TPC-DS 2.0: A complex and comprehensive benchmark built on TPCDS 1.0 supporting emerging platforms like Hadoop. Industry's first standard for SQL based Big Data systems [14–16].
- TPCx-BB: A comprehensive Big Data benchmark in the TPC Express benchmark category leveraging existing workloads including TPC-DS, TPCx-HS, HiBench, etc. [20].
- TPC-IoT: A new committee with the mission of exploring standards for Internet of Things workloads [22].

3 TPCTC Conference Series

To keep pace with these rapid changes in technology, in 2006, the TPC initiated the conference series on performance analysis and benchmarking. The TPCTC has been challenging Industry experts and researchers to develop innovative techniques for performance evaluation, measurement, and characterization of hardware and software systems. Over the years it has emerged as a leading forum to present and debate the latest and greatest in the world of benchmarking. The topics of interest included:

- Big Data
- Data Analytics
- Cloud Computing
- In-memory databases
- Social media infrastructure
- Security

- Complex event processing
- Internet of Things
- Database Optimizations
- Disaster tolerance and recovery
- Energy and space efficiency
- Hardware innovations
- Hybrid workloads
- Virtualization
- Lessons learned in practice
- Enhancements to TPC workloads
- Data Integration

A short summary of TPCTC conference proceedings are listed below.

The first TPC Technology Conference on Performance Evaluation and Benchmarking (TPCTC 2009) was held in conjunction with the 35th International Conference on Very Large Data Bases (VLDB 2009) in Lyon, France from August 24th to August 28th, 2009. The keynote speaker was Michael Stonebraker. [1, 3]

The second TPC Technology Conference on Performance Evaluation and Benchmarking (TPCTC 2010) was held in conjunction with the 36th International Conference on Very Large Data Bases (VLDB 2010) in Singapore from September 13th to September 17th, 2010. The keynote speaker was C. Mohan. [4]

The third TPC Technology Conference on Performance Evaluation and Benchmarking (TPCTC 2011) was held in conjunction with the 37th International Conference on Very Large Data Bases (VLDB 2011) in Seattle, Washington from August 29th to September 3rd, 2011. The keynote speaker was Umeshwar Dayal. [5, 23]

The fourth TPC Technology Conference on Performance Evaluation and Benchmarking (TPCTC 2012) was held in conjunction with the 38th International Conference on Very Large Data Bases (VLDB 2012) in Istanbul, August 27th to August 31st, 2012. The keynote speaker was Michael Carey. [6, 24]

The fifth TPC Technology Conference on Performance Evaluation and Benchmarking (TPCTC 2013) was held in conjunction with the 39th International Conference on Very Large Data Bases (VLDB 2013) in Riva del Garda, Trento, Italy, August 26th to August 30st, 2013. The keynote speaker was Raghu Ramakrishnan. [7]

The sixth TPC Technology Conference on Performance Evaluation and Benchmarking (TPCTC 2014) was held in conjunction with the 40th International Conference on Very Large Data Bases (VLDB 2014) in Hangzhou, China, September 1st to September 5th, 2014. [8]

TPCTC has had significant positive impact to the TPC. TPC is able to attract new members from industry and academia to join the TPC. The formation of the Workshop Series on Big Data Benchmark (WBDB) was inspired by TPCTC [26]. TPCTC also triggered development of benchmark standards in virtualization, data integration and Big Data. The formation of a working group on IoT was a direct result of TPCTC conferences.

4   Big Data and the Internet of Things [25]

Industry and technology landscapes are changing rapidly. Two of the technologies that will change the world in the next decade years are expected to be Big Data and the Internet of things (IoT).

Big Data: Big Data is a popular term now that describes the exponential growth of data, often defined by the 5Vs, associated technologies like storage, and how to effectively process and drive business values. The Big Data technology and services market represents one of the fast-growing, multi-billion dollar, worldwide market that is expected to grow to a $60 billion marke, driving $300 billion in worldwide IT spending directly or indirectly by 2020.

Foreseeing the importance, in 2014 the TPC developed the TPC Express Benchmark HS (TPCx-HS) to provide the industry with verifiable performance, price-performance, and availability metrics of hardware and software systems dealing with Big Data. This standard can be used to assess a broad range of system topologies and implementation of Hadoop systems in a technically rigorous and directly comparable, and vendor-neutral manner. This is the first major step while the TPC continues to enhance and develop new standards in this area such as TPC-DS with support for Hadoop and TPC-Big Bench.

Internet of Things (IoT): IoT has emerged in the last few years, poised to transform virtually every major market segment which contains a complex mix of technologies and products, from data collection and data curation to complex analytics exploiting the data generated by an exploding number of connected devices. According to IDC, the global IoT market will grow from $665 billion in 2014 to $1.7 trillion in 2020. To put that in perspective, it's an absolutely enormous figure; only 16 economies in the world had gross domestic products exceeding $1 trillion in 2014.

As the IoT ecosystem evolves in the enterprises, it is eminent to have a set of standards that enable effective comparison of hardware and software systems and topologies in a technology and vendor-neutral manner. Continuing its commitment to bring relevant standards to the industry, today the TPC announced the formation of the TPC-IoT benchmark committee, tasked with developing industry standard benchmarks for benchmarking hardware and software platforms associated with IoT [25].

5   Outlook and Acknowledgements

Over the last few years the TPC has truly reinvented itself by investing in the Technology Conference Series, Express benchmark initiatives, and new areas including Big Data and the Internet of Things. TPC remains committed to developing relevant standards in collaboration with industry and research communities, and to continue to enable fair comparison of technologies and products in terms of performance, cost of ownership and energy efficiency.

Developing benchmark standards requires a huge effort to conceptualize, research, specify, review, prototype, and verify the benchmark. The authors acknowledge the work and contributions of past and present members of the TPC.

References

1. Stonebraker, M.: A new direction for TPC? In: Nambiar, R., Poess, M. (eds.) TPCTC 2009. LNCS, vol. 5895, pp. 11–17. Springer, Heidelberg (2009)
2. Nambiar, R., Poess, M.: Keeping the TPC relevant! PVLDB **6**(11), 1186–1187 (2013). Nambiar, R., Wakou, N., Masland, A., Thawley, P., Lanken, M., Carman, F., Majdalany, M.: Shaping the Landscape of Industry Standard Benchmarks: Contributions of the Transaction Processing Performance Council (TPC), TPCTC 2011, pp. 1–9
3. Nambiar, R., Poess, M.: Performance Evaluation and Benchmarking. LNCS, vol. 5895. Springer, Heidelberg (2009). ISBN 978-3-642-10423-7
4. Nambiar, R., Poess, M.: Performance Evaluation, Measurement and Characterization of Complex Systems. LNCS, vol. 6417. Springer, Heidelberg (2011). ISBN 978-3-642-18205-1
5. Nambiar, R., Poess, M.: Topics in Performance Evaluation, Measurement and Characterization. LNCS, vol. 7144. Springer, Heidelberg (2012). ISBN 978-3-642-32626-4
6. Nambiar, R., Poess, M.: Selected Topics in Performance Evaluation and Benchmarking. LNCS, vol. 7755. Springer, Heidelberg (2013). ISBN 978-3-642-36726-7
7. Nambiar, R., Poess, M.: Performance Characterization and Benchmarking. LNCS, vol. 8391. Springer, Heidelberg (2014). ISBN 978-3-319-04935-9
8. Nambiar, R., Poess, M.: Performance Characterization and Benchmarking. Traditional to Big Data. LNCS, vol. 8904. Springer, Heidelberg (2015). ISBN 978-3-319-15349-0
9. Huppler, K., Johnson, D.: TPC express – a new path for TPC benchmarks. In: Nambiar, R., Poess, M. (eds.) TPCTC 2013. LNCS, vol. 8391, pp. 48–60. Springer, Heidelberg (2014)
10. Nambiar, R., Poess, M.: Transaction performance vs. Moore's law: a trend analysis. In: Nambiar, R., Poess, M. (eds.) TPCTC 2010. LNCS, vol. 6417, pp. 110–120. Springer, Heidelberg (2011)
11. TPC-C Specification
12. TPC-H Specification
13. TPC-E Specification
14. TPC-DS Specification
15. Nambiar, R., Poess, M.: The making of TPC-DS. In: VLDB 2006, pp. 1049–1058 (2006)
16. Nambiar, R., Poess, M.: Why you should run TPC-DS: a workload analysis. In: VLDB 2007, pp. 1138–1149 (2007)
17. TPC-VMS Specification
18. TPC-xHS Specification
19. Nambiar, R., Poess, M., Dey, A., Cao, P., Magdon-Ismail, T., Qi Ren, D., Bond, A.: Introducing TPCx-HS: the first industry standard for benchmarking big data systems. In: Nambiar, R., Poess, M. (eds.) TPCTC 2014. LNCS, vol. 8904, pp. 1–12. Springer, Heidelberg (2015)
20. Chaitanya, K., et al.: Discussion of BigBench: a proposed industry standard performance benchmark for big Data. In: Nambiar, R., Poess, M. (eds.) TPCTC 2014. LNCS, vol. 8904, pp. 44–63. Springer, Heidelberg (2015)
21. Bond, A., Johnson, D., Kopczynski, G., Taheri, H.: Architecture and performance characteristics of a PostgreSQL implementation of the TPC-E and TPC-V workloads. In: Nambiar, R., Poess, M. (eds.) TPCTC 2013. LNCS, vol. 8391, pp. 77–92. Springer, Heidelberg (2014)
22. Nambiar, R.: Vendor-neutral benchmarks drive tech innovation. http://data-informed.com/vendor-neutral-benchmarks-drive-tech-innovation/

23. Dayal, U., Wilkinson, K., Simitsis, A., Castellanos, M., Paz, L.: Optimization of analytic data flows for next generation business intelligence applications. In: Nambiar, R., Poess, M. (eds.) TPCTC 2011. LNCS, vol. 7144, pp. 46–66. Springer, Heidelberg (2012)
24. Carey, M.J., Ling, L., Nicola, M., Shao, L.: EXRT: towards a simple benchmark for XML readiness testing. In: Nambiar, R., Poess, M. (eds.) TPCTC 2010. LNCS, vol. 6417, pp. 93–109. Springer, Heidelberg (2011)
25. Nambiar, R.: Benchmarking Internet of Things (IoT). http://blogs.cisco.com/datacenter/industry-standards-for-benchmarking-iot
26. Baru, C., Bhandarkar, M., Nambiar, R., Poess, M., Rabl, T.: Benchmarking big data systems and the big data top 100 list

Pocket Data: The Need for TPC-MOBILE

Oliver Kennedy$^{(\boxtimes)}$, Jerry Ajay, Geoffrey Challen, and Lukasz Ziarek

University at Buffalo, Buffalo, NY 14260, USA
{okennedy,jerryant,challen,ziarek}@buffalo.edu
http://odin.cse.buffalo.edu/research/

Abstract. Embedded database engines such as SQLite provide a convenient data persistence layer and have spread along with the applications using them to many types of systems, including interactive devices such as smartphones. Android, the most widely-distributed smartphone platform, both uses SQLite internally and provides interfaces encouraging apps to use SQLite to store their own private structured data. As similar functionality appears in all major mobile operating systems, embedded database performance affects the response times and resource consumption of billions of smartphones and the millions of apps that run on them—making it more important than ever to characterize smartphone embedded database workloads. To do so, we present results from an experiment which recorded SQLite activity on 11 Android smartphones during one month of typical usage. Our analysis shows that Android SQLite usage produces queries and access patterns quite different from canonical server workloads. We argue that evaluating smartphone embedded databases will require a new benchmarking suite and we use our results to outline some of its characteristics.

Keywords: Sqlite · Client-side · Android · Smartphone · Embedded database

1 Introduction

The world's 2 billion smartphones represent the most powerful and pervasive distributed system ever built. Open application marketplaces, such as the Google Play Store, have resulted in a vibrant software ecosystem comprising millions of smartphone and tablet apps in hundreds of different categories that both meet existing user needs and provide exciting novel capabilities. As mobile apps and devices become even more central to the personal computing experience, it is increasingly important to understand and improve their performance.

A common requirement of mobile apps and systems is persisting structured private data, a task that is frequently performed using an *embedded database* such as SQLite [18]. Android, the open-source and widely-used smartphone platform, provides interfaces that simplify the process of accessing private SQLite databases, and many apps make use of SQLite for this purpose. In addition, Android platform services themselves make heavy use of SQLite, as do built-in

© Springer International Publishing Switzerland 2016
R. Nambiar and M. Poess (Eds.): TPCTC 2015, LNCS 9508, pp. 8–25, 2016.
DOI: 10.1007/978-3-319-31409-9_2

apps (Mail, Contacts), popular apps (Gmail, Maps), and libraries (Google Play Services) distributed by Google. As a result, the large and growing number of mobile apps using embedded databases represent a new and important class of database clients.

Unsurprisingly, mobile app usage of embedded databases is quite different from the workloads experienced by database servers supporting websites or big data applications. For example, while database servers are frequently tested and tuned for continuous high-throughput query processing, embedded databases experience lower-volume but bursty workloads produced by interactive use. As another example, enterprise database servers are frequently provisioned to have exclusive access to an entire machine, while apps using embedded databases compete for shared system resources with other apps and may be affected by system-wide policies that attempt to conserve limited energy on battery-constrained mobile devices. So while the fundamental challenges experienced by mobile apps using embedded databases—minimizing energy consumption, latency, and disk utilization—are familiar ground for database researchers, the specific tradeoffs produced by this domain's specific workload characteristics are far less well understood.

In this paper, we present results drawn from a one-month trace of SQLite activity on 11 PHONELAB [16] smartphones running the Android smartphone platform. Our analysis shows that the workloads experienced by SQLite on these phones differ substantially from the database workloads expressed by popular database benchmarking suites. We argue that a new benchmark for mobile embedded databases is required to effectively measure their performance, and that such a benchmark could spur innovation in this area.

Our specific contributions are as follows: (a) A month-long trace of SQLite usage under real world conditions (details in Sect. 2), (b) An in-depth analysis of the complexity (Sect. 3) and runtime (Sect. 4) characteristics of SQL statements evaluated by SQLite during this trace, (c) A comparison of these characteristics to existing benchmarking strategies (Sect. 5), and (d) An overview of the requirements for a new "pocket data" benchmark: TPC-MOBILE (Sect. 6).

2   Experimental Setup

To collect and analyze SQLite queries generated by Android, we used the unique capabilities of the PHONELAB smartphone platform testbed located at the University at Buffalo (UB). Approximately 200 UB students, faculty, and staff use instrumented LG Nexus 5 smartphones as their primary device and receive discounted service in return for providing data to smartphone experiments. PHONELAB participants are balanced between genders and distributed across ages, and thus representative of the broader smartphone user population. PHONELAB smartphones run a modified version of the Android Open Source Platform (AOSP) 4.4.4 "KitKat" including instrumentation and logging developed in collaboration with the mobile systems community. Participating smartphones log experimental results which are uploaded to a central server when the device is charging.

We instrumented the PHONELAB AOSP platform image to log SQLite activity by modifying the SQLite source code and distributing the updated binary library as an over-the-air (OTA) platform update to PHONELAB participants. Our logging recorded each SQL statement that was executed, along with its resulting runtime and the number of rows returned as appropriate. All current PHONELAB instrumentation including our SQLite logging statements are documented at https://phone-lab.org/experiment/data/. To protect participant privacy, our instrumentation removes as much personally-identifying information as possible, as well as recording prepared statement arguments only as hash values.

Our trace data-set is drawn from publicly-available data provided by 11 PHONELAB developers who willingly released[1] complete trace data for their phones for March 2015. Of the eleven participants, seven had phones that were participating in the SQLite experiment every day for the full month, with the remaining phones active for 1, 3, 14, and 19 days. A total of 254 phone/days of data were collected including 45,399,550 SQL statements. Of these, we were unable to interpret 308,752 statements (∼0.5 %) due to a combination of data corruption and the use of unusual SQL syntax. Results presented in this paper that include SQL interpretation are based on the 45,090,798 queries that were successfully parsed.

3   Query Complexity

In this section we discuss the query complexity we observed during our study and illustrate typical workloads over pocket data. Figure 1 summarizes all 45 million statements executed by SQLite over the 1 month period. As might be expected, SELECT forms almost three quarters of the workload by volume. UPSERT statements (*i.e.*, INSERT OR REPLACE) form a similarly substantial 16 % of the workload — more than simple INSERT and UPDATE statements combined. Also of note is a surprising level of complexity in DELETE statements, many of which rely on nested sub-queries when determining which records to delete.

Figure 2 shows the 10 most frequent and 10 least frequent clients of SQLite over the one month trace. The most active SQLite clients include internal Android services that broker access to data shared between apps such as personal media, calendars, and address books; as well as pre-installed and popular social media apps. There is less of a pattern at the low end, although several infrequent SQLite clients are themselves apps that may be used only infrequently, especially on a phone-sized device. We suspect that the distribution of apps would differ significantly for a tablet-sized device.

3.1   Database Reads

Of the 45 million queries analyzed, 33.47 million were read-only SELECT queries. Figure 3 shows the distribution of SELECT queries by number of tables accessed by

---

[1] https://phone-lab.org/static/experiment/sample_dataset.tgz.

Operation	SELECT	INSERT	UPSERT	UPDATE	DELETE	Total
Count	33,470,310	1,953,279	7,376,648	1,041,967	1,248,594	45,090,798
Runtime (ms)	1.13	2.31	0.93	6.59	3.78	
Features Used						
OUTER JOIN	391,052				236	391,288
DISTINCT	1,888,013			25	5,586	1,893,624
LIMIT	1,165,096				422	1,165,518
ORDER BY	3,168,915				194	3,169,109
Aggregate	638,137			25	3,190	641,352
GROUP BY	438,919			25		438,944
UNION	13,801				65	13,866

Fig. 1. Types and numbers of SQL statements executed during the trace, and query features used in each.

Client App	Statements Executed		Client App	Statements Executed
Google Play services	14,813,949		Weather	12
Media Storage	13,592,982		Speedtest	11
Gmail	2,259,907		KakaoStory	8
Google+	2,040,793		MX Player Pro	4
Facebook	1,272,779		Quickoffice	4
Hangouts	974,349		VLC	4
Messenger	676,993		Barcode Scanner	2
Calendar Storage	530,535		Office Mobile	2
User Dictionary	252,650		PlayerPro	2
Android System	237,154		KBS kong	2
(a)			(b)	

Fig. 2. Apps that executed the (a) 10 most and (b) 10 fewest SQL statements.

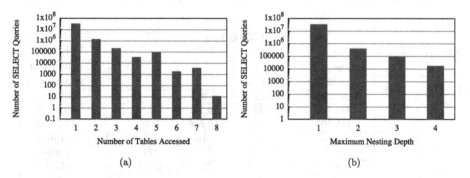

(a)   (b)

Fig. 3. SELECT queries by (a) number of tables accessed and (b) maximum nesting depth.

the query, as well as the maximum level of query nesting. Nesting includes from-nesting (*e.g.*, SELECT ... FROM (SELECT ...)), as well as expression-nesting (*e.g.*, SELECT ... WHERE EXISTS (SELECT ...)). Even at this coarse-grained view of query complexity, the read-only portion of the embedded workload distinguishes itself from existing TPC benchmarks.

Like TPC-C [6], the vast majority of the workload involves simple, small requests for data that touch a small number of tables. 29.15 million, or about 87 % of the SELECT queries were simple select-project-join queries. Of those, 28.72 million or about 86 % of all queries were simple single-table scans or look-ups. In these queries, which form the bulk of SQLite's read workload, the query engine exists simply to provide an iterator over the relationally structured data it is being used to store. Conversely, the workload also has a tail that consists of complex, TPC-H-like [8] queries. Several hundred thousand queries involve at least 2 levels of nesting, and over a hundred thousand queries access 5 or more tables. As an extreme example, our trace includes 10 similar SELECT queries issued by the Google Play Games Service[2], each of which accesses up to 8 distinct tables to combine developer-provided game state, user preferences, device profile meta-data, and historical game-play results from the user.

Simple SELECT Queries. We next examine more closely a class of *simple look-up* queries, defined as any SELECT query that consists exclusively of selections, projections, joins, limit, and order by clauses, and which does not contain any nested sub-queries or unions. Figure 4 shows queries of this class, broken down by the number of tables involved in the query (Join Width) and the complexity of the where clause, as measured in number of conjunctive terms (Where Clauses). For example, consider a query of the form: SELECT R.A FROM R, S WHERE R.B = S.B AND S.C = 10 This query would have a join width of 2 (R, S) and 2 conjunctive terms (R.B = S.B and S.C = 10). For uniformity, NATURAL JOIN and JOIN ON (*e.g.*, SELECT R.A from R JOIN S ON B) expressions appearing in the FROM clause are rewritten into equivalent expressions in the WHERE clause.

	Join Width					
Where Clauses	1	2	3	4	6	**Total**
0	1,085,154					**1,085,154**
1	26,932,632	9,105				**26,941,737**
2	1,806,843	279,811	5,970			**2,092,624**
3	384,406	80,183	29,101	1		**493,691**
4	115,107	70,891	10,696	939		**197,633**
5	28,347	15,061	1,162	17	11	**44,598**
6	212	524	591	471	3	**1,801**
7	349	22,574	333	1,048	8	**24,312**
8	35	18			6	**59**
9		541	2,564	4		**3,109**
10	159					**159**
11	545					**545**
Total	**30,353,789**	**478,708**	**50,417**	**2,480**	**28**	**30,885,422**

Fig. 4. Number of simple look-up queries subdivided by join width (number of tables) and number of conjunctive terms in the WHERE clause.

---

[2] https://developers.google.com/games/services/.

Expression Type	Expression Form	Count
Exact Lookups	Const = Expr	26,303,579
Membership Test	Expr [NOT] IN (List)	331,788
Inequality on 1 constant	Const θ Expr	93,816
Patterned String Lookup	Expr [NOT] LIKE Pattern	72,289
Disjunction	[NOT] Expr $\vee$ Expr	61,541
Other Inequality	Expr θ Expr	38,714
Validity Test	Expr IS [NOT] NULL	17,305
No-op Clause	Const or (Const = Const)	6,710
Boolean Column Cast	[NOT] Column	5,358
Other Equality	Expr = Expr	1,471
Function Call	Function(Expr)	43
Range Test	Expr BETWEEN Const AND Const	18

Fig. 5. The WHERE clause structure for single-tabled simple lookup queries with a single conjunctive term in the WHERE clause.

The first column of this table indicates queries to a single relation. Just over 1 million queries were full table scans (0 where clauses), and just under 27 million queries involved only a single conjunctive term. This latter class constitutes the bulk of the simple query workload, at just over 87 % of the simple look-up queries. Single-clause queries appear to be the norm. Recall that an N-way equi-join requires N-1 conjunctive terms; Spikes occur in the number of queries with one more term than strictly required to perform a join, suggesting a constraint on at least one relation.

Narrowing further, we examine simple look-up queries referencing only a single source table and a single conjunctive term in the WHERE clause. Figure 5 summarizes the structure of the predicate that appears in each of these queries. In this figure, constant terms (Const) are any primitive value term (*e.g.*, a quoted string, an integer, or a float), or any JDBC-style parameter (?). For simple relational comparators, we group together *in*equalities (*i.e.*, $<$, $\leq$, $>$, $\geq$ and $\neq$) under the symbol θ, and explicitly list equalities. Other relational operators such as LIKE, BETWEEN, and IN are also seen with some frequency. However, the majority (85 % of all simple look-ups) are exact match look-ups. Not surprisingly, this suggests that the most common use-case for SQLite is as a relational key-value store. As we show shortly through a per-app analysis of the data (Sect. 3.1), 24 out of the 179 apps that we encountered posed no queries other than exact look-ups and full table scans.

Other SELECT Queries. Figure 6 shows a similar breakdown for all 33.5 million SELECT queries seen. As before, the table shows the form of all expressions that appear as one of the conjunctive terms of a WHERE clause, alongside the number of queries where the expression appears at least once. 31.0 million of these queries contain an exact lookup. 1.6 million queries contain at least one multi-attribute equality expression such as an equi-join constraint, lining up nicely with the 1.7 million queries that reference at least two tables.

Expression Type	Expression Form	Count
Exact Lookups	Const = Expr	30,974,814
Other Equality	Expr = Expr	1,621,556
Membership Test	Expr [NOT] IN (List or Query)	1,041,611
Inequality on 1 constant	Const θ Expr	677,259
Disjunction	[NOT] Expr $\vee$ Expr	631,404
Bitwise AND	Expr & Expr	480,921
Other Inequality	Expr θ Expr	442,164
Boolean Column Cast	[NOT] Column	302,014
No-op Clause	Const or (Const = Const)	229,247
Patterned String Lookup	Expr [NOT] LIKE Pattern	156,309
Validity Test	Expr IS [NOT] NULL	87,873
Functional If-Then-Else	CASE WHEN ...	2,428
Range Test	Expr BETWEEN Const AND Const	2,393
Function Call	Function(Expr)	1,965
Subquery Membership	[NOT] EXISTS (Query)	1,584

Fig. 6. WHERE clause expression structures, and the number of SELECT queries in which the structure appears as a conjunctive clause.

App developers make frequent use of SQLite's dynamic typing: Where clauses include bare column references (*e.g.*, WHERE A, implicitly equivalent to WHERE A <> 0) as well as bare bit-wise AND expressions (*e.g.*, A&0xc4). This latter predicate appearing in a half-million queries suggests extensive use of bit-arrays packed into integers.

Functions. Functions extend the basic SQL syntax, providing for both specialized local data transformations, as well as computation of aggregate values. Figure 7 shows all functions appearing in SELECT queries during our trace, organized by the number of times that each function is used. All functions that we saw are either built-in SQLite functions, or in the case of PHONE_NUMBERS_EQUAL are Android-specific extensions; No user-defined functions appeared in the trace.

Overall, the most common class of function was aggregate functions (*e.g.*, SUM, MAX, COUNT), followed by string operations (*e.g.*, LENGTH and SUBSTR). The most commonly used function was GROUP_CONCAT, an aggregate operator that

Function	Call Sites	Function	Call Sites	Function	Call Sites
GROUP_CONCAT	583,474	CAST	38,208	STRFTIME	1,147
SUM	321,387	UPPER	20,487	IFNULL	657
MAX	314,970	MIN	19,566	JULIANDAY	587
COUNT	173,031	COALESCE	3,494	DATE	44
LENGTH	102,747	LOWER	3,110	AVG	15
SUBSTR	88,462	PHONE_NUMBERS_EQUAL	2,017		

Fig. 7. Functions appearing in SELECT queries by number of times the function is used.

constructs a string by concatenating its input rows. This is significant, as it means that the most commonly used aggregate operator is holistic — its output size is linear in the number of input rows.

Per-Application Analysis. We next break the SELECT workload down by the calling application (app). Due to limitations of the logging infrastructure, 4.32 million queries (just over 12.9 % of the workload) could not be associated with a specific application, and our app-specific analysis excludes these queries. Additionally, system services in Android are often implemented as independent apps and counted as such in the numbers presented.

Over the course of the one-month trace we observed 179 distinct apps, varying from built-in Android applications such as *Gmail* or *YouTube*, to video players such as *VLC*, to games such as *3 Kingdoms*. Figure 8a shows the cumulative distribution of apps sorted by the number of queries that the app performs. The results are extremely skewed, with the top 10 % of apps each posing more than 100 thousand queries over the one month trace. The most query-intensive system service, *Media Storage* was responsible for 13.57 million queries or just shy of 40 queries per minute per phone. The most query-intensive user-facing app was *Google+*, which performed 1.94 million queries over the course of the month or 5 queries per minute. At the other end of the spectrum, the bottom 10 % of apps posed as few as 30 queries over the entire month.

We noted above that a large proportion of SELECT queries were exact look-ups, suggesting that many applications running on the device might be using SQLite as a simple key-value store. This suggestion was confirmed in our app-level analysis. For example, approximately half of one specific app's query workload consisted of the following two queries:

```
INSERT OR REPLACE INTO properties(property_key,property_value) VALUES (?,?);
SELECT property_value FROM properties WHERE property_key=?;
```

In this query, ? is a prepared statement parameter that acts as a place holder for values that are bound when the prepared statement is evaluated.

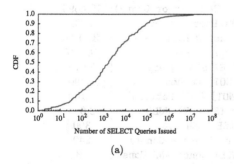
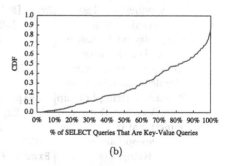

Fig. 8. Breakdown of SELECT queries by app. (a) Cumulative distribution of applications by the number of SELECT queries issued (note the logarithmic scale). (b) Cumulative distribution of applications by the percent of the app's SELECT queries that are full table scans or exact look-ups.

To broaden the scope of our analysis of key/value queries, we define a key-value look-up query as a SELECT query over a single relation that either performs a full table scan, or performs an exact look-up on a single attribute. Figure 8b shows the cumulative distribution of apps sorted by the fraction of each app's queries that are key-value lookup queries. For 24 apps (13.4 %), we observed *only* key-value queries during the entire, month-long trace.

3.2 Database Writes

Write statements, INSERT, INSERT OR REPLACE (here abbreviated as UPSERT), UPDATE, and DELETE, together constitute 11.6 million statements or about 25 % of the trace. As shown in Fig. 1, the most prevalent operation is the UPSERT. INSERT and UPSERT together account for 9.3 million operations, of which 7.4 are UPSERTs. In many of these cases, the use of UPSERTS appears to be defensive programming on the part of wrapper libraries that make use of SQLite (*e.g.*, Object Relational Mappers, or ORMs). UPSERTS are also the canonical form of update in key-value stores, further supporting the argument that a large fragment of SQLite's traffic is based on key-value access patterns.

DELETE Statements. The trace includes 1.25 million DELETE statements. This was by far the most expensive class of statement, with an average DELETE taking just under 4 ms to complete. A significant portion of this cost is attributable to the use of DELETE as a form of bulk erasure. As shown in Fig. 9, 323 thousand DELETEs have no exact match condition in their WHERE clause, while 528 thousand do include a range predicate. DELETE predicates can become quite complex; 46,122 DELETEs (just under 3.7 %) use nested SELECT queries, and touch as many as 7 separate tables (in 616 cases). This suggests extensive use of DELETE as a

Expression Type	Expression Form	Count
Exact Lookups	Const = Expr	926,042
Other Inequality	Expr θ Expr	527,517
Membership Test	Expr [NOT] IN (List or Query)	190,695
Disjunction	[NOT] Expr ∨ Expr	48,534
Inequality on 1 constant	Const θ Expr	31,128
Other Equality	Expr = Expr	10,037
Subquery Membership	[NOT] EXISTS (Query)	9,079
Boolean Column Cast	[NOT] Column	6,490
Patterned String Lookup	Expr [NOT] LIKE Pattern	6,109
Validity Test	Expr IS [NOT] NULL	2,693
Functional If-Then-Else	CASE WHEN ...	390
No-op Clause	Const or (Const = Const)	249
Range Test	Expr BETWEEN Const AND Const	18

Fig. 9. WHERE clause expression structures, and the number of DELETE statements in which the structure appears.

Expression Type	Expression Form	Count
Exact Lookups	Const = Expr	1,013,697
Disjunction	[NOT] Expr ∨ Expr	84,937
Inequality on 1 constant	Const θ Expr	18,146
Membership Test	Expr [NOT] IN (List or Query)	14,146
Other Inequality	Expr θ Expr	9,443
Boolean Column Cast	[NOT] Column	1,640
Validity Test	Expr IS [NOT] NULL	1,517
Other Equality	Expr = Expr	221
Patterned String Lookup	Expr [NOT] LIKE Pattern	59

Fig. 10. WHERE clause expression structures, and the number of UPDATE statements in which the structure appears.

form of garbage-collection or cache invalidation, where the invalidation policy is expressed through SQL.

UPDATE Statements. Slightly over 1 million statements executed by SQLite over the course of the month were UPDATE statements. Figure 10 breaks down the predicates used to select rows to be updated. Virtually all UPDATE statements involved an exact look-up. Of the million updates, 28 thousand did not include an exact look-up.

193 of the UPDATE statements relied on a nested SELECT statement as part of their WHERE clause, including 56 that involved 2 levels of nesting. Of the 193 UPDATEs with nested subqueries, 25 also involved aggregation.

Although the WHERE clause of the updates included a variety of expressions, *every single setter* in every UPDATE statement in the trace assigned a constant value; Not a single UPDATE expression attempted to compute new values using SQL, suggesting a strong preference for computing updated values in the application itself. This is not entirely unexpected, as the database lives in the address space of the application. Consequently, it is feasible to first perform a SELECT to read values out of the database and then perform an UPDATE to write out the changes, a tactic used by many ORMs. An unfortunate consequence of this tactic is that ORMs cache database objects at the application layer unnecessarily, suggesting that a stronger coupling between SQL and Java (*e.g.*, through language primitives like LINQ [2] or StatusQuo [4]) could be of significant benefit to Android developers.

Per-Application Analysis. Figure 11a illustrates app-level write workloads, sorting applications by the number of INSERT, UPSERT, UPDATE, and DELETE operations that could be attributed to each. The CDF is almost perfectly exponential, suggesting that the number of write statements performed by any given app follows a long-tailed distribution, a feature to be considered in the design of a pocket data benchmark.

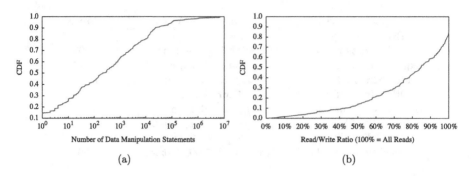

Fig. 11. App-level write behavior. (a) Cumulative distribution of applications by number of data manipulation statements performed (note the logarithmic scale). (b) Cumulative distribution of applications by read/write ratio.

Figure 11b breaks apps down by their read/write ratio. Surprisingly, 25 apps (14 % of the apps seen) did not perform a single write over the course of the entire trace. Manual examination of these apps suggested two possible explanations. Several apps have reason to store state that is updated only infrequently. For example, *JuiceSSH* or *Key Chain* appear to use SQLite as a credential store. A second, far more interesting class of apps includes apps like *Google Play Newsstand, Eventbrite, Wifi Analyzer*, and *TuneIn Radio Pro*, which all have components that query data stored in the cloud. We suspect that the cloud data is being encapsulated into a pre-constructed SQLite database and being pushed to, or downloaded by the client applications. This type of behavior might be compared to a bulk ETL process or log shipment in a server-class database workload, except that here, the database has already been constructed. Pre-caching through database encapsulation is a unique feature of embedded databases, and one that is already being used in a substantial number of apps.

4   Runtime Characteristics

Next, we look at overall runtime characteristics of the query workload observed during our study. We examine how often queries arrive, how long they run, and how many rows they return—all important inputs into designing the TPC-Mobile embedded database benchmark.

General Characteristics. Figure 12 shows query interarrival times, runtimes, and returned row counts (for SELECT statements) for all users, applications, and non-informational query types (SELECT, UPDATE, INSERT, DELETE) included in our dataset. Given that each mobile application is really generating an isolated workload to its own embedded database, we measure query interarrival time only between queries issued by the same application.

Examining the interarrival times shown in Fig. 12a, it is interesting to observe that many queries seem to arrive much more quickly than the minimum query

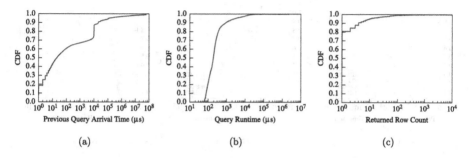

Fig. 12. Summary Statistics for Android SQLite Queries. Distributions of (a) inter-query arrival times, (b) query runtimes, and (c) rows returned per query.

runtime shown in Fig. 12b. Part of this may be due to apps that use multiple separate databases, which is not yet captured by our analysis. However, our logging is also done above any locking performed by SQLite, and so this may demonstrate that there are many cases where multiple application threads are issuing overlapping queries in parallel, even if the queries are eventually serialized before results are returned. Figure 12a also shows that, in addition to a standard long-tailed distribution of query inter-arrival times, about 20 % of the workload is very periodic, arriving at a rate of 0.01 Hz.

The runtime CDF shown in Fig. 12b shows while overall query runtimes show variation over several orders of magnitude, a large fraction of queries are executed in between 100 and 1000 μs. Further investigation into the small fraction of extremely slow queries may discover areas for database or application improvement. Finally, the row count CDF shown in Fig. 12c shows that 80 % of queries return only one row, further supporting our observation that many applications seem to be using the SQLite database almost as a key-value store.

Runtime Characteristics by Query Type. Figure 13 shows runtime characteristics for each of the four types of SQL statement. Figure 13a and b in particular show the time since the last query to be issued and the time until the next query is issued (respectively), while Fig. 13c shows the distribution of runtimes for each type of query. Examining the differences between Fig. 13a and b, we observe that INSERT queries are far more likely to arrive shortly before another query than shortly after. Almost 80 % of INSERTs are followed by another query within 100 μs. A similar, but far more subdued pattern can be seen for UPDATE statements. Conversely, both SELECT and DELETE statements are slightly more likely to arrive shortly before, rather than shortly after another query. Figure 13c shows significant deviations from the global average runtime for DELETE and UPDATE statements. UPDATE statements in particular have a bimodal distribution of runtimes, spiking at 100 μs and 10 ms. We suspect that this performance distribution is related to SQLite's use of filesystem primitives for locking and write-ahead logging [10,11]. This could also help to explain the 0.01 Hz query periodicity we observed above.

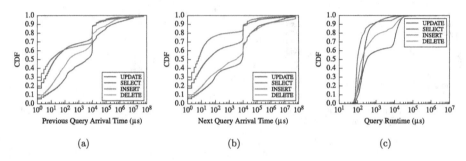

Fig. 13. By-Query-Type Statistics for Android SQLite Queries. Distribution of times since the query (a) immediately preceding, and (b) immediately following the query in question. (c) Distribution of runtimes for each query.

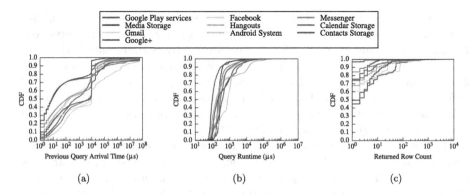

Fig. 14. Per-App Summary Statistics for Android SQLite Queries. Distributions of (a) inter-query arrival times, (b) query runtimes, and (c) rows returned per query.

Runtime Characteristics by Application. Figure 14 shows query interarrival times, runtimes, and returned row counts for ten of the most active SQLite clients. As seen in Fig. 14a, the 0.01 Hz periodicity is not unique to any one application, further suggesting filesystem locking as a culprit. Two of the most prolific SQLite clients, *Google Play services* and *Media Storage* appear to be very bursty: 70 % of all statements for these applications are issued within 0.1 ms of the previous statement. Also interesting is the curve for queries issued by the *Android System* itself. The interarrival time CDF appears to be almost precisely logarithmic for rates above 10 μs, but has a notable lack of interarrival times in the 1 ms to 10 ms range. This could suggest caching effects, with the cache expiring after 1 ms. As seen in Fig. 14b, most apps hold to the average runtime of 100 μs, with several notable exceptions. Over 50 % of the *Android System*'s statements take on the order of 1 ms. Just under 20 % of *Hangouts* statements take 10 ms, suggesting an update-heavy workload. Also, *Contacts Storage* has a heavier-duty workload, with 30 % of statements taking between 100 μs and 1 ms. Figure 14c shows that the *Android System* and *Media Storage* issue almost exclusively single-row lookup queries. The remaining apps issue a large number of single-row queries — Even *Contacts Storage* has a workload consisting of 45 % single-row reads — the number of rows returned in general varies much more widely. Many of these apps' user interfaces have both a list and a search view that show multiple records at a time, suggesting that these views are backed directly by SQLite. Although all apps have long tails, two apps in particular: *Gmail* and *Google+* are notable for regularly issuing queries that return on the order of 100 rows.

5   Pocket Data and Related Work

In spite of the prevalence of SQL on mobile devices, and an increasing interest in so-called "small data" [9], relatively little attention has been paid to the rapidly growing *pocket data* space. In this section, we first explore some existing research on mobile databases, with a focus on how the authors evaluate their solutions. Then, we turn to existing benchmarking suites and identify specific disconnects that prevent them from being applied directly to model pocket data. In the process, we explore aspects of these benchmarks that could be drawn into a potential pocket data benchmark.

5.1   Pocket Data Management

Kang et al. [11] explored the design of a flash-aware transactional layer called X-FTL, specifically targeting limitations of SQLite's redo logging on mobile devices. To evaluate their work, the authors used the TPC-C benchmark in conjunction with a series of micro-benchmarks that evaluate the file system's response to database write operations. This workload is appropriate for their target optimizations. However, as we discuss below, TPC-C is not sufficiently representative of a pocket data workload to be used as a general-purpose mobile database benchmark.

Jeong et al. [10] noted similar limitations in SQLite's transactional layer, and went about streamlining the IO-stack, also primarily for the benefit of mobile devices. Again, micro-benchmarks played a significant role in the author's evaluation of their work. To evaluate their system's behavior under real-world conditions, the authors ran the *Twitter* and *Facebook* apps, simulating user behavior using a mobility trace generated by MobiGen [1]. This is perhaps the most representative benchmarking workload that we encountered in our survey of related work.

Many of the same issues with IO and power management that now appear in mobile phones have also historically arisen in sensor networks. Madden et al.'s work on embedded databases with TinyDB [15] is emblematic of this space, where database solutions are driven by one or more specific target application domains. Naturally, evaluation benchmarks and metrics in sensor networks are typically derived from, and closely tied to the target domain.

5.2   Comparison to Existing Benchmarks

Given the plethora of available benchmarking software, it is reasonable to ask what a new benchmark for pocket-scale data management brings to the table. We next compare the assumptions and workload characteristics behind a variety of popular benchmarking suites against a potential TPC-MOBILE, and identify concerns that this benchmark would need to address in order to accurately capture the workload characteristics that we have observed.

Existing Mobile Benchmarks and Data Generators. Although no explicit macro-benchmarks exist for mobile embedded databases, we note two benchmark data generators that do simulate several properties of interest: AndroBench [12] and MobiGen [1]. AndroBench is a micro-benchmark capable of simulating the IO behavior of SQLite under different workloads. It is primarily designed to evaluate the file-system supporting SQLite, rather than the embedded database itself. However, the structure of its micro-benchmark workloads can just as effectively be used to compare two embedded database implementations.

The second benchmark, MobiGen has little to do with data management directly. Rather, it generates realistic traces of environmental inputs, simulating the effects of a phone being carried through a physical space. Replaying these traces through a virtual machine running a realistic application workload could generate realistic conditions (*e.g.*, as in the evaluation of X-FTL [10]). However, it can not simulate the effects of user interactions with apps running on the device.

TPC-C. One macro-benchmark suite that bears a close resemblance to the trace workload is TPC-C [6], which simulates a supply-chain management system. It includes a variety of transactional tasks ranging from low-latency user interactions for placing and querying orders, to longer-running batch processes that simulate order fulfillment. A key feature of this benchmark workload is the level of concurrency expected and required of the system. Much of the data is neatly partitioned, but the workload is designed to force a non-trivial level of cross-talk between partitions, making concurrency a bottleneck at higher throughputs. Conversely, mobile SQLite databases are isolated into specialized app-specific silos. In our experiments, throughput remained at very manageable levels from a concurrency standpoint. The most intensive database user, *Google Play services* had 14.8 million statements attributable to it, just under half of which were writes. This equates to about one write every 3 seconds, which is substantial from a power management and latency perspective, but not from the standpoint of concurrency.

YCSB. We observed many applications using SQLite as a simple key/value store. Indeed, 13 % of the applications we observed had a read workload that consisted exclusively of key/value queries, and over half of the applications we observed had a workload that consisted of at least 80 % key/value queries.

The Yahoo Cloud Services benchmark [5] is designed to capture a variety of key/value query workloads, and could provide a foundation for a pocket-scale data benchmark in this capacity. However, it would need to be extended with support for more complex queries over the same data.

Analytics. These more complex queries include multiple levels of query nesting, wide joins, and extensive use of aggregation. As such, they more closely resemble analytics workload benchmarks such as TPC-H [8], The Star-Schema Benchmark [17], and TPC-DS [7]. This resemblance is more than passing; many of the more complex queries we encountered appeared to be preparing application runtime state for presentation to the user. For example the *Google Play Games* service tracks so-called *events* and *quests*, and participating *apps*. One of the most complex queries that we encountered appeared to be linking and summarizing these features together for presentation in a list view. We note that the presence of analytics queries in pocket data management is likely to increase further, as interest grows in smartphones as a platform for personal sensing [3,13,14].

TPC-E. The TPC-E benchmark emulates a brokerage firm, and includes a mix of reporting and data mining queries alongside stream-monitoring queries. It models decision support systems that involve a high level of CPU and IO load, and that examine large volumes of rapidly changing data. SQLite does not presently target or support streaming or active database applications, although such functionality may become available as personal sensing becomes more prevalent.

6   Why TPC-MOBILE?

Our primary observation was that a pocket data workload includes a mix of both OLTP and OLAP characteristics. The majority of operations performed by SQLite were simple key-value manipulations and look-ups. However, a substantial fraction of the (comparatively read-heavy) workload consisted of far more complex OLAP-style operations involving wide, multi-table joins, nested sub-queries, complex selection predicates, and aggregation.

Many of these workload characteristics appeared to be motivated by factors unique to embedded databases. For example, SQLite uses single-file databases that have a standard, platform-independent format. As a consequence, we saw indications of entire databases, indexes and all, being transported in their entirety through web downloads or as attachments to other files [9]. This is suggestive of a pattern where cloud services package fragments of their state into SQLite databases, which are then downloaded and cached by the app for both lower-latency and offline access.

Query optimization goals also differ substantially for pocket data workloads. For example, latency is a primary concern, but at vastly different scales. Over our one-month trial, the average SQL statement took 2 ms to evaluate, and even complex SELECT queries with 4-level deep nesting only took an average of 120 ms.

Finally, unlike typical server-class benchmark workloads, where throughput is a key factor, embedded databases have smaller workloads — on the order of hundreds of rows at most. Moreover, embedded databases need to share computing resources fairly with other processes on the same device. This means that in stark contrast to server-class workloads, an embedded database is idle more frequently. Periods of low-utilization are opportunities for background optimization, but must be managed against the needs of other applications running on the device, as well as the device's limited power budget.

Pocket data workloads represent a growing, and extremely important class of database consumers. Unfortunately, research and development on embedded databases (e.g., [10,11]) is presently obligated to rely on micro-benchmarks or anecdotal observations about the needs and requirements of embedded database engines. We believe that a new TPC-MOBILE benchmark that captures the characteristics observed in this paper can provide a principled, standardized way to evaluate advances in mobile database technology, which will in turn, help to drive the development of such advances.

7   Conclusions

In this paper, we identified embedded databases on smartphones as the foundation of a new class of *pocket data* workloads. We have presented the preliminary results for a long-running study of SQLite embedded database usage on Android smartphones, and identified numerous ways in which pocket data workloads differ from big data workloads. Through this study, we hope to be able to create a benchmark that will spur further research and development on pocket data and embedded databases.

References

1. Ahmed, S.: MobiGen: a mobility generator for environment aware mobility model (2009). http://arrow.monash.edu.au/hdl/1959.1/109933
2. Box, D., Hejlsberg, A.: LinQ: NET language-integrated query. MSDN Developer Centre 89 (2007)
3. Campbell, A.T., Eisenman, S.B., Lane, N.D., Miluzzo, E., Peterson, R.A., Lu, H., Zheng, X., Musolesi, M., Fodor, K., Ahn, G.-S.: The rise of people-centric sensing. IEEE Internet Comput. 12(4), 12–21 (2008)
4. Cheung, A., Arden, O., Madden, S., Solar-Lezama, A., Myers, A.C.: StatusQuo: making familiar abstractions perform using program analysis. In: CIDR (2013)
5. Cooper, B.F., Silberstein, A., Tam, E., Ramakrishnan, R., Sears, R.: Benchmarking cloud serving systems with YCSB. In: SOCC. ACM, New York, NY, USA (2010)
6. Transaction Processing Performance Council. TPC-C specification. http://www.tpc.org/tpcc/
7. Transaction Processing Performance Council. TPC-DS specification. http://www.tpc.org/tpcds/

8. Transaction Processing Performance Council. TPC-H specification. http://www.tpc.org/tpch/
9. Dittrich, J.: The case for small data management. In: CIDR (2015)
10. Jeong, S., Lee, K., Lee, S., Son, S., Won, Y.: I/O stack optimization for smartphones. In: USENIX ATC, pp. 309–320. USENIX Association, Berkeley, CA, USA (2013)
11. Kang, W.-H., Lee, S.-W., Moon, B., Gi-Hwan, O., Min, C.: X-FTL: Transactional FTL for SQLite databases. In: SIGMOD (2013)
12. Kim, J.-M., Kim, J.-S.: AndroBench: benchmarking the storage performance of android-based mobile devices. In: Sambath, S., Zhu, E. (eds.) Frontiers in Computer Education. AISC, vol. 133, pp. 667–674. Springer, Heidelberg (2012)
13. Klasnja, P., Consolvo, S., McDonald, D.W., Landay, J.A., Pratt, W.: Using mobile & personal sensing technologies to support health behavior change in everyday life: lessons learned. In: AMIA (2009)
14. Lam, S.C.K., Wong, K.L., Wong, K.O., Wong, W., Mow, W.H.: A smartphone-centric platform for personal health monitoring using wireless wearable biosensors. In: ICICS, December 2009
15. Madden, S.R., Franklin, M.J., Hellerstein, J.M., Hong, W.: TinyDB: an acquisitional query processing system for sensor networks. ACM TODS $30(1)$, 122–173 (2005)
16. Nandugudi, A., Maiti, A., Ki, T., Bulut, F., Demirbas, M., Kosar, T., Qiao, C., Ko, S.Y., Challen, G.: PhoneLab: a large programmable smartphone testbed. In: SenseMine, pp. 4:1–4:6 (2013)
17. O'Neil, P., O'Neil, E., Chen, X., Revilak, S.: The star schema benchmark and augmented fact table indexing. In: Nambiar, R., Poess, M. (eds.) TPCTC 2009. LNCS, vol. 5895, pp. 237–252. Springer, Heidelberg (2009)
18. Owens, M., Allen, G.: SQLite. Springer, Heidelberg (2010)

SparkBench – A Spark Performance Testing Suite

Dakshi Agrawal[1], Ali Butt[2], Kshitij Doshi[5], Josep-L. Larriba-Pey[3], Min Li[1(✉)], Frederick R. Reiss[1], Francois Raab[4], Berni Schiefer[1], Toyotaro Suzumura[1], and Yinglong Xia[1]

[1] IBM Research, San Jose, USA
{agrawal,minli,frreiss,tsuzumura,yxia}@us.ibm.com,
schiefer@ca.ibm.com
[2] Virginia Tech, Blacksburg, USA
butta@cs.vt.edu
[3] Universitat Politècnica de Catalunya BarcelonaTech, Barcelona, Spain
larri@ac.upc.edu
[4] InfoSizing, Manitou Springs, USA
francois@sizing.com
[5] Intel, Mountain View, USA
kshitij.a.doshi@intel.com

Abstract. Spark has emerged as an easy to use, scalable, robust and fast system for analytics with a rapidly growing and vibrant community of users and contributors. It is multipurpose—with extensive and modular infrastructure for machine learning, graph processing, SQL, streaming, statistical processing, and more. Its rapid adoption therefore calls for a performance assessment suite that supports agile development, measurement, validation, optimization, configuration, and deployment decisions across a broad range of platform environments and test cases.

Recognizing the need for such comprehensive and agile testing, this paper proposes going beyond existing performance tests for Spark and creating an expanded Spark performance testing suite. This proposal describes several desirable properties flowing from the larger scale, greater and evolving variety, and nuanced requirements of different applications of Spark. The paper identifies the major areas of performance characterization, and the key methodological aspects that should be factored into the design of the proposed suite. The objective is to capture insights from industry and academia on how to best characterize capabilities of Spark-based analytic platforms and provide cost-effective assessment of optimization opportunities in a timely manner.

1 Introduction

Spark's brisk evolution and rapid adoption outpace the ability of developers and deployers of solutions to make informed tradeoffs between different system designs, workload compositions, configuration optimizations, software versions, etc. Designers of its core and layered capabilities cannot easily gauge how wide ranging the potential impacts can be when planning and prioritizing software changes. While Spark-perf [16]

© Springer International Publishing Switzerland 2016
R. Nambiar and M. Poess (Eds.): TPCTC 2015, LNCS 9508, pp. 26–44, 2016.
DOI: 10.1007/978-3-319-31409-9_3

can be used to calibrate certain categories of operations, a Spark-specific, comprehensive and extensible performance evaluation alternative is essential for ferreting out inefficiencies and anomalies. This proposal is intended to be a starting point for a community driven development of such a testing suite. With this proposal we plan to open discussion and solicit feedback and participation from the community at the very beginning of designing such a performance testing suite.

1.1   Objective

The objective is to develop a far-reaching performance testing suite that enables performance comparisons between different levels of Spark offerings, including Spark libraries and Spark core. The suite is intended to facilitate evaluation of technologies and be relevant to Spark adopters and solutions creators. We anticipate that the implementation and execution of this suite will benefit from efforts of many groups of professionals – Spark operators, workload developers, Spark core developers, and vendors of Spark solutions and support services.

The following sections present the use cases, the fundamental requirements of the performance testing suite, the design of data models and data generators, the chosen workloads covering the Spark ecosystem, the execution and auditing rules, and the performance metrics. Finally, we conclude the proposal and indicate some areas for future work.

1.2   Related Work

Benchmarks and performance testing suites serve many different communities. They are valuable tools for software engineering teams to assess the performance impact of design trade-offs, to refine choices in system architectures, to inform implementation choices and to identify performance bottlenecks. They can be used by researchers to evaluate new concepts and algorithms. They are excellent vehicles for assessing the performance impact of new hardware or different hardware topologies. They can be used by users and system integrators to gain a deeper understanding of the capabilities offered by competing technologies. No one performance test can ever perfectly serve the needs of all constituencies, but the TPC and SPEC benchmarks, as well as open source benchmarks like DOTS [13] have proven track records in providing value to a broad spectrum of constituencies.

Overall, the focus of benchmarks and testing suites can span a spectrum from low-level (e.g. SPEC CPU2006 [7]) to high-level (e.g. TPC-E [6], SAP SD, LDBC SNB [11]) functions. In the big data application domain, existing performance testing suites and benchmarks can be grouped into three categories: component-level testing, technology-specific solutions and technology-agnostic solutions.

Component-level tests (sometimes called micro-benchmarks) focus on stressing key system primitives or specifically targeted components using a highly synthetic workload. Examples of big data component-level testing include the suite of Sort Benchmarks [17], YCSB [23] and AMP Lab Big Data [21].

Technology-specific solutions involve a set of representative applications in the targeted domains and generally mandate the use of a specific technology to implement the solution. The goal is to test the efficiency of a selected technology in the context of a realistic operational scenario. Examples of technology-specific solutions testing for big data are MRBench [29], PigMix [28], HiBench [18, 19] and SparkBench [24].

Technology-agnostic solutions aim at creating a level playing field for any number of technologies to compete in providing the most efficient implementation of a realistic application scenario within the targeted application domain. No assumption is made about which technology choice will best satisfy the real world demands at a solution level. Benchmarks such as BigDataBench [20], BigBench [22] and TPC-DS [6] fall into this category.

The Spark performance testing suite introduced in this paper is designed to fall into the category of technology-specific solutions. It aims at providing a Spark specific, comprehensive and representative set of workloads spanning the broad range of application types successfully implemented within the Spark ecosystem. While other benchmarks such as BigBench [22], BigDataBench [20] and HiBench [18] each cover a small number of Spark-enabled workloads, they are far from including a comprehensive coverage of the full set of application types supported under Spark. Spark-Bench [24] and Spark-perf [16] provide good initial starting points, yet they fall short of covering the full Spark picture. In particular Spark-perf is a performance testing suite developed by DataBricks to test the performance of MLlib, with extensions to streaming, SQL, data frame and Spark core currently under development. In contrast the Spark performance testing suite proposed in this paper incorporates a broader set of application types including text analytics, Spark R and ETL, with realistic and scalable data generators to enable testing them in a more real-world environment.

2   Targeted Dimensions

A distinctive aspect of the Spark performance testing suite proposed here is that it will simultaneously target the following three dimensions of performance analysis within the Spark ecosystem.

- **Quantitative Spark Core Engine Evaluation,** by enabling comparative analysis of core Spark system ingredients, such as caching policy, memory management optimization, and scheduling policy optimization, between baseline (standard) Spark release and modified/enhanced variations. It anticipates in-depth performance studies from multiple perspectives, including scalability, workload characterization, parameter configurations and their impacts, and fault tolerance of Spark systems.
- **Quantitative Spark Library Evaluation,** by allowing quantitative comparison of different library offerings built on top of the Spark core engine. These include the categories of SQL, streaming, machine learning, graph computation, statistical analysis, and text analytics. We envision interest in comparisons among different levels/versions of Spark libraries, as well as alternative libraries from vendors.
- **Quantitative Staging Infrastructure Evaluation,** by providing insight toward analysis relative to a fixed software stack, two examples of which are

(a) comparison across different runtimes and hardware cluster setups in private datacenters or public clouds, and with use of Spark data services, (b) gaining of configuration and tuning insights for cluster sizing and resource provisioning, and accelerated identification of resource contentions and bottlenecks.

In summary, the Spark performance testing suite is intended to serve the needs and interests of many different parties, and aims to cover the technology evaluation of the Spark ecosystem by exercising its key components comprehensively.

3   Requirements

Measurement is the key to improvement, in computing as in many other spheres. The Transaction Processing Performance Council [6] and the SPEC [7] are among the most prominent performance benchmarking organizations. Supplementing them are efforts like LDBC, for more specific yet significant areas like graph and RDF technologies benchmarking [27]. Application level benchmarks from vendors like SAP [14] and Infor Baan [15] play a key role in influencing solution choice, workload balancing and configuration tuning. Open source communities have created a rich variety of performance test suites, DOTS [13] being just one example. From these and other efforts we recognize an established set of core attributes that any new performance testing suite should possess.

From Huppler [3] we have the following attributes

- Relevant
- Repeatable
- Understandable
- Fair
- Verifiable
- Economical

In the context of a 21st century Spark performance testing suite we can further refine these timeless attributes as follows:

- **Simple, Easy-to-use and Automated**: The suite needs to be simple to understand, deploy, execute, and analyze in an automated fashion, requiring only modest configuration. Considering the rapidly evolving nature of Spark ecosystem, automation is essential.
- **Comprehensive**: The performance testing suite should be comprehensive and representative of the diversity of applications supported by Spark. Different Spark operations can put pressure on different resources, in different ratios. Since a benchmark suite cannot capture all such operations, it is important that the chosen representatives reflect both the diversity of Spark uses at the application level and the variant stresses put on the computing resources at the systems level. For example, the suite should include workloads that have high resource demands for specific system resources to test extreme cases for a provisioned system as these workloads will be one of several uses of Spark.

- **Bottleneck Oriented**: Frequently a role of performance testing is to spur technology advancement. The concept of bottleneck (or choke point) analysis appears with the LDBC benchmark effort and is a good means to shape workloads, and thereby provide impetus for innovation by drawing attention to tough, but solvable, challenges.

- **Extensible**: Due to the rapid evolution of Spark, the Spark performance testing suite needs to be able to evolve, which includes allowing users to easily add new or extend/expand existing capabilities. A successful Spark benchmark will successfully address the many parts of the Spark taxonomy and be flexible to extend to new capabilities that the community may develop. This is illustrated in Fig. 1 Spark Taxonomy, derived from Databricks [1], starting with the Spark Core Engine as a base with several workload-focused extensions on top.

- **Portable**: The benchmark suite should run on a broad range of open systems and be designed to be readily portable to other operating systems if required.

- **Scalable:** To allow scaling of tests to large distributed or cloud environments, the suite should facilitate generation of data that is sufficiently voluminous and varied that it exercises systems under test in statistically significant ways. The rate at which new data needs to be generated also needs to create meaningful stresses.

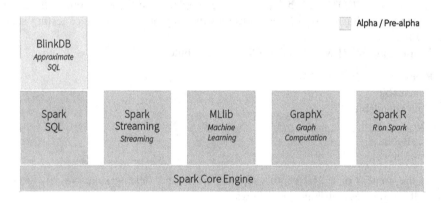

Fig. 1. Spark Taxonomy (https://databricks.com/Spark/about)

4 Data Model

Ideally we will want to develop a unified data model that allows integrating the multiple varieties of data, (relational tables, resilient distributed datasets, semi-structured data, graphs, arrays, and unstructured data such as text) that arise in Spark usages. A possible approach could be to start with an existing, largely traditional, relational data model and then extend it to the emerging domains. This has been popularized by the BigBench benchmark [8] which started with TPC-DS [6] and extended its data model to the SQL/MR and Mahout machine learning areas. An interesting possibility is to build on top of the LDBC Social Network Benchmark (SNB) [11] which already covers a number of the Spark ecosystem domains, and to extend it further.

We believe it would be effective to use this extension approach for the Spark performance testing suite. As the design and overall implementation of the Spark performance testing suite is refined, the choice between TPC-DS, SNB or some other option can be made. Since any kind of relational model would support SQL, the data model for that domain is quite straightforward. Streaming can use the relational tables both as sources and as targets. Work to recast the Mahout-based machine learning with Spark MLlib [2] is already underway. For graph computation, understanding the link between the Social Network Benchmark of LDBC and how it could contribute to the testing suite will be a challenge [25]. Finally, defining a data model across various specialized Spark features and spanning text analytics, and SparkR for a unified performance testing suite appears feasible in principle, but more investigation is needed.

5   Data Generator

Scalable, efficient, and realistic data generation plays a crucial role in the success of a data intensive testing suite. The built-in scalable data generator of TPC-H made it very compelling, as recounted in a retrospective of TPC-H [4]. TPC-DS further refined this notion and added non-uniform distributions and correlation. Multiple research efforts (e.g., Myriad [9] from TU Berlin, Parallel Data Generation Framework (PDGF) from Bankmark [10], and DATAGEN from the LDBC Social Network Benchmark [11]) are addressing these well appreciated needs for scalability and for reflecting real-world characteristics into synthetic data generation. We recognize similarly that while it may require significant development effort, rapid generation of representative data for use in large scale clusters will be critical in the adoption of the proposed Spark performance testing suite. We expect that the definition, design and validation of a powerful data generator is a key work item as we proceed with the implementation of this Spark performance testing suite.

5.1   Properties of Data Generator

A data generator must have multiple key attributes in order to be successful; in particular, it will need to be:

- Open source and transparent: to allow users to view and modify the code to enhance it or alter its behavior
- Scalable: to allow users to use it in a variety of environments, from small single node servers with only a few GB of data to the largest clusters with hundreds or even thousands of nodes and Petabytes of data.
- Parallel and distributed: as practical generation of petabytes of data will require many multi-core servers
- Incremental: to allow data to grow in iterations one must be able to generate data in "chunks" rather than in one monolithic start to finish method
- Realistic: Although synthetic, data must strive to be realistic; i.e., representative of real data sets. Following are some of the common properties of real life data:

- • Correlation
- • Non-uniform distributions representing high levels of skew
- • Fields/columns with both low and high cardinality
- • Varying numeric fields
- • Text fields of varying length
- • Able to represent relationships: as capturing connections across multiple tables/data sets is essential for advanced analytics.
- • Random but predictable: The data must be sufficiently random to challenge the system-under-test with unknown input sets. And yet, the output of data processing must be sufficiently predictable to permit validation of results and to determine which sets of input may trigger comparable levels of processing by the workload.

6 Workloads

6.1 Machine Learning

Several subtasks in the Machine Learning (ML) category are desirable for inclusion in the proposed suite, and are described further below. For each, the Spark performance testing suite should contain a reference implementation based on the most recent Spark MLlib capabilities. The suite should include a written specification for each machine learning subtask. It should be easy to substitute a different ML algorithm or implementation, provided that the replacing algorithm meets the specifications identically with reference implementation. The specification should therefore be at a sufficiently high level to permit alternative implementations, and be sufficiently strict to ensure that variant implementations produce useful outputs leading to quality results from a data science perspective.

It is important for the data generator for the machine learning tasks to cover a broad range of data characteristics which affect the behavior of ML algorithms. Input data should include dense, sparse, and hybrid (some attributes dense, others sparse) inputs. Algorithms should run against both small and large numbers of features.

In order to be able to draw broadly accepted conclusions and to drive innovation towards continuously improved machine learning, the generated data should also be robust and highly representative of real world data. In machine learning, processing speed is important but certain levels of quality are even more important. In a nutshell, generated data should not be so well-conditioned as to favor optimization algorithms that are not usable in practice with real-world data. We believe that substantial work is required to construct a robust, realistic data generator for the performance testing suite assessing Spark machine learning implementations.

Based on the above criteria, a Spark performance testing suite could augment the features tested in Spark-perf [16] and supplement [16] with extensions in the areas of logistic regression, support vector machine and matrix factorization. These are widely used regression, classification and recommendation algorithms for machine learning applications.

6.1.1   ML Subtasks

Logistic Regression. Logistic regression, as a machine learning classifier can be used to predict continuous or categorical data. For example, it is used to predict whether a patient has a given cancer based on measured characteristics such as various blood test, family disease history, age, sex, etc. The algorithm uses the stochastic gradient descent to train the classification model. The input data sets are kept in memory through RDD abstractions, and the parameter vector is calculated, updated, and broadcast in each iteration.

Support Vector Machine. A support vector machine (SVM) model is trained by constructing a set of hyper-planes in a high, or even infinite, dimension space for classification. Compared with linear and logistic classification, SVMs can implicitly map inputs into a high dimensional feature space and efficiently conduct nonlinear classifications.

Matrix Factorization. Matrix factorization, typically used by recommendation systems, is a collaborative filtering technique that fills in the missing entries of a user-item association matrix. Matrix factorization in Spark currently supports model based collaborative filtering and can be configured to use either explicit or implicit feedback from users.

Random Forest Classification. A random forest classifier uses a large set of relatively simple decision trees to perform classification tasks. The classifier combines the results of the individual classifiers to produce a consensus result. Random forests have shown to be effective in a number of machine learning tasks beyond their primary uses in classification. Since building a random forest involves training many small models in parallel, the task involves different communication patterns from other types of training tasks. MLlib exposes a random forest classifier implementation via the `mllib.tree.RandomForest` API.

6.2   Graph Computation

Graph is a very widely utilized data model. Consequently, a comprehensive Spark performance testing suite needs to include graph processing. The graph packages supported under Spark include GraphX and Dato. Additional projects are underway.

Graph computations to be included in the testing suite need to be representative of common types of graphs and graph analytics operations, and graph properties should reflect those in practical applications. Therefore, the data generator should be able to generate graphs of different types, such as the social graphs and man-made graphs (e.g. road-network) where a sensitive metric (say, vertex degree distribution) can be varied to obtain a wide range of analytics impact. Where practical, we want to be able to link graph data with other data generated for other components of the Spark performance testing suite. We propose to draw considerably from the LDBC Social Network Benchmark [25, 26] and need to examine how best to adapt their benchmarks to the Spark ecosystem and the Spark performance testing suite infrastructure. Different types of work, such as static structure-based traversal, graph structure morphing/property updates, and the processing of property-rich graphs, are highly desirable to include in the graph analytics operations of the testing suite.

The following subtasks are proposed according to the above criteria.

6.2.1   Graph Generator Subtask

The Linked Data Benchmark Council (LDBC [27]) has created two benchmarks. One of them is the LDBC Social Network Benchmark [25, 26] (SNB) whose correlated graph generation, graph querying tests, complex graph dependencies and scalable benchmark drivers reflect landmark innovation in graph benchmarking. Its data generator (ldbc_snb_datagen) uses experimentally extracted metrics and correlations to produce scalable datasets mimicking real world social networks. LDBC introduced a new choke-point driven methodology for developing benchmark workloads, which combines user input with that from expert systems architects.

The SNB analytics workload [26] includes General Statistics, Community Detection, Breath First Search, Connected Components and Graph Evolution; a list that will grow in the near future with the addition of new algorithms. We propose to select workloads from this benchmark for the Spark performance testing suite and develop additional workloads to cover various aspects of graph computing as detailed in the next subsection.

Graph500 [12] is a graph benchmark focusing on data-intensive workloads and particularly on large graphs. It is based on a breadth first search in a synthetically generated large undirected graph with power-law property based on the Kronecker model with average degree of 16. It measures performance in TEPS (for Traversed Edges Per Second) and its problem size can be changed by varying a SCALE parameter that determines the total number of vertices as 2^{SCALE}. Thus its generated graphs can be of various sizes, suitable for benchmarking software or platforms at different scales. It consists of three phases: construction, computation, and validation.

A dataset generator for Belief Propagation should be included as it would make rich property graph analytics possible, and it should produce directed acyclic graphs (DAG) with (conditional) probability distributions of various scales.

6.2.2   Graph Analytics Subtask

Primitive operations for graph analytics, such as creating/reading/updating/deleting (CRUD) vertices, edges, and properties, are nearly universal. Tests calibrating these graph analytics building blocks are therefore essential to include in the suite. The metrics would cover throughput (e.g., number of edges traversed per second), latency, and scalability.

Graph construction for large scale property graph is another key subtask to cover. The metrics would be running time, and scalability, akin to a subset of Graph500 [12].

Graph query is of interest as it involves both structural information and property information [11].

Pagerank exercises graph structure traversal with fixed active working set; *Triangle counting* stresses similarly. In such graph computations, each vertex iterates through tasks of gathering information (say, rank score) from its (partial) neighbors (say, predecessors), updating local information, and propagating it to the other neighbors (say, successors); and the iterations continue until convergence or certain termination conditions are reached.

Breadth-first Search (BFS) represents another type of graph traversal where only the vertices on the traversal frontier are affected, and the workload can vary from one iteration to another.

Single Source Shortest Path (SSSP) with a maximum traversal depth represents a type of graph traversal similar to BFS (e.g., Bellman Ford algorithm), but it only touches a local subgraph, instead of engaging the entire graph. This workload can evaluate if a graph processing framework on Spark can efficiently address local or subgraph computations.

Belief Propagation on a Bayesian network represents property-rich graph processing, and is a type of graph analytics operation that occurs in many cognitive computing applications. For example, Loopy Belief Propagation on a Bayesian network traverses graph iteratively, but when vertex or edge properties are updated, it can become a multi-pattern and computationally intensive graph structure operation.

Graph Triangulation (a.k.a. Chordization) represents a type of graph processing workload where the structure is dynamically changed. It is used to find graph cliques (dense subgraphs) and/or the hyper graph representation. It is an iterative graph processing algorithm that modifies topology in each iteration. It can be used to determine whether graph dynamics can be efficiently captured by the system.

Collaborative Filtering finds a lot of application, especially in recommendation systems. It involves a number of local graph searches on a bipartite graph, possibly in parallel, and is suitable for evaluating the concurrent local traversal capacity of a graph analytic system.

Graph Matching and motif searching are similarly used extensively. When the target graph lacks an index, these operations are challenging and possibly involve significantly high local traversals.

Various *Graph Centrality* metrics, such as the betweenness, degrees, closeness, clustering coefficient should also be considered due to their wide use in many real graph processing solutions.

6.3   SQL Queries

SQL continues to be an enduring query language due to its ubiquity, the broad ecosystem of tools that supports it, and its ability to evolve and support new underlying infrastructure and new requirements, such as advanced analytics and data sampling.

One area where a different approach might be warranted is in the construction of the queries. Historically, different vendors have proposed queries that combined a variety of SQL processing constructs, such as the TPC-D/H/DS benchmarks. In such case, the coverage was often not obvious initially. There has been some good analysis of the TPC-H query set [6].

We propose that we introduce a set of elemental or atomic queries that assess basic scan, aggregation, and join properties, then a set of intermediate queries that add challenges both to the query optimizer and to a runtime engine, and finally some complex and very challenging queries, representing ROLAP concepts and advanced analytic processing.

6.4   Streaming Applications

Streaming applications can be characterized along three dimensions: latency, throughput, and state size. Ideally, the Spark performance testing suite would exercise each of these dimensions at three representative values - high, medium, and low - giving a total of twenty-seven use cases. However, guided by applicability in the real world scenarios, the number of use cases can be pruned down to a more manageable count initially, and grow as more diverse workloads migrate to Spark over time.

6.4.1   Streaming Subtasks

The following are some of the use cases covering a subset of the twenty seven combinations posed above.

Real-time Model Scoring. The emphasis in this use case is on small and medium latency ranges. Low latency is defined as response time in seconds and sub-second values[1]. An example is sending an SMS alert to a prepaid mobile customer notifying them of their leftover account balance and potentially inserting a marketing message in the SMS alert after a model evaluation. In this use case, a latency in the range of 20 ms to a few seconds is desired with lower latencies offering a larger payoff – for example, a 50 ms delay does not force the customer to take a second look at the phone screen to get the marketing message while a delay exceeding 10 s may lead to customer pocketing the phone without getting the marketing message. Other examples in this area are cybersecurity, fraud detection for online transactions, and insertion of ads in webpages, where latency requirements are considerably more stringent (possibly 100 ms or less).

In all use cases of real-time model scoring, state management is an independent dimension. The state could be as simple as a single quantity (e.g., in the example above, minutes of calls left) which gets updated based only on the current record, with the model scored on this simple state. Or, the state could be a very complex assemblage of hundreds of attributes across millions of entities, updated by incoming records; with the model evaluation proceeding over a selection of such entities (e.g., a fraud detection application which maintains a profile with hundreds of attributes for each customer, updates it based on incoming records and scores a model on the profile.)

Near Real-time Aggregations. Near real-time aggregates are required for a number of scenarios in which a physically distributed system is monitored for its health using the key performance indicators of its elements. Examples include monitoring of traffic congestion on roads, monitoring of communication networks and energy grids.

In these usages either sliding or tumbling window aggregates are computed from streaming records. Incoming records may be enriched by joining them with reference information. The aggregation window size could be from one minute up to an hour. In a typical case, records arrive out of order and are delayed, and contain a timestamp which should be used for aggregate computation.

---

[1] Current Spark Streaming is not recommended for sub-second response time, however, we discuss this here in the anticipation of future improvements.

For near real-time aggregations, throughput is an independent dimension. The volumes could range from a few hundred GB a day (enriched Twitter data) and range up to 500 TB a day (e.g., telecommunication call data records).

Another independent dimension is the number of aggregation buckets - which themselves can vary from 100's of millions (one bucket for each mobile user) to several thousands (monitoring of different metropolitan cities within US).

The two subtasks listed above could be used to produce four use cases that could become part of the Spark performance testing suite.

6.5   SparkR

R is a widely used language for statistical analysis, and the SparkR project will allow practitioners to use familiar R syntax in order to run jobs on Spark. In the short term we propose following SparkR subtasks for inclusion in the performance testing suite, with future additions as SparkR capabilities evolve.

6.5.1   SparkR Subtasks

Data Manipulation. This covers SparkR DataFrame functions, and operations that can be performed in a purely distributed fashion and includes all "record-at-a-time" transformations such as `log()`, `sin()`, etc.

Segmented or Subpopulation Modeling. This is a technique in which the data is broken down into subpopulations, such as by age and gender, and a separate model is built for each segment of the data. Assuming each segment is of a "reasonable" size, R's existing ML libraries can be used to build the models.

Ensemble Modeling. This is a technique in which the data is broken down into randomly selected sub-samples, each of which is a "reasonable" size. R's existing ML libraries can be used to build the component models of the ensemble; however, the code that constructs the ensembles has to be written. This code could be in Scala or maybe in R.

Scoring R Models. This is applying an existing model. In essence, it is a "record-at-a-time" transformation.

6.6   Spark Text Analytics

Text analytics is an extremely broad topic, encompassing all types of analysis for which natural language text is one of the primary inputs. To give the benchmark broad coverage of this domain, we propose including a wide variety of text-related subtasks described in the section that follows. For each subtask, the benchmark should include a reference implementation based on an open-source NLP software stack (e.g., Stanford NLP toolkit) consistent with the open-source license under which the performance test suite is released.

Different commercial vendors have proprietary implementations of these subtasks and will want to substitute their own implementations for the reference implementation. Each subtask should include a specification that is sufficiently detailed to permit vendors to perform such substitutions. For example, it should be possible to perform the "rule-based information extraction" subtask using IBM's System T engine. In general, proprietary implementations should be required to produce the same answer as the reference implementations. For tasks with an element of randomization, the result of a proprietary implementation should be of equal utility compared with the reference result. For example, in the "deep parsing" subtask, any deep parser that produces substantially the same parse trees as the reference implementation (say, 90 % or greater overlap) would be acceptable.

Data for the subtasks should consist of English-language documents that a human being could read and understand. The data generator should work either by taking a random sample from an extremely large "canned" collection of documents, or by mixing together snippets of English text drawn from a suitably large database. A range of document sizes from 100 bytes up to 1 MB should be supported.

6.6.1   Text Subtasks

Rule-based Information Extraction. Information extraction, or IE, is the process of identifying structured information inside unstructured natural language text. IE is an important component of any system that analyzes text. In some cases, IE is used to identify useful features for other NLP tasks. In other cases, it is the primary NLP component of a processing pipeline. Rule-based IE systems use a collection of fixed rules to define the entities and relationships to extract from the text. These systems are widely used in practice, particularly in feature extraction applications, because they deliver high throughput and predictable results. The rule-based IE task will stress Spark by producing large amounts of structured information from each input document.

Information Extraction via Conditional Random Fields. A number of supervised statistical techniques are used in NLP as an alternative to using manually curated rules. Conditional Random Fields (CRF) is currently the most popular of these techniques. A CRF is a graphical model, similar to a hidden Markov model, but with greater expressive power. CRF-based information extraction involves transforming each input document into a graph with missing labels; then a collection of labeled training data is used to compute the maximum likelihood estimate for each missing label. The CRF-based extraction task will stress Spark due to its very high memory requirements.

Deep Parsing. Deep parsing involves computing the parse trees of natural language sentences according to a natural language grammar. Deep parsing is an important component of advanced feature extraction tasks such as sentiment determination. The deep parsing task will stress Spark due to its high CPU requirements and large output sizes.

Online Document Classification. Automatically classifying a stream of incoming documents into two or more categories is a very common NLP task, arising in applications such as publish-subscribe systems and spam filtering.

Batch Topic Clustering. Topic clustering is a family of supervised learning techniques for identifying important topics within a corpus of text, while simultaneously classifying documents according to the topics. The resulting topics and clusters can be used to understand the corpus at a high level, or serve as features for other machine learning tasks.

6.7 Resilient Distributed Dataset (RDD) Primitives

Since the main programming abstraction in Spark is RDDs, offering RDD primitive facilitates end users to gain micro-level understanding of how RDD performs within Spark framework. The reference test suite implementation of RDD primitives should be based on the latest version of Spark core and make it easy to substitute a different RDD implementation, add new RDD operations and remove obsolete RDD operations.

While RDDs supports a wide variety of transformations and actions, the testing suite should cover the key operations broadly. In particular, the RDD primitives should include IO related, shuffle, set and compute RDD operations. We choose not to include set operations with `RDD.subtract` and `RDD.intersection` because their characteristics are a combination of compute and shuffle RDD operations.

The testing suite should provide a data generator which produces synthetic data sets to exercise the various RDD primitives. Considering that data skew is known to commonly exist in data analytics workloads, the data generator needs to be able to generate data sets with different types of statistical distribution representing different levels of data skew. Note that whereas this type of workloads is aimed at micro-level RDD performance, the data generator needs not to generate realistic data sets.

6.7.1 RDD Primitives Subtasks

IO Related RDD Operations. This set of operations identify how fast Spark reads and writes data from/to local or distributed file system and creates/removes RDDs for the targeted data set with various size. Examples of RDD actions include `SparkContext.textFile, RDD.unpersist`.

Shuffle RDD Operations. This set of operations focus on stressing the shuffle behavior of RDD operations. They quantify how fast shuffle RDD operations can perform given different data set sizes. Examples of RDD transformations include `RDD.union, RDD. zipPartition, RDD.reduceByKey, RDD.groupByKey,` and `RDD. treeAggregate`.

Compute RDD Operations. This set of operations exercise how fast the compute RDD operations can perform. Examples of RDD transformations include `RDD.map, RDD. flatMap`. We choose to specify trivial map function such as `sleep` within compute RDD operations so that we can isolate the evaluation of the overhead of Spark framework.

Check-pointing RDD Operations. This set of operations assesses how fast the check pointing RDD operations can perform. This is a key factor which helps encourage the adoption of Spark framework seeing that failure is a common phenomenon in large scale data centers and check-pointing and lineage are the fundamental failure recovery mechanisms within Spark.

The key evaluation metrics for RDD primitives are as follows: (1) throughput: how many RDD transformations and actions can Spark conducts within a given time window; (2) scalability: how does the execution time change when the RDD data set size increases; (3) efficiency of failure recovery: how fast can Spark recover from a RDD data partition lost.

7 Execution and Auditing Rules

In this section we discuss the outline of the proposed execution and auditing rules of the testing suite. These rules typically govern the preparation of the testing environment, the execution of the testing suite, and the evaluation, validation and reporting of the test results.

During test environment preparation, a user first identifies the targeted workload(s) and accordingly chooses a benchmarking profile. To reduce the performance testing overhead, the testing suite provides a set of benchmarking profiles. Each profile includes a subset of workloads from the entire testing suite, along with corresponding data generation configurations and sequence(s) of workload execution. For example, the testing suite has one benchmark profile for each workload described in Sect. 6. If the testing focuses on machine learning, the machine learning benchmarking profile can be used, eliminating the overhead of running the other workloads.

The execution rules also require both single user and multi-user execution scenarios. A single user scenario executes the workloads included in the benchmarking profile one after another with a focus on evaluating and collecting per-workloads metrics. A multi-user scenario runs multiple benchmarking profiles concurrently with profile launching time following a certain statistical distribution. The multi-user scenario also could support running the profiles against different data sets instead of reusing the same data sets. This gives the users a better understanding of the performance implication of the targeted system under a multi-user scenario.

Having selected a benchmarking profile, the testing environment can be set up. This includes provisioning a set of connected machines and installing the software stack needed for running the testing suite's profile.

Once the testing environment is ready, the testing suite's data generator is used to generate needed datasets and loading them into the storage component of the tested system. The user is then ready to proceed with running the benchmark with a workload execution sequence defined by the chosen benchmarking profile. To check whether a benchmark run is valid, all the workload execution should report successful return status and pass the validation phase.

The testing suite includes an output quality evaluation and validation phase to evaluate the correctness of the execution. While this varies by workloads, a user can get an initial result indicating the validity and performance level of a test run from the result log generated by the testing suite.

Another important aspect of the execution and auditing rules is the requirement to provide sufficient reporting about the testing to allow others to reproduce the results. The system details needed in the disclosure report includes the hardware configurations such as CPU, memory, network, disk speed, network controller, switches; and software information such as the OS name and version, other software names and versions relevant to the testing suite, and the parameters used to generate input datasets. The full set of result logs generated by the testing suite should also be provided online and in a format that is easy to reproduce.

8 Metrics

Whenever a set of somewhat independent measurements are performed, a question always arises – how should the results be aggregated into a single metric, a simple and comparable measure of composite "goodness"? Historically, geometric mean has been chosen for some benchmarks [8, 9], while it has been argued later that a geometric mean is inappropriate [6]. Several other options, viz. an arithmetic mean, a weighted arithmetic mean, a harmonic mean, a weighted harmonic mean, etc. may also be applicable candidates for devising a figure of merit.

Different components of the proposed suite have widely diverse origins, and are likely to be accorded dissimilar measures of importance by different people. Thus arriving at a consensus single metric is particularly challenging in this case. For the purpose of this paper we therefore defer any specific recommendations. We understand and accept that a simple single figure of merit for any set of measurements is highly desirable.

Overall, we believe that most tests are best characterized by multi-user throughput. However, as the community-based approach to evolve and finalize the ideas presented in this paper gets underway, we expect considerable open discussion before a final metric is settled upon.

9 Preliminary Work

Preliminary work [24] has been done in the design of a benchmarking suite focusing on targeted dimensions of quantitative Spark Core and the staging of infrastructure evaluation. In this work ten diverse and representative workloads were chosen, covering four types of applications supported by Spark – machine learning, graph computation, SQL and streaming workloads. The ten chosen workloads were characterized using synthetic data sets and demonstrating distinct patterns with regards to resource consumption, data flow and communication features affecting performance. The work also demonstrated how the benchmarking suite can be used to explore the performance implications of key system configuration parameters such as task parallelism.

10   Conclusion, Ongoing, and Future Work

As Spark is increasingly embraced by industries and academia, there is a growing need for a comprehensive set of Spark performance tools. Such tools should enable developers, integrators and end users within the Spark and big data community to identify performance bottlenecks, explore design trade-offs, assess optimization options and guide hardware and software choices with a focus on key workload characteristics. While early work has been done in this area, the Spark ecosystem, being a relatively new data analytics platform, lacks a far reaching set of performance tools. This paper introduces a framework for the creation of a comprehensive Spark performance testing suite to address this need. It identifies several key factors such a performance testing suite should consider, a set of Spark workloads consistent with those factors, and the requirements for their reference implementations and corresponding data generators.

Currently we are focusing on machine learning and graph processing workloads. More specifically, we are identifying real world data sets as seeds for data generator. They exemplify the data characteristics that need to be preserved in order to generate realistic data sets at selected scale factors. We are also looking into meaningful metrics for each workload with a focus on setting apart high performing algorithms and implementations from less efficient ones. In the future, we plan to add additional workloads to the identified set. For instance, as a necessary step between the data generation process and the analytics workflow, we identify extract-transform-load (ETL) as another key workload within the Spark ecosystem. We also plan to explore the possibility of supporting a Python interface within the performance testing suite. Moreover, we recognize the need for a formal definition of the testing suite's detailed execution and auditing rules, along with the selection of representative metrics that create an environment where true apples-to-apples comparisons can be made and alternative choices can be fairly evaluated.

Acknowledgements. The authors would like to acknowledge all those who contributed with suggestions, ideas and provided valuable feedback during earlier drafts of this document. In particular we would like to thank Alan Bivens, Michael Hind, David Grove, Steve Rees, Shankar Venkataraman, Randy Swanberg, Ching-Yung Lin, and John Poelman.

References

1. DataBricks. https://databricks.com/
2. Mahout. http://mahout.apache.org/
3. Huppler, K.: The art of building a good benchmark. In: Nambiar, R., Poess, M. (eds.) TPCTC 2009. LNCS, vol. 5895, pp. 18–30. Springer, Heidelberg (2009)
4. Boncz, P., Neumann, T., Erling, O.: TPC-H analyzed: hidden messages and lessons learned from an influential benchmark. In: Nambiar, R., Poess, M. (eds.) TPCTC 2013. LNCS, vol. 8391, pp. 61–76. Springer, Heidelberg (2014)

5. Jacob, B., Mudge, T.N.: Notes on calculating computer performance. University of Michigan, Computer Science and Engineering Division, Department of Electrical Engineering and Computer Science (1995)
6. Transaction Processing Performance Council. http://www.tpc.org/
7. Standard Performance Evaluation Corporation. https://www.spec.org/
8. Ghazal, A., Rabl, T., Hu, M., Raab, F., Poess, M., Crolotte, A., Jacobsen, H.-A.: BigBench: towards an industry standard benchmark for big data analytics. In: Proceedings of the 2013 ACM SIGMOD International Conference on Management of Data, SIGMOD 2013, pp. 1197–1208. ACM, New York, NY, USA (2013)
9. Alexandrov, A., Tzoumas, K., Markl, V.: Myriad: scalable and expressive data generation. Proc. VLDB Endow. 5(12), 1890–1893 (2012)
10. Rabl, T., Frank, M., Sergieh, H.M., Kosch, H.: A data generator for cloud-scale benchmarking. In: Nambiar, R., Poess, M. (eds.) TPCTC 2010. LNCS, vol. 6417, pp. 41–56. Springer, Heidelberg (2011)
11. Linked Data Benchmark Council Social Network Benchmark (LDBC-SNB) Generator. https://github.com/ldbc/ldbc_snb_datagen
12. Graph500 generator. http://www.graph500.org/specifications
13. DOTS: Database Opensource Test Suite. http://ltp.sourceforge.net/documentation/how-to/dots.php
14. SAP. http://www.sap.com
15. Infor LN Baan. www.infor.com/product_summary/erp/ln/
16. Spark-perf. https://github.com/databricks/spark-perf
17. Sort Benchmark. http://sortbenchmark.org/
18. Huang, S., Huang, J., Dai, J., Xie, T., Huang, B.: The HiBench benchmark suite: characterization of the MapReduce-based data analysis. In 26th IEEE ICDEW, pp. 41–51, March 2010
19. Performance portal for Apache Spark. http://01org.github.io/sparkscore/plaf1.html
20. Wang, L., Zhan, J., Luo, C., Zhu, Y., Yang, Q., He, Y., Gao, W., Jia, Z., Shi, Y., Zhang, S., Zheng, C., Lu, G., Zhan, K., Li, X., Qiu, B.: Bigdatabench: a big data benchmark suite from internet services. In: IEEE 20th HPCA, pp. 488–499, February 2014
21. AMPLab Big Data Benchmark. https://amplab.cs.berkeley.edu/benchmark/
22. Ghazal, A., Rabl, T., Hu, M., Raab, F., Poess, M., Crolotte, A., Jacobsen, H.-A.: Bigbench: towards an industry standard benchmark for big data analytics. In: Proceedings of the 2013 ACM SIGMOD, pp. 1197–1208 (2013)
23. Cooper, B.F., Silberstein, A., Tam, E., Ramakrishnan, R., Sears, R.: Benchmarking cloud serving systems with YCSB. In: Proceedings of the 1st ACM SOCC, pp. 143–154 (2010)
24. Li, M., Tan, J., Wang, Y., Zhang, L., Salapura, V.: SparkBench: a comprehensive benchmarking suite for in memory data analytic platform Spark. In: Proceedings of the 12th ACM International Conference on Computing Frontiers, CF 2015, Article 53, ACM, New York, NY, USA (2015)
25. Erling, O., Averbuch, A., Larriba-Pey, J.L., Chafi, H., Gubichev, A., Prat, A., Pham, M.-D., Boncz, P.: The LDBC social network benchmark: interactive workload. In: Proceedings of SIGMOD 2015, Melbourne (2015)
26. Capotă, M., Hegeman, T., Iosup, A., Prat, A., Erling, O., Boncz, P.: Graphalytics: a big data benchmark for graph-processing platforms. In: Proceedings of GRADES2015, co-located with ACM SIGMOD/PODS (2015)

27. Angles, R., Boncz, P.A., Larriba-Pey, J.-L., Fundulaki, I., Neumann, T., Erling, O., Neubauer, P., Martínez-Bazan, N., Kotsev, V., Toma, I.: The linked data benchmark council: a graph and RDF industry benchmarking effort. SIGMOD Record **43**(1), 27–31 (2014)
28. PigMix. https://cwiki.apache.org/confluence/display/PIG/PigMix
29. Kim, K., Jeon, K., Han, H., Kim, S.,x Jung, S., Yeom, H.Y.: MRBench: a benchmark for MapReduce framework. In: IEEE ICPADS (2008)

NUMA-Aware Memory Management
with In-Memory Databases

Mehul Wagle[1]([✉]), Daniel Booss[2], Ivan Schreter[2], and Daniel Egenolf[3]

[1] Sybase an SAP Company, Magarpatta City, Pune 411028, India
mehul.wagle@sap.com
[2] SAP SE, Dietmar-Hopp-Allee 16, 69190 Walldorf, Germany
{daniel.booss,ivan.schreter}@sap.com
[3] Heidelberg University, Grabengasse 1, 69117 Heidelberg, Germany
egenolf@stud.uni-heidelberg.de

Abstract. Writing enterprise grade software for multi-processor systems is an interesting challenge since such a system primarily involves a multitude of hardware components that exhibit conflict due to simultaneous access by unorganized software threads of user applications. The problem is particularly compounded with In-Memory paradigm that includes potential applications like Data Management in the modern era. With an emergence of distributed hardware trends like Non-Uniform Memory Access (NUMA), where access times to a system's physical address space depend on relative location of Memory w.r.t CPU, it is crucial to rethink about placement of a user process' workable memory with respect to executing threads. We present a few novel techniques from our Heap management work with SAP HANA as part of our goal towards building a strong NUMA awareness with in-memory databases. Our work primarily focuses on providing a robust and well-performant Memory Management framework on Linux OS by handling the associated complexity and challenges seen with enabling enterprise software to live on a distributed memory landscape. One of the important outcomes of our approach is to build a rich set of kernel APIs that provide fine-granular control to higher DBMS layers like Store and Query for educated placements of their relational data structures. However the generality of our techniques allows them to be readily applied to other domains that need to deal with NUMA performance penalty.

Keywords: Memory management · Heap manager · In-Memory databases · NUMA · Linux · Data locality · Performance

1 Introduction

1.1 Shared Memory Architectures

Traditional hardware systems have a shared memory architecture based on Uniform Memory Access (UMA). On such an SMP system (Fig. 1), the memory is typically accessed by processors via shared bus which provides similar access times for any CPU. Inter-communication between CPUs is also channeled through this shared bus, which

© Springer International Publishing Switzerland 2016
R. Nambiar and M. Poess (Eds.): TPCTC 2015, LNCS 9508, pp. 45–60, 2016.
DOI: 10.1007/978-3-319-31409-9_4

can quickly become congested with requests from multiple cores. The number of DRAM chips manageable by a single controller is limited, which limits the memory capacity supported by the system architecture. All in all such a design does not scale well for the ever expanding multi-processing landscape [1, 2].

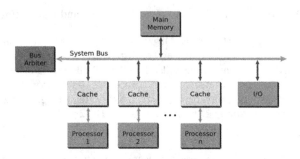

Fig. 1. Typical components of SMP system

1.2 Non-uniform Memory

To address the above limitations, modern CPU architectures have embraced a distributed memory model called NUMA, where computer memory lives across a number of processors and where each processor is able to access some locations (*local memory*) faster than others (*remote memory*). A few examples of such sub-systems include the AMD Opteron, IBM Power5, HP Superdome and SGI Altix [1]. The primarily goal of this design is to surpass the scalability limits of shared memory architectures. The system memory is typically partitioned into multiple physical Nodes (or Sockets), each with its own processing units and a fast dedicated access path to its private memory (as outlined in Fig. 2). All the nodes in such a system are glued together using a communication link called "interconnect" that doubles up to provide access to inter-node memory as well as to implement the Cache Coherency protocol (i.e. ccNUMA). Such hardwares were built since the late 80's, and early operating systems designed for it were optimized for access locality. It first became commercially available with Linux distributions in 2004 with SLES9 and RHEL4 [3].

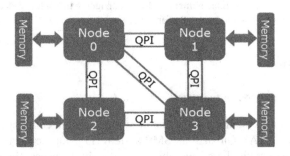

Fig. 2. Typical layout of a NUMA system

1.3 Processing Hierarchy of NUMA and Misgivings

Today's generation of processor is so agile that it usually requires physical memory to be directly attached to the socket of residence. Processing time in the life of such a system is typically clogged inside hardware sensitive factors like shared cache contention, remote memory latency, memory controller and interconnect contention, together of which contribute to significant degradation in application workloads. The moving pieces of hardware interaction are neatly captured in Fig. 3.

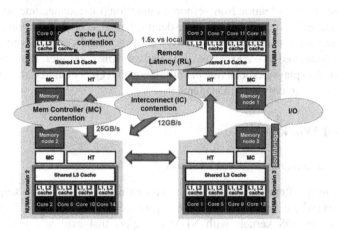

Fig. 3. Typical bottlenecks in a NUMA system [4]

The contention on last-level processor cache is a bottleneck experienced during multi-processing with shared data access patterns. Processing units on the sameCPU coreusually talk through a shared L1/L2 cache (~ 1–2 cycles), while processing units residingon different CPU cores, but contained in a chip,talk through a shared L3 (~ 10–20 cycles). Finally processing units residing on separate chips communicate either by sharing memory or through a cache-coherence protocol (~ hundreds of cycles). Cache-line contention can be a significant impediment in scaling large NUMA configurations,and its effects may be broadly classified as either "false cacheline sharing" or "cache-line ping-ponging" [5]. The "false cache-line sharing" is the unintendedco-residency of unrelated variables in the samecache-line, while"cache-line ping-ponging" is the change in exclusive ownership of a cache-lineas different CPUs write to it. The penalty is aggravated multi-folds when the contention is not self-contained within a single socket and is further intensified by the cache-coherency policy (e.g. broadcast-based global policies are hurtful). This is due to the need to traverse inter-node links to handle the cache-to-cache traffic to resolve cache-line contention. An example of false cache sharing is a poor datastructure layout whereby a single L3 cache-line contains a location (frequently written) and another location (only read). In this situation, a read will trigger an expensive cache coherency operation to demote the cache-linefrom exclusive to shared state in the directory. Once identified, false cache sharing can often be remedied by isolating the write-mostly variable into a separate cache locality. The processor's prefetch mechanism and usage of atomic operations additionally contribute to false cache contention [6]. An example of cachelineping-pong on the other hand is that of multiple-reader single-writer lock synchronization which contains a contending variable (read-lock count). Each read_lock() and read_unlock()changes the count and dirties the cache-line containing the lock. Thus, an actively used lock object is continually bounced across the entire system.

As a side-effect of NUMA hierarchy, a memory access from a given socket to its neighbor incurs an additional hop. This is the penalty of remote memory access and is typically ~ 1.2–1.5x in modern NUMA systems. However as seen from prior studies [4, 8], the overheads of contention from resource saturation (interconnect/memory controllers) are far more significant than raw wire delays. Unbalanced distribution of memory requests increase the memory access latency on overloaded controllers to as high as 1000 cycles, compared to ~ 200 cycles on a relatively idle controller. Proper placement of application data plays a crucial role in optimizing both Query latency and Throughput achieved with In-Memory data management.

2 Related Work

2.1 Application Agnostic Considerations

The performance differences of memory were first noticeable on large-scale systems (e.g. SGI Altix) where data paths were spanning motherboards or chassis. These systems required modified OS kernels with NUMA support that explicitly understood the system's topological properties to avoid the excessively long signal path lengths and achieve High-Performance computing and scalability [2, 5]. Several techniques and strategies have ever since been proposed by research community for application unaware NUMA optimizations. The processor caching bottlenecks (from Fig. 3) are partly solved with software techniques like *"thread clustering"* [7] that perform efficient thread scheduling keeping in mind the application's data sharing pattern. The remote access and resource saturation penalties are considered by OS-based scheduling techniques like *Automatic NUMA Balancing* in Linux kernel [9], *DINO* [4] and *Carrefour* [8]. The crux of these algorithms is that they migrate data and threads closer to each other. The Auto-Numa feature, available in recent kernels since Linux v3.8 +, allows applications to transparently adapt to non-uniform hardware behavior by supporting dynamic schemes like *"CPU-follows-memory"* and *"Memory-follows-CPU"*. These policies are internally triggered by watching hardware statistics like Page Faults with special heuristics like *Quadratic Filter* to migrate a page only when accessed by the same remote node more than a specific threshold. The page migration in fact uses a lazy technique to move pages present in the fault path [9, 10].

Some NUMA systems (e.g. AMD Opteron) may even be configured by firmware to globally interleave their virtual address space across nodes. Such a technique is called hardware interleaving [2] and is a quick and easy solution not entailing modification of program source. It does avoid the worse-case performance penalties seen with centralized bandwidth bottlenecks, but suffers from a lot of remote memory accesses and hence may not always be an optimal choice. The DINO and Carrefour scheduling algorithms [4, 8] take both remote latency and resource contention into account during NUMA guided decision-making. These approaches use contention-sensitive thread ranking based on hardware metrics like LLC miss rate, Memory read ratio, DRAM accesses per μs, and Local memory access ratio. These algorithms employ not just thread and memory migration techniques, but are supplemented with advanced capabilities like memory replication (with modified kernel and Page Table mgt.) to reduce both remote accesses and resource contention. Such application neutral strategies are useful but not fully optimal for applications like relational DBMS with a wide spectrum of access characterizations ranging from weakly parallel (point) transactional updates to highly parallel (dense) analytical scans. For example, running a whole DBMS process in interleaved mode may not be optimal and most likely not an option in real world [11]. It is desirable to incorporate a fair degree of intelligence in DB kernel with respect to Memory Management and Thread Scheduling capabilities for deeper hardware considerations.

2.2 Application Guided NUMA Awareness

There is substantial prior work in this field. For instance the authors [11, 12] deal with executing join algorithms efficiently, while [13, 14] generalize the scope to other relational operators. This is immensely useful to understand the different ways of coordinating and collocating threads along with their working data set during query execution. But it does not deal with the specifics and complexity of the underlying memory infrastructure needed to create the hardware sensitive placement leveraged by algorithms in higher spaces.

Prior work in the area of NUMA-aware Heap Managers by Kaminski et al. [15] is one of the earliest works known to us on such low-level considerations. The authors acknowledge the need for programmer's usage of heap memory libraries (C/C ++ runtime) to avoid the expensive context switches between user and kernel space. Their work is based on extending the TCMalloc allocators [16] to be NUMA-sensitive. TCMalloc is an open source project available as part of the google-perftools package under BSD license. It typically allocates memory in very large memory blocks, splits them into smaller chunks and manages the client requests with minimal memory fragmentation. To achieve this goal it maintains a separate memory pool per thread used for tiny allocations which greatly helps to reduce the lock contention as well as OS API call overheads. The authors even extend this existing fairly-scalable heap manager to work efficiently on NUMA by using the 3rd party library 'libnuma' and showcase the performance benefits with respect to traditional heap managers like glibc's PtMalloc [19]. However there are a couple of inherent weaknesses in their design, which need careful consideration and are neatly solved by our proposal.

3   OS Allocation Policies and NUMA-Aware Heap Decisions

3.1   Policy of First Touch

Most operating systems use a well-established memory management paradigm called *"Policy of First Touch"*. When an application requests memory, the virtual address is initially not mapped to real memory. When the threads of user process first access the memory during initialization (using 'memset') or read/write of addresses, the OS will allocate a physical memory region and map the virtual address to the physical range to make it resident. The OS typically allocates physical memory from the same NUMA node as holding the CPU executing the page faulting thread. This concept of Demand Paging is used by most modern operating systems such as Microsoft Windows and Linux. The OS thereby retains complete control over which physical address range to use and user applications are completely abstracted [2, 17].

3.2 APIs to Control Location of Physical Memory

For data intensive algorithms one needs to consider where to place the consumed data. Operating systems are typically aware of NUMA architectures. Linux for instance partitions memory into NUMA zones, one for each socket [2]. For each NUMA zone, the kernel maintains separate management data structures. Unless explicitly bound to a specified socket (NUMA zone) through a special system call ('mbind'), the Linux kernel allocates memory on the socket of first touch. The kernel tries to satisfy the allocation from current zone, but in case of insufficient zone memory, it may select next zone with free memory. System calls like 'mbind' thus help programmers with better control of their process' resident memory assignment.

Linux provides a 3rd party user-space library 'libnuma' [23] for NUMA-aware programming which provides a convenient wrapper around the low level system calls for target node binding and NUMA topology access. Similar APIs are available on other OS flavors, although the focus of our present work is restricted to Linux only. The 'libnuma' library is generally installed with corresponding RPM packages 'libnuma-devel' and 'numactl-devel' on SUSE and RHEL distributions respectively [1]. The library APIs for heap locality currently support 3 different policy flavors as described in Table 1. The default OS decision corresponds to "First Touch" policy.

Table 1. Memory Policies to control allocation locality [1, 17]

Name	Description
Default	System default is to allocate on local node running the thread (*first touch*)
Bind	Allocate strictly on a given set of nodes
Preferred	Hint to allocate on a given set of nodes and fallback to other nodes if needed
Interleave	Interleave in round-robin on a set of nodes

The "BIND" policy is a strict specification to the kernel to restrict the physical allocations from a specified set of nodes only. Although this provides a reliable and high precision guarantee of memory acquisition, the behavior turns out to be overly restrictive during resource hit situations like Node-level OOMs where this policy forces OS to reclaim the local memory within target node(s). This may even cause undesired effects like VM swapping as a result of which the user process is sometimes chosen as victim by resource daemons like Linux OOM killer [26]. Unfortunately this is also the de-facto policy of 'libnuma' public APIs for node binding (e.g. numa_alloc_onnode(< size > , < node >)). This is clearly not even an option for production-grade In-Memory systems like SAP HANA [22] which need to deal with high concurrency and memory-intensive situations with resource demand pressures.

The "PREFERRED" policy is a best-effort mechanism allowing user applications to provide a hint to OS to provide the backing physical memory from a specified list of nodes. This renders rich flexibility to Modern Operating Systems to transparently fall-back to other nodes from topology in the event of memory pressures. It provides a best of both worlds (i.e. location affinity of Strict Binding and flexibility of First Touch) and is the approach chosen by our NUMA-aware heap [18].

The "INTERLEAVE" policy directs the kernel to effect a round-robin distribution of underlying physical pages across the specified subset of nodes with OS page stripe (e.g. 4 KB on x86). This provides a powerful mechanism to balance the memory band-width and effectively reduce the controller contention [17]. In the relational context, the data striping is a useful philosophy especially for shared Data Structures and Store components that are accessed from multiple nodes e.g. Temporary structures of table joins. This is an alternative choice for DB layers by our NUMAdesign [18].

3.3 NUMA Policy Hierarchy

Linux allows policies to be set either at the level of processes or memory regions. Policies set per memory region are called VMA policies and allow a process to set policy for a block of memory in its address space [17]. *Memory region policies* have a higher priority than *Process policy* (see Fig. 4). The main advantage of memory region policy is it can be set up before an allocation happens and hence we use it [18].

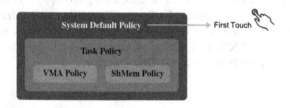

Fig. 4. Memory policy hierarchyof OS

3.4 Heap Manager Decisions with Libnuma

It must be noted that the allocation routines of 'libnuma' round up all allocations to kernel page granularity and are relatively expensive. The cost is amortized when used for large memory objects that exceed the CPU cache sizes and where NUMA-aware policy is likely to help. Our design [18] amortizes and absorbs the internal overheads by restricting usage of library APIs to request sizes exceeding a few 100 Megabytes.

Linux introduces three new system calls for NUMA awareness: (i) 'mbind', (ii) 'set_mempolicy', and (iii) 'get_mempolicy'. Normally user applications should not have to invoke the system calls directly and instead use the higher libnuma interfaces.

The 'mbind' is the most important system call to bind memory to a node and our design uses a high-level libnuma wrapper around this call. The 'get_mempolicy' retrieves the memory policy of a given VMA. This system call is used by our design to publish API for higher DB layers to query node of actual physical allocations. This metadata can be used to guide scheduling decisions of relational worker tasks/threads.

The most important contribution of our Distributed Memory aware design is to abstract the gory complexity of NUMA-driven management decisions from DBMS client layers by exclusively dealing with contracts of the external library (and even OS). This is achieved by publishing the frequently needed infrastructure services for clients to be able to place and locate their in-Memory objects efficiently. Our design [18] does not completely eliminate the lock synchronization overheads but manages to bring down intra-node memory fragmentation to a bare minimum.

4   Memory Management in DBMS [18]

4.1   Existing Design

The basic principle of any scalable user-space memory allocator like PtMalloc of linux glibc ([19], TcMalloc [16] and Hoard [20]) is to use slab-based allocations based on multiple slab classes along with tiered caching hierarchy like Thread vs Local vs Global Heaps [25]. In similarity our Memory Manager is a user-level memory alloca servicing the object sized allocations using buffer pools partitioned per logical core. As a consequence, threads executing on different logical processing units naturally do not need synchronization. Whenever a DBMS worker thread needs to allocate a few chunks of memory, the Memory Manager handles it by forwarding to designated allocator object assigned to thread's execution core. The slab allocation philosophy is coupled since each Allocator object has four pre-defined sub-allocators based on request size (see Fig. 5 for concept). The 'SMALL' allocator deals with tiny pre-defined slabs upto 4 KB, the 'MEDIUM' deals upto 32 KB, while 'BIG' allocator can handle upto half GB. The rest are forwarded directly to OS through 'HUGE' allocator.

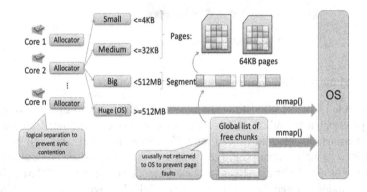

Fig. 5. Existing memory manager architecture

The 'BIG' allocator is the crucial piece since it handles the segment allocations of very large VMA regions by requesting OS to map them as anonymous pages. The large span of the reserved memory region are then carved into chunks of 64 KB pages and further into smaller pieces (<= 4 KB) which eventually get cached in the 'MEDIUM' and 'SMALL' allocators respectively. The memory chunks allocated by the 'BIG' allocator originate from a global list of free chunks, and hence once a chunk is de-allocated it turns completely free and returned to the global freelist. However, the chunks are never returned to OS and instead retained within the process's address space, which helps reduce expensive context switches and associated page faults.

As is apparent, the above design is lock-free and also makes sure that the memory fragmentation overheads are minimized since after a particular memory is released, the adjacent free virtual addresses in internal caches are combined and compacted wherever possible. There may be lock waits in the scenario of more threads than processing units, but this problem is partially addressed by our DBMS Task Scheduler [21] which fits thread parallelism to available computing units. Our present design of memory allocators is robust, efficient and scalable, but sub-optimal for NUMA.

4.2 Limitations of Existing Design from NUMA Perspective

The present design does not necessarily guarantee that allocated memory will live on NUMA socket of the executing thread! Since we use 'mmap' call to reserve large segments from Linux, we are bound by the "First Touch" policy (Sect. 3.1). Load balancing by OS schedulers in multi-threaded environments may lead to context switches, and increase likelihood of a situation where the memory touching thread runs on a different socket Vs allocating thread

Since a single NUMA node may have multiple cores and our existing heap model creates a per-core allocator, this does not eliminate the possibility of memory fragmentation. A thread might run OOM [26] with a particular CPU's allocator and switch to another CPU's cache reserves (possibly on a very distant NUMA node)

4.3 NUMA-Conscious Heap Memory Design

API Perspective. The fundamental step towards becoming NUMA-friendly primarily begins by creating a binding of physical memory immediately after VMA reservation. As already discussed in Sect. 3.2, we choose to avoid the "BIND" policy and instead support the "PREFERRED" and "INTERLEAVED" policies as a best effort to set the physical page affinity on NUMA systems. We feel this is an important difference with respect to earlier work prescribed on NUMA-aware heap allocators [15] that implicitly relies on the strong binding guarantees of 'libnuma', bringing into picture the perils of Node-level OOM and swapping during high memory demands. Our design creates a robust NUMA heap manager by using a safe combination of the appropriate library routines on Linux platform (explained in next section). With a best-effort approach, we entrust OS with the responsibility of fallback decisions pertaining to physical memory placement in event of low memory situations on the requested node. As per the library documentation of "PREFERRED" policy behavior [23], the OS will automatically choose an optimal neighbor when the target node is unable to bind the requisite physical memory. This creates a neat abstraction for application modules around the OS-dependent gory rigors of physical memory management.

Below are APIs published by our Heap Manager to higher DB modules (aka Data Store & Query Processor) to strategize their data structure and object placement (Table 2).

Table 2. Data placement APIs for allocating modules

Memory Manager API	Purpose
ALLOC_ON_NUMA_NODE(< N>)	hint to allocate on NUMA node < N>
ALLOC_ON_CURRENT_NODE	hint to allocate on node of the executing thread
ALLOC_ON_NUMA_INTER-LEAVED	hint to interleave memory with OS page granularity in round-robin fashion across all available nodes

Below are additional APIs useful for lower-level DBMS operations (aka Job Scheduling) to guide placement decisions of relational worker threads (Table 3).

Table 3. Resource lookup APIs for task scheduling modules

Memory Manager API	Purpose
GET_NUMA_NODE_OF_ADDR (< addr >)	Determine physical memory mapping of given virtual address (< addr >) to its node of residence. This internallyinvokes the get_mempolicy() system call
GET_NUMA_DISTANCE (< N_1 >, <N_2 >)	Determine relative distance in multiples of 10 from SLIT ACPI tables (linux kernel) to quantify # of hops between nodes < N_1 > and < N_2>
GET_NEAREST_NEIGHBOR (< N>)	Determine the node closest to node < N > in the NUMA Topology based on inter-node distances
GET_FREE_MEMORY_ON_NODE (< N>)	Determine total free memory (OS + Allocator caches) available with node < N>. The OS portion is determined with numa_node_size64() routine of libnuma, while the Allocatorcache is tracked by our Memory Manager

A Peek into Design Internals. The data placement APIs are further understood by looking at the numbered steps in life of a NUMA-aware allocation workflow from Client module to OS (Fig. 6).

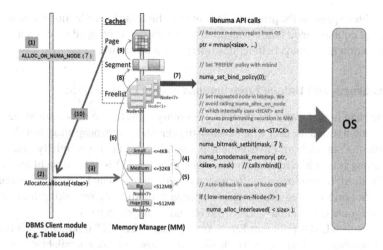

Fig. 6. Low-level interactions of NUMA-aware heap and OS

(1) Client thread calls placement API to allocate on a particular node (say Node# 7)
(2) Call by client to allocate < size > bytes of data object
(3) Entry into Memory Manager module where the decision is cleverly taken to use the Memory Pool of executing core from target node and appropriate slab allocator of the Pool that best fits the incoming request size
(4) 'SMALL' allocator satisfies request or forwards to 'MEDIUM' allocator
(5) 'MEDIUM' allocator satisfies request or forwards to 'BIG' allocator
(6) 'BIG' allocator of Node# 7 satisfies request or consults Global free list of segments
(7) Global Freelist of Node# 7 consults its internal caches or calls libnuma APIs...
   – Mmap call to reserve memory segment of requested < size > (as in earlier design)
   – Specify 'PREFERRED' policy (Table 1) via call to numa_set_bind_policy API
   – Prepare the allocation bitmask for binding and turn on bit for Node# 7
   – Bind the reserved memory to Node# 7 with libnuma API 'numa_to_node-mask_memory' which internally invokes the 'mbind' system call
(8) (9)Add reserved segment into Freelist and carve out desired sized chunks (segments/pages) and add them to slab allocator caches. In case memory is not available in Step# 7, we borrow from pools of adjacent cores co-located in same node
(10) Return VMA pointer of allocated memory to the requestor

Obviously one of the important considerations is also how Memory is released to OS to meet the high demand pressures in high concurrency scenario. This is achieved with the help of internal statistics/watermarks to track free memory available and used in decision making to free up large segments. Remember our buffers do not otherwise return memory to OS. At reclaim time, the selected chunks are unmapped and released to OS. With the help of periodic memory reclaim triggered by appropriate events, our design is able to prevent the process footprint from bloating in production environments. This may of course punch holes in an otherwise contiguous mapped memory arena, but our compaction algorithms help reduce internal fragmentation.

4.4   Challenges and Unique Contributions of Our Proposal [18]

Our basic heap model overrides the C/C ++ library APIs (e.g. malloc, calloc, new) and intercepts them to call the user wrappers that trigger our custom heap allocators. Working with 'libnuma' in such an environment is bound to result in potentially undesirable programming issues like reentrancy and stack overflow. This is because libnuma APIs internally need to malloc/calloc temporary allocations, which triggers a recursive behavior. Solving this requires a unique approach of suitably reworking routines like numa_alloc_onnode(), numa_node_size64() and numa_distance().

The default NUMA policy of Linux kernel uses "STRICT" binding which is prone to severe problems. Transparently dealing with low memory availability at actual commit time (or "page touch") at OS level requires applications to use "PREFERRED" policy to spill over "non-fitting" allocations into other (remote) nodes. This is achievable with special calls like 'numa_set_bind_policy(0)' [23].

Process-managed heap memory in multi-threaded environment requires more effort for NUMA-awareness since it typically involves internally cached data structures which are either "process-global" or "thread-private". These structures are used to buffer the OS-allocated segment chunks. With the concept of NUMA-aware heap, such internally cached pools need to be "topology-sensitized". This may include borrowing memory from other CPU's caches within socket boundaries (or closer nodes).

5   OS Settings and Their Adverse Effects on NUMA Systems

As mentioned earlier, the behavior during physical memory allocation at touch is heavily dependent on the running Linux kernel flavor. With the "PREFERRED" scheme of allocations, it is experimentally observed that the below system factors significantly impact the %NUMA awareness (locality hit) of physical memory.

5.1   Transparent Huge Pages (or THP)

The "PREFERRED" policy (see Sect. 3.2) sometimes selects remote NUMA node although specified node has free memory. Using advanced linux tools like '/proc/ < PID >/numa_maps', '/proc/zoneinfo' and '/proc/pagetypeinfo', we isolated the root cause of this behavior as due to Huge Pages feature on Linux.

The Transparent Huge Pages (THP) feature was introduced to solve performance penalty of page fault rates and TLB accesses during virtual address translations, but introduces the side-effect of memory fragmentation. The fragmentation is particularly severe when requested target node has enough memory to satisfy the node binding, but no continuous huge page range (e.g. 2 MB). In such situations, the OS tries the other (remote) nodes, because it is cheaper than trying to defragment the free memory using compaction. In some cases, it may even decide to demote to 4 KB page allocations, but that usually happens only if the huge page allocation failed on remote node and compaction also did not help. This is a highly OS-specific behavior and may trigger remote allocations. Prior work in [24] also highlights the performance degradation in memory accesses of THP owing to adverse effects like poor data locality and imbalance of data distribution on NUMA systems. Based on discussions with Linux kernel team, we would advise to disable THP on large topologies.

```
echo never > /sys/kernel/mm/transparent_hugepage/enabled
(as root)
```

5.2 Filesystem Page Cache

Linux typically uses unused memory for file system buffers. In situations when the page file cache grows to significant proportions without periodic reclaim, this might cause a given NUMA node to appear low on memory, when may be far from reality! The problem we observed in the context of "PREFERRED" policy is that remote nodes were sometimes being chosen, because the default OS behavior is to skip requested node if most of its free memory resides within page caches.

In Linux 2.6.16 a form of local reclaim was introduced [3]. Zone reclaim begins to do light-weight reclaim of local nodeby removing pages of unmapped page cache. By default the system tunable (/proc/sys/vm/zone_reclaim_mode) is set to '0' by Linux team for performance reasons, since it is found unwise to trigger a local reclaim across every NUMA system. However on very large topologies with significant inter-node distance, the parameter may be automatically activated by OS. Based on discussions with kernel team, our recommendation is to enable the local reclaim feature.

```
echo 1 > /proc/sys/vm/zone_reclaim_mode (as root)
```

Another option is to periodically free the system-wide cache, but this is expensive.

```
echo 3 > /proc/sys/vm/drop_caches (as root)
```

6 Performance and Scalability

6.1 Hardware Setup

Our hardware comprises of NUMA server with 8 sockets each of 15-core Intel Xeon E7-8880 v2 2.50 GHz (Ivybridge-EX) processors. Each core consists of 2 hardware threads with 32 KB L1, 256 KB L2 cache, and the cores in a socket share ~ 38 MB L3 cache. Each socket shares 2 memory controllers configured in independent mode for the highest throughput. Each controller supports 2 Intel SMI interfaces, each SMI supporting 2 memory channels, with up to 3 DDR3 DIMM attached on each channel. Each channel has one 16 GB DDR3 (1600 MHz) DIMM. Each socket has 3 Intel Quick-Path Interconnect (QPI), each with 16 GB/s bandwidth that supports data requests and directory-based cache coherence protocol. A remote hop is ~ 1.1–1.2x slower than a local hop.

6.2   Workload Scenario- I

The first workload was purely to measure raw speed of allocation requests of random sizes (8B–130B) concurrently fired from multiple threads of user-space allocators (Fig. 7).

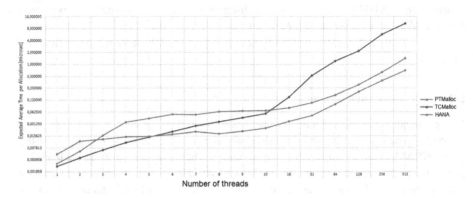

Fig. 7. Scalability of NUMA-aware allocators for pure allocation workload

Our approach shows good scalability with increasing number of parallel threads compared to some of the popular allocators like PtMalloc and TCMalloc [25]. The break-even happens at ~ 5 threads, which is a less popular scenario in commercial DBMS (Fig. 8).

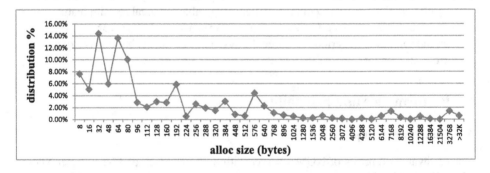

Fig. 8. Distribution of allocation frequency per size class

6.3   Workload Scenario - II

For a real-world usecase, we ran an OLTP workload on SAP HANA with 40 users concurrently updating a columnar table of 50 columns and 4 Million rows. Each user updates an entire row and touches nearly 2 % of the entire dataset. We found an end-to-end improvement of +9 % with our proposal of NUMA-aware allocators compared to

OS default approach. The improvement may be correlated to the 1-hop latency of underlying hardware. It may be noted that the default approach uses OS policy of first touch, and hence incurs remote access overhead (Fig. 9).

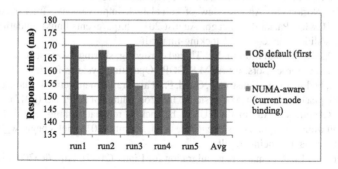

Fig. 9. Response time speedup in OLTP (updates) with NUMA-aware allocations

7 Conclusion

In this paper, we demonstrated some techniques to create a scalable multi-threaded Heap Memory Allocator optimized for NUMA architectures. Some of the earlier studies of distributed memory systems have either used application agnostic approaches or employ higher-level relational optimizations. None of the prior work focuses on creating a deeper programming framework for NUMA-awareness suitable for DB kernels. In our contribution, we use an appropriate mix of Linux library and system calls to create the infrastructural pieces of Heap Management needed for higher layers to efficiently place their internal data structures and data stores and also schedule their relational operator execution threads. Our approach sustains minimal fragmentation overheads with hierarchical slab-based technique and helps showcase good performance scalability on large multi-cores with respect to competitive approaches. We additionally conduct a study of Linux kernel settings unsuitable for large NUMA.

Acknowledgements. The authors would like to thank Norman May, Tobias Scheuer, Iraklis Psaroudakis, Abdelkader Selami, Vipin Vishvkarma, Harshada Khandekar, Amit Saonerkar and the entire project team for their valuable contributions. The authors also thank Alexander Boehm, Werner Thesing and senior leadership for their valuable guidance.

References

1. Kleen, A.: A NUMA API for linux (Technical whitepaper by SUSE Labs), April 2005. http://www.novell.com/docrep/2009/11/4621437_en.pdf
2. Lameter, C.: NUMA(non-uniform memory access): an overview. ACM Queue **11**(7), 40 (2013)
3. Lameter, C.: Local and remote memory: memory in a Linux/NUMA System (June 2006)

4. Blagodurov, S., Zhuravlev, S., Fedorova, A., and Kamali, A.: A case for NUMA-aware contention management on multicore systems. In: Proceedings of PACT (2010)
5. Bryant, R., Barnes, J., Hawkes, J., Higdon, J., and Steiner, J.: Scaling Linux to the extreme. In: Proceedings of the 2004 Ottawa Linux Symposium, July 2004
6. Bueso, D., Norton, S.: An overview of kernel lock improvements. In: LinuxCon North America, Hewlett-Packard, Chicago, August 2014. http://events.linuxfoundation.org/sites/events/files/slides/linuxcon-2014-locking-final.pdf
7. Tam, D., Azimi, R., and Stumm, M.: Thread clustering: sharing-aware scheduling on SMP-CMP-SMT multiprocessors. In: ACM SIGOPS Operating Systems Review (2007)
8. Dashti, M., Fedorova, A., Funston, J., Gaud, F., et al.: Traffic management: a holistic approach to memory placement on NUMA systems. In: Proceedings of ASPLOS (2013)
9. Riel, R., Chegu, V.: Automatic NUMA balancing. red hat summit, April 2014. http://events.linuxfoundation.org/sites/events/files/slides/summit2014_riel_chegu_w_0340_automatic_numa_balancing_0.pdf
10. Schermerhorn, L.: Automatic page migration for Linux (2007). http://lca2007.linux.org.au/talk/197.html
11. Lang, H., Leis, V., Albutiu, M.-C., Neumann, T., Kemper, A.: Massively parallel NUMA-aware Hash joins. In: Jagatheesan, A., Levandoski, J., Neumann, T., Pavlo, A. (eds.) IMDM 2013/2014. LNCS, vol. 8921, pp. 3–14. Springer, Heidelberg (2015)
12. Albutiu, M., Kemper, A., Neumann, T.: Massively parallel sort-merge joins in main memory multi-core database systems. PVLDB 5(10), 1064–1075 (2012)
13. Li, Y., Pandis, I., Müller, R., Raman, V., Lohman, G.: NUMA-aware algorithms: the case of data shuffling. CIDR (2013)
14. Leis, V., Boncz, P., Kemper, A., Neumann, T.: Morsel-driven parallelism: a NUMA-aware query evaluation framework for Many-Core age. In: SIGMOD (2014)
15. Kaminski, P.: NUMA-aware heap memory manager
16. Ghemawat, S., Menage, P.: TCMalloc: thread-caching malloc. http://goog-perftools.sourceforge.net/doc/tcmalloc.html
17. Drepper, U.: What every programmer should know about memory, November 2007
18. Wagle, M., Booss, D., Schreter, I.: US patents with SAP Ref. No: 150150US01 (Title: NUMA-Aware Memory Allocation) and SAP Ref. No: 150423US01 (Title: NON-Uniform Memory Access (NUMA) database management system) (2015)
19. Gloger, W.: PTMalloc. http://www.malloc.de/en/
20. Berger, E., McKinley, K., Blumofe, R., Wilson, P.: Hoard: a scalable memory allocator for multithreaded applications. In: Proceedings of ASPLOS (2000)
21. Psaroudakis, I., Scheuer, T., May, N., Ailamaki, A.: Task scheduling for highly concurrent analytical and transactional main-memory workloads. ADMS@VLDB (2013)
22. Färber, F., May, N., Lehner, W., Große, P., Muller, I., Rauhe, H., Dees, J.: The SAP HANA database–an architecture overview. IEEE Data Eng. Bull. **35**, 28–33 (2012)
23. libnuma–3rd party library for NUMA Policy control. http://linux.die.net/man/3/numa
24. Gaud, F., Lepers, B., Decouchant, J., Funston, J., Fedorova, A., Quéma, V.: Large pages may be harmful on NUMA systems. In: Proceedings of USENIX ATC (2014)
25. Ferreira, T.B., Matias, R., Macedo, A., Araujo, L.B.: An experimental study on memory allocators in multicore and multithreaded applications. In: Proceedings of PDCAT (2011)
26. Sentosa, M.: When Linux runs out of memory (2006). http://www.linuxdevcenter.com/pub/a/linux/2006/11/30/linux-out-of-memory.html

Big-SeqDB-Gen: A Formal and Scalable Approach for Parallel Generation of Big Synthetic Sequence Databases

Rim Moussa[✉]

ENICarthage Engineering School of Carthage, Carthage, Tunisia
rim.moussa@esti.rnu.tn

Abstract. The recognition that data is of big economic value and the significant hardware achievements in low cost data storage, high-speed networks and high performance parallel computing, foster new research directions on large-scale knowledge discovery from *big sequence databases*. There are many applications involving *sequence databases*, such as customer shopping sequences, web clickstreams, and biological sequences. All these applications are concerned by the big data problem. There is no doubt that fast mining of billions of sequences is a challenge. However, due to the non availability of big data sets, it is not possible to assess knowledge discovery algorithms over big sequence databases. For both privacy and security concerns, Companies do not disclose their data. In the other hand, existing synthetic sequence generators are not up to the big data challenge.

In this paper, *first* we propose a formal and scalable approach for *Parallel Generation of Big Synthetic Sequence Databases*. Based on *Whitney numbers*, the underlying *Parallel Sequence Generator* (*i*) creates billions of distinct sequences in parallel and (*ii*) ensures that *injected sequential patterns* satisfy user-specified *sequences' characteristics*. *Second*, we report a scalability and scale-out performance study of the *Parallel Sequence Generator*, for various sequence databases' sizes and various number of *Sequence Generators* in a shared-nothing cluster of nodes.

Keywords: Big synthetic data · Sequence database · Sequential pattern · Parallel generator · Whitney numbers

1 Introduction

There are many applications involving *sequence databases*, namely customer shopping sequences, web clickstreams, biological sequences, and sequences of events in science and engineering. Jiawei Han, Micheline Kamber and Jian Pei define a *Sequence Database* as it *consists of sequences of ordered elements or events, recorded with or without a concrete notion of time* [1]. Problems addressed within sequence databases, include mining the frequently occurring patterns [2–6], mining for outliers patterns [7,8], building efficient sequence databases and indexes for sequence data [9,10], mining compressing sequential patterns [11,12] and comparing sequences for similarity [13]. Most published papers in the literature address

© Springer International Publishing Switzerland 2016
R. Nambiar and M. Poess (Eds.): TPCTC 2015, LNCS 9508, pp. 61–76, 2016.
DOI: 10.1007/978-3-319-31409-9_5

the *Frequent Sequential Pattern Mining problem.* The latter was introduced by Agrawal and Srikant in 1995 [2] and is defined as follows: *Given a database of sequences, where each sequence consists of a list of transactions ordered by transaction time and each transaction is a set of items, sequential pattern mining is to discover all sequential patterns with a user-specified minimum support.* An example of a sequential pattern is that *customers typically rent video Star Wars, then Empire Strickes Back, then Return of the Jedi.* Elements of a sequential pattern might be sets of items (i.e., itemsets), with a sequential pattern which looks as *customers typically rent video Star Wars, then the triplet Return of the Jedi, Lord of Ring and Alien movies.*

Experiences with mining big data ascertain that *more data usually beats better algorithms* [14]. All pattern mining algorithms over sequence databases are concerned by the big data challenges. Big data adds a further level of complexity to any knowledge discovery algorithm. However, due to the non availability of big real data sets, it is not possible to assess sequential patterns' mining algorithms over big sequence databases. For both privacy and security concerns, companies do not disclose and share their data. It is also complex to encode real data sets, while preserving their characteristics. On the other hand, available synthetic sequence generators such as *IBM Quest Synthetic Data Generator* [15] are not up to the big data challenge. Hence, in this paper, we propose a formal and scalable approach based on *Whitney numbers* for *Parallel Generation of Big Synthetic Sequence Databases* satisfying both user-specified *sequences' characteristics* and *velocity* requirements.

In this paper, we make the following contributions,

- We propose a new efficient and fast approach based on *Whitney numbers* for a parallel generation of big sequence databases,
- We assess by performance measurements the scalability and the scale-out of the proposed *Parallel Sequence Generator* on a GRID5000 cluster of shared-nothing nodes [16]. Performance measurements report the throughput in terms of MBps and in terms of number of sequences created and stored per second for various number of *sequence generators* (termed *workers* in distributed computing) and various *number of injected sequential patterns.* The latter grows linearly with the sequence database size.

The paper is organized as follows, Sect. 2 overviews existing sequence generators. Section 3 presents basic concepts of *sequence databases.* Section 4 details our proposed *Parallel Sequence Generator* (for short *PSG*), precisely the requirements it fulfills and its computational model. Section 5 presents a thorough performance study of *PSG.* Finally, Sect. 6 concludes the paper and presents future research.

2   Related Work

The most known generator of sequential patterns is the *IBM Quest Synthetic Data Generator* [15,17,18]. A second testbed for patterns' mining is described in [19], although the testbed is not available for download. After a performance study of distributed implementations [18] of *GSP* [3] and *PrefixSpan* [6] algorithms, we investigated the source code of the *IBM Quest Synthetic Data Generator*. The generator reveals the shortcomings enumerated below,

1. First issue is related to the fact that the benchmark is not documented. The original source code is no longer available through IBM web site[1]. Available implementations address portability and compatibility issues.
2. Second issue is related to sequences' generation. Indeed, regards generated sequences, no evident correlation could be drawn from input parameters, and particularly how do they should scale with the sequence database size. A random process is used for generating sequences and corrupting base sequential patterns used for populating the sequence database [15,17,18]. This process does not guarantee that a sequential pattern repeats a number of times proportional to the database size.
3. Third issue is related to capacity and velocity requirements, the *IBM Quest Synthetic Data Generator* was not designed for *fast* generation of *big* sequence databases.

Most data mining benchmarks relate to small test datasets. Many big data benchmarks exist, but have different objectives. For instance, the *TeraSort* benchmark [20] measures the time to sort 1 TB (10 billions of 100 Bytes records) of randomly generated data. The *Parallel Data Generator Framework* (PDGF) [21,22] allows parallel generation of big relational databases. The *BigDataBench* [23] proposes several benchmarks specifications to model five important application domains, including search engine, social networks, e-commerce, multimedia data analytics and bioinformatics.

To the best of our knowledge, the *Parallel Sequence Generator* is the first synthetic sequence generator addressing big data and velocity requirements. Our contribution is then three fold (*i*) a computational approach based on *Whitney numbers* allowing the generation of billions of data sequences, (*ii*) an efficient implementation and an experimental assessment of the scalability and the scale-out of the proposed *Parallel Sequence Generator*, finally (*iii*) an open-source code, available for download in order to help researchers in benchmarking knowledge discovery algorithms over big sequence databases [18].

3   Sequence Databases: Concepts and Primitives

Given a database of customer purchase histories, one would like to mine and predict the behaviors of customers. A customer buying A and then B is likely to buy C, D and E. A marketing manager can then send advertisements of products C, D and E to clients who have bought A and then B. $\langle \{A\}\{B\}\{C, D, E\} \rangle$ is termed a *sequential pattern*.

---

[1] URL: http://www.research.ibm.com/labs/almaden/index.shtml#assocSynData does not point to the benchmark homepage.

Sequence ID	Sequence
s_1	$\langle\{1\}\{1,2,3\}\{1,3\}\{1,4\}\{3,6\}\rangle$
s_2	$\langle\{1,4\}\{3\}\{2,3\}\{1,5\}\rangle$
s_3	$\langle\{5,6\}\{1,2\}\{4,6\}\{3\}\{2\}\rangle$
s_4	$\langle\{5\}\{7\}\{1,6\}\{3\}\{2\}\{3\}\rangle$

Fig. 1. Example of $\mathcal{S}$-a database of sequences.

Figure 1 illustrates a *sequence database* $\mathcal{S}$ composed of four sequences, which abstract customer-shopping sequences. The set of items in $\mathcal{S}$ is $\{1,2,3,4,5,6,7\}$. The *count* of a sequence s, denoted by *count(s)*, is defined as the number of sequences that contain s. For instance for $s = \langle\{1\}\{3\}\{3\}\rangle$, $count(s) = 2$. Indeed, s is a *subsequence* of both s_1 and s_2, denoted as $s \sqsubseteq s_1$ and $s \sqsubseteq s_2$. Inversely, s_1 and s_2 are *supersequences* of s. A sequence contributes only one to the count of a sequential pattern, for instance $count(\langle\{1\}\{1\}\rangle) = 2$. The support of a sequence s, denoted by *support(s)*, is defined as *count(s)* divided by the total number of sequences seen. If $support(s) \geq \tau$, where τ is a user-supplied minimum support threshold, then we say that s is a *frequent sequential pattern*. For $\tau = 0.75$, $s' = \langle\{1\}\{3\}\{2\}\rangle$ is a frequent sequential pattern. Indeed, s' is a subsequence of all of s_2, s_3 and s_4. Finally, the *length* of a sequence s, denoted by $|s|$ is the sum all its itemsets' lengths, and a *k-sequence* is a sequence of length k. For instance, s_1 is a 9-sequence and $\langle\{1\}\{3\}\{3\}\rangle$ is a 3-sequence.

The major approaches for mining of sequential patterns [2–6] are based on the The *Apriori property*. The latter states that *all non empty subsets of a frequent itemset must also be frequent*, including frequent items. This property is also denoted *antimonotonicity*. If a sequence is infrequent, all of its supersequences must be infrequent, and if a sequence is frequent, all of its subsequences must be frequent. For instance for $\tau = 0.75$, all of $\langle\{1\}\{3\}\rangle$, $\langle\{1\}\{2\}\rangle$, $\langle\{3\}\{2\}\rangle$, are subsequences of $s' = \langle\{1\}\{3\}\{2\}\rangle$ and are frequent sequential patterns. For more details, readers are invited to check the seminal paper on *Sequential Patterns Mining* by Agrawal R. and Srikant R. [2].

4   Parallel Generation of a Sequence Database

Very early, the Database community proposed synthetic benchmarks, which handle big data and variety of workloads. Our work is mainly inspired by [24], the TPC benchmarks [25], and PDGF [21,22]. In the sequel, first, we define goals that the proposed *Parallel Sequence Generator* (for short *PSG*) fulfills. Second, we detail a formal method based on *Whitney enumerators* for the enumeration of *sequential patterns*, denoted as *source sequences* in this paper.

4.1   Requirements

The *Parallel Sequence Generator* is designed so that it fulfills well known requirements of benchmarking [25,26], namely,

- *Relevance*: *PSG* implements *Whitney Enumerators* a computational method which efficiently enumerates in parallel distinct *source sequences* to be injected in the *sequence database*,
- *Repeatability*: for multiple runs with same input parameters, *PSG* outputs a sequence database with same characteristics, namely sequence database volume, sequence size, number of sequences, average number of items per sequence, average number of itemsets per sequence, and *source sequences* with lengths and quotas equal to input parameters,
- *Economy*: *PSG* is open-source and is hardware and platform independent,
- *Fairness*: the generator does not overfit a particular algorithm of sequential pattern mining, and provides directions to generate a sequence database for testing the mining capacity of algorithms through variation of database size and sequential patterns size.
- *Performance*: *PSG* reports metrics demonstrating its velocity for synthetic sequence generation. Experiments are carried out in order to assess scalability and scale-out performance of *PSG*.

4.2   *Whitney Enumerators* for the Enumeration of *Source Sequences*

Raissi and Pei used *Whitney numbers* in order to bound the number of frequent sequential patterns [27]. *PSG* implements *Whitney Enumerators* a computational method based on *Whitney numbers* which efficiently enumerates in parallel distinct *source sequences*. *PSG* is based on the *Apriori property*: given a finite set of items $\mathcal{I}$, which cardinality is n; *PSG* generates distinct *source sequences* of a given length k, to be injected in the *sequence database*. Next, we show how to enumerate *source sequences* using *Whitney enumerators*.

Enumerating the k-*sequences* is described in the recurrence relation introduced in Eq. 1. $\mathcal{WE}_k$ stands for *Whitney Enumerator* of *source sequences* of length k and $\mathcal{E}\binom{n}{i}$ stands for *Combination Enumerator*.

$$\mathcal{WE}_k = \bigcup_{i=0}^{k-1} \mathcal{E}\binom{n}{k-i} \times \mathcal{WE}_i \ with \begin{cases} n = |\mathcal{I}| \\ \mathcal{WE}_0 = \varnothing \\ \mathcal{WE}_1 = \mathcal{E}\binom{n}{1} \end{cases} \tag{1}$$

For instance, for $\mathcal{I} = \{1, 2\}$,

- $\mathcal{WE}_1 = \mathcal{E}\binom{2}{1} = \{1\}, \{2\}$
- $\mathcal{WE}_2 = \bigcup_{i=0}^{1} \mathcal{E}\binom{2}{2-i} \times \mathcal{WE}_i = \mathcal{E}\binom{2}{2} \times \mathcal{WE}_0 \cup \mathcal{E}\binom{2}{1} \times \mathcal{WE}_1 = \{1,2\} \times \varnothing \cup$
$\{1\}, \{2\} \times \{1\}, \{2\} = \{1,2\}, \{1\}\{1\}, \{1\}\{2\}, \{2\}\{1\}, \{2\}\{2\}.$

Figure 2 illustrates compositions of *source sequences* obtained from $\mathcal{WE}_5$ and $\mathcal{I}$, such that $|\mathcal{I}| = 10$. Notice that each branch allows the enumeration of a number of *source sequences* presented in blue. For instance, the last branch

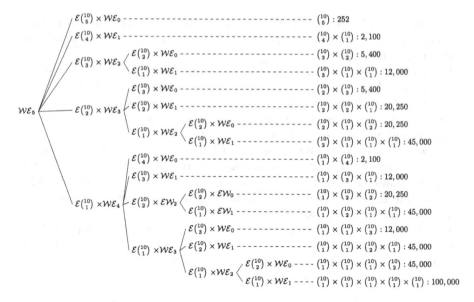

Fig. 2. *Source sequence* enumeration and count for $\mathcal{WE}_5$ ($k = 5$) and $n = 10$ (Color figure online).

allows the enumeration of 10^5 *source sequences*, such that each is composed of five singletons, while the first branch's capacity is only 252 sequences, and each *source sequence* is a single itemset which contains five items. For small values: $k = 5$ and $n = 10$, one could enumerate $392,002$ *source sequences*.

Equation 2 introduced by Raissi and Pei [27] allows the count of each *Whitney number* in terms of number of *source sequences*. Table 1 presents capacities of *Whitney numbers* while varying k for $|\mathcal{I}| = 50$, as well as the count of single itemset sequences and k itemsets sequences. Notice that, for $|\mathcal{I}| = 50$, $\mathcal{WE}_5$ allows the enumeration of more than one billion of *source sequences*, and $\mathcal{WE}_{10}$ enumerates more than two and half trillions of *source sequences* (one trillion $= 10^{18}$). For higher values of k and $|\mathcal{I}|$, enumerating and storing all possible *source sequences* can turn into high storage costs and memory leaks. Next, we detail an efficient enumeration procedure.

$$
\mathcal{W}_k = \sum_{i=0}^{k-1} \binom{n}{k-i} \times \mathcal{W}_i \quad with \begin{cases} n = |\mathcal{I}| \\ \mathcal{W}_0 = 1 \\ \mathcal{W}_1 = n \end{cases} \tag{2}
$$

4.3 Efficient Enumeration of *Source Sequences*

Hereafter, we describe how *Parallel Sequence Generator* enumerates in parallel variety of *source sequences* at less cost.

Table 1. Whitney numbers' capacities for $|\mathcal{I}| = 50$.

W_k	Nbr. of source sequences	Nbr. of k itemsets source sequences	Nbr. of single itemset source sequences
W_1	50	50	50
W_2	3,725	2,500	1,225
W_3	267,100	125,000	19,600
W_4	19,128,425	6,250,000	230,300
W_5	1,370,262,510	312,500,000	2,118,760
W_6	98,160,302,325	15,625,000,000	15,890,700
W_7	7,031,803,751,400	781,250,000,000	99,884,400
W_8	503,729,624,143,775	39,062,500,000,000	536,878,650
W_9	36,085,128,550,756,000	1,953,125,000,000,000	2,505,433,700
W_{10}	2,584,990,924,265,820,000	97,656,250,000,000,000	10,272,278,170

Enumerate *Source Sequences* at Less Cost. We propose algorithms for the enumeration of a *Combination* contents as well as for the *Cross product of Combinations*. Our algorithms save a *current context*, which is composed of a *current combination* and a *current cross of combinations*. The enumeration is then performed through successive calls of *next sequence method*. The source code of *Whitney numbers* and *Whitney enumerators* manipulations for *source sequences*' enumeration is available for download [18].

Figure 3 demonstrates the enumeration process. Starting with the first source sequence of the 10th branch of $\mathcal{WE}_5$, which is $\{0\}\{0,1,2\}\{0\}$, the next source sequence is obtained by shifting third combination to next value in order to obtain source sequence $\{0\}\{0,1,2\}\{1\}$. Successive calls of *next sequence method* continue so, until we reach source sequence $\{0\}\{0,1,2\}\{9\}$. The next source sequence is obtained by reset of third combination and shift of second combination to next value, in order to obtain source sequence $\{0\}\{0,1,3\}\{0\}$. The enumeration procedure is generalized to cross products of multiple combinations [18].

Enumerate Variety of *Source Sequences*. As illustrated in Fig. 2, *source sequences* of same length k have different number of itemsets. The first branch is composed of a single itemset, while the last branch is composed of k itemsets *source sequences*. A depth-first traversal of the tree will enumerate source sequences branch by branch. Within each branch, *source sequences* feature the same number of itemsets and the same number of items for each itemset. For the example illustrated in Fig. 2, the enumeration of the first 10,000 *source sequences* stops at the third branch, and does not include any *source sequence* beyond this branch. This might have an impact on the mining process. Thus, in order to variate generated *source sequences*, we preponderate the number of source sequences to be generated along each branch capacity of the tree. Likewise, the

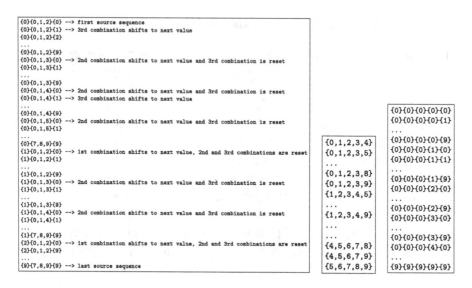

Fig. 3. Excerpt of enumerated source sequences in (a) 10th branch: $\binom{10}{1} \times \binom{10}{3} \times \binom{10}{1}$, (b) 1st branch: $\binom{10}{5}$, (c) *last* branch: $\binom{10}{1} \times \binom{10}{1} \times \binom{10}{1} \times \binom{10}{1} \times \binom{10}{1}$, for $\mathcal{WE}_5$ and $\mathcal{I} = \{0, 1, 2, 3, ..., 9\}$.

10,000 *source sequences* will be generated from each of the 16 branches with the following quotas, $[6, 54, 137, 307, 137, 517, 516, 1148, 53, 307, 516, 1148, 306, 1148, 1147, 2553]$.

PSG allows generation of other specific compositions of *source sequences*, namely,

- *Source sequences with a single itemset*, which are typical data sets for frequent itemsets mining algorithms (a.k.a. market basket analysis) (see 2nd box in Fig. 3),
- *Source sequences composed of singletons*, which are typical event type sequences (see 3rd box in Fig. 3),
- *Source sequences of different lengths* through the use of different *Whitney enumerators*. Each *Whitney enumerator* has its own source of items i.e. $\mathcal{I}$, so that source sequences generated using smaller Whitney enumerators are not subsequences of source sequences generated using bigger Whitney enumerators.

Emit Sequences. We vary sequences' contents as follows: initially each source sequence is composed of a number of itemsets in the range 1 to k itemsets and of exactly k frequent items. All frequent items are in $\mathcal{I}$. In order to mimic real datasets, we add more itemsets and we append to each sequence random items, which do not belong to $\mathcal{I}$. *Padded items* are distributed among all itemsets of the sequence. Each sequence s is finally emitted a number of times which depicts the *count(s)*. All of the input parameters, *number of* *padded items, number of itemsets* and *sequence support* follow a Poisson distribution. For instance, $\langle\{0\}\{0,1,2\}\{0\}\rangle$ is a *source sequence* for both following sequences $\langle\{\mathbf{0},70,80\}\{180,200\}\{\mathbf{0,1,2},53,65,103\}\{\mathbf{0},1000\}\rangle$ and $\langle\{1003\}\{78,309\}$ $\{\mathbf{0}\}\{407,509\}\{\mathbf{0,1,2},5000\}\{507,809\}\{\mathbf{0},3000\}\{67,89\}\rangle$.

Enumerate in Parallel. For parallel generation of distinct source sequences, *Whitney numbers* are communicated to a pool of M *Sequence Generators*. Each *Sequence Generator* has a logical identifier in the range: $0\ldots M-1$. *Sequence Generators* generate simultaneously generate distinct source sequences using the same Whitney numbers. For so, for each new branch of a Whitney Enumerator, each *Sequence Generator* identified by sg_j skips j *source sequences*. Then, each time it processes a *source sequence*, it skips M sources sequences, simulating a round robin distribution scheme [18]. Notice that this way, sequences having the same source sequence are clustered. For declustering purpose, all *Sequence Generators* may emit the same *source sequence* with different padding patterns.

5   Implementation and Performance Measurements

We implemented the *Parallel Sequence Generator* (PSG) using *MapReduce framework* [28] of Apache Hadoop 2.4 YARN. The generation load is evenly distributed among all *Sequence Generators*. Each *Sequence Generator* (Mapper in MapReduce framework terminology) is responsible for the creation of sequences using x *source sequences*, such that x is equal to the *number of source sequences for injection* divided by the *number of Sequence Generators*. For so, it creates a single file and writes into generated sequences. Finally, the *Sequence Generator* emits the volume of data sequences as well as the number of generated sequences. A Reducer aggregates summaries of generation results, it calculates the total volume and the total number of sequences written into *Hadoop Distributed File System* (HDFS).

A performance study was conducted in a shared-nothing cluster of nodes to demonstrate the scalability of the proposed *Parallel Sequence Generator*. The hardware system configuration used for performance measurements are Suno nodes located at Sophia site of french HPC platform GRID5000 [16]. Each Suno node has 32 GB of memory, its CPUs are Intel Xeon E5520, 2.27 GHz, with 2 CPUs per node and 4 cores per CPU. All nodes are connected by a 10 Gbps Ethernet.

The primary goal of carried-out experiments is to assess the scalability and the scale out of *PSG*. We are interested in two metrics, namely (1) the *Throughput in terms of Mega Bytes per second* (MBps), and (2) *the Throughput in terms of sequences per second* (#Seqs/sec). We report these metrics for different experiment settings, namely,

- *Hadoop cluster size*: the hadoop cluster is composed of one *master* and 2, 5 or 10 *slave nodes*. The Hadoop block size is set to 256 MB and the replication factor is set to 1 in order to reduce data redundancy overhead, and determine the maximum allowed throughput rates.

– *Number of sequence generators*: each *slave node* sets up a number of *sequence generators*, which also corresponds to the number of output data files. This parameter denotes the degree of parallelism in sequence generation and writing to HDDs. *Sequence generators* run in parallel in order to increase write throughput performances.

– *Number of source sequences injected in the database*: the size of the sequence database grows linearly with the number of injected source sequences (see Fig. 12). For experiments, a sequence is 420 bytes. This size relates to 5-sequences type (i.e., $\mathcal{WE}_5$), with an average of 25 items padded to each source sequence distributed over an average of 15 itemsets. Each source sequence repeats in average 5 % of the number of source sequences injected.

Experiments compare *PSG* to *TestDFSIO*. The latter is a distributed I/O benchmark tool, part of the Hadoop distribution. Each mapper in *TestDFSIO-write workload* creates a file and a 1 MB buffer and repeatedly writes the buffer into the output file until the file size reaches a user-specified value. For instance, a workload example of *TestDFSIO* could be create 10 files, such that each file is 10 GB. *TestDFSIO* reports average throughput per node, to be multiplied by the cluster size in order to obtain the aggregated write throughput. We compare throughput performances of *PSG* to *TestDFSIO*, in order to highlight the sequence generation overhead.

Figure 4 presents performance measurements of *PSG* compared to *TestDFSIO* for a 3 nodes' cluster. The cluster is composed of one master and 2 slave nodes. It sets up 10 *Sequence Generators*, which create sequences independently from each other. *PSG* creates a sequence database of over 450 GB with more than 2 billions of sequences, it succeeds to write 1.2 millions of sequences per second at a throughput of 287 MBps. The throughput is measured for various *number of injected source sequences* in the range 1,000 .. 200,000. A maximum throughput of 315 MBps is recorded, which results from the injection of 90,000

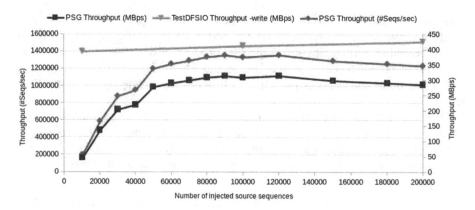

Fig. 4. *PSG* throughput performance results for a 3 nodes' cluster for 10 *sequence generators*, compared to *TestDFSIO* benchmark with 10 mappers.

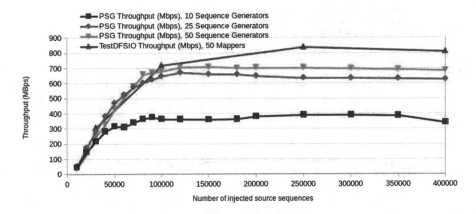

Fig. 5. *PSG* throughput performance results (MBps) for a 6 nodes' cluster and 10, 25, 50 *Sequence Generators*, compared to *TestDFSIO -write workload* benchmark with 50 Mappers.

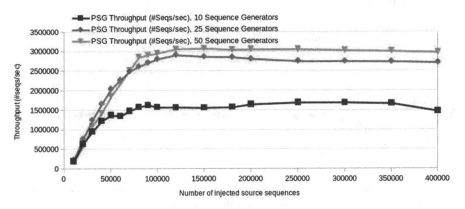

Fig. 6. *PSG* throughput performance results in terms of sequences per second for a 6 nodes' cluster and various number of *Sequence Generators*.

source sequences. This corresponds to a 91 GB Sequence Database, composed of more 400 millions of sequences.

Figures 5 and 6 present throughput performance measurements of *PSG* respectively in terms of MBps and #Seqs/sec for a 6 nodes' cluster. The cluster is composed of one master and 5 slave nodes. It sets up various number of *Sequence Generators*, which create sequences in parallel independently from each other. *PSG* creates a sequence database of over 1.8TB with more than 8 billions of sequences, it succeeds to write 3 millions of sequences per second at a throughput of 694 MBps. The throughput is measured for various number of *source sequences* in the range 10,000 .. 400,000. For each experiment, whether for 10, 25 or 50 *Sequence Generators*, the throughput increases for a number of *source sequences* less than 100,000, then it is invariant, and finally slightly

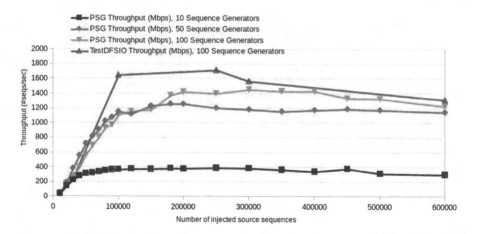

Fig. 7. PSG throughput performance results in terms of MBps for 11 nodes' cluster and 10, 25, 50 *Sequence Generators*, compared to *TestDFSIO -write workload* benchmark with 100 Mappers.

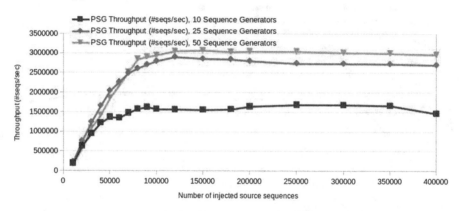

Fig. 8. *PSG* throughput performance results in terms of sequences per second for a 11 nodes' cluster and various number of *Sequence Generators*.

decreases due to the saturation of HDDs of slave nodes. It reaches a maximum value of 741.61 MBps for 50 *Sequence generators* and 180,000 source sequences. This corresponds to a 365 GB Sequence Database composed of more than one billion and half of sequences.

Figures 7 and 8 present respectively throughput performance measurements of *PSG* respectively in terms of MBps and #Seqs/sec for an 11 nodes' cluster. The cluster is composed of one master and 10 slave nodes. It sets up various numbers of *Sequence Generators*, which create sequences in parallel independently from each other. *PSG* creates a sequence database of over 4TB with more than 18 billions of sequences, it succeeds to write 5.3 millions of sequences per second at a throughput of 1.2 GBps(1230 MBps). The throughput is measured for various number of *injected source sequences* in the range 10,000 .. 600,000. The throughput increases for a number of *source sequences* less than 100,000, then it is almost invariant, and finally slightly decreases due to the saturation of HDDs of slave nodes. It reaches a maximum value of 1.45 GBps (1481.51 MBps) for 100 *Sequence Generators* and 300,000 *injected source sequences*.

Notice that we could not create bigger databases for HDDs' space constraints. Indeed, for an 11 nodes' cluster (one master and 10 slave nodes), the exception message when creating a sequence database with 700,000 *source sequences* is *Error: org.apache.hadoop.ipc.RemoteException (java.io.IOException): File/sequences/sequences_97.seq could only be replicated to 0 nodes instead of min-Replication (=1). There are 10 datanode(s) running and no node(s) are excluded in this operation.*

In conclusion, the sequence generation is proved efficient, especially for big Sequence databases. Comparisons with *TestDFSIO* shows that for big sequence databases, HDFS IO operations which consist in appends to data files are much more expensive than enumeration costs of *source sequences*. Figures 9 and 10

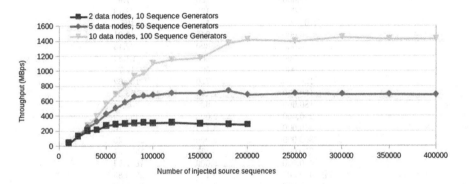

Fig. 9. Comparison of *PSG* Throughput (MBps) performance evaluation for various number of hadoop data nodes.

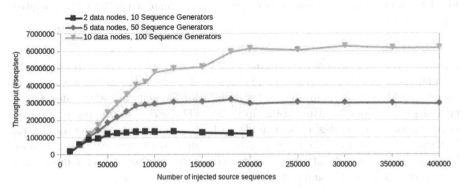

Fig. 10. Comparison of *PSG* Throughput (#Seqs/sec) performance evaluation for various number of hadoop data nodes.

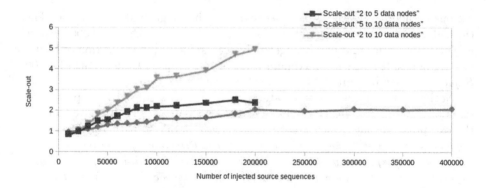

Fig. 11. *PSG* Scale-out Tests.

# source sequences	# sequences (×10⁶)	Sequence DB (GB)
10,000	5	1.12
20,000	20	4.50
30,000	45	10.10
40,000	80	17.97
50,000	125	28.18
60,000	180	40.56
70,000	245	55.21
80,000	320	72.13
90,000	405	91.34
100,000	500	112.71
120,000	720	162.62
150,000	1,125	253.54
180,000	1,620	364.76
200,000	2,000	450.69
250,000	3,125	704.10
300,000	5,000	1014.20
350,000	6,125	1379.91
400,000	8,000	1802.52
450,000	10,125	2280.85
500,000	12,500	2816.97
600,000	180,000	4056.40

Fig. 12. Average *number of sequences* (millions) and *volume* (Giga Bytes) of generated *Sequence DBs*.

illustrate best performance measurements obtained for each cluster size. Figure 11 calculates the *scale-out* factor for the three cluster size settings, for a *number of injected source sequences* limited by the generation capacity of each cluster. Comparisons to a 3 nodes' cluster holds up to 200,000 *injected source sequences*, and comparisons to a 6 nodes' cluster holds up to 400,000 *injected source sequences*. Pairwise comparisons of the three cluster sizes shows that the *scale out* is almost ideal for big sequence databases. Indeed, *n times* the number of data nodes results in *n times* the write throughput.

6 Conclusions and Future Work

Starting from unavailability of synthetic big sequence databases for mining sequential patterns. *First*, this paper proposes a scalable and formal approach for *Parallel Generation of Big Synthetic Sequence Databases* satisfying both user-specified *sequences' characteristics* and *velocity* requirements. Experiments prove that the underlying *Parallel Sequence Generator* (*i*) creates billions of different sequences in parallel, (*ii*) ensures that injected source sequences satisfy the user requirements especially sequential pattern length characteristic. *Second*, the paper reports a scalability and scale-out performance study of the *Parallel Sequence Generator*, for various sequence databases' sizes and various number of *Sequence Generators* in a shared-nothing cluster of nodes.

Future work is mainly oriented towards three different directions. *First*, we aim to conduct thorough performance study of *GSP** and *PrefixSpan**: our proposed parallel implementations of *GSP* [3] and *PrefixSpan* [6] algorithms, using big sequence databases generated using *PSG*. *Second*, we aim to propose sophisticated algorithms with lessons learned from the performance studies of *GSP** and *PrefixSpan**. *Third*, we aim to customize *Parallel Sequence Generator* in order to generate datasets close to real data sets particularly for event sequences of computer logs, where large clusters emit millions of log entries per second.

Acknowledgements. We acknowledge with thanks a VLDB travel fellowship.

References

1. Han, P.J., Kamber, M., Pei, J.: Data Mining: Concepts and Techniques. The Morgan Kaufmann Series in Data Management Systems, 3rd edn. Morgan Kaufmann, Burlington (2011)
2. Agrawal, R., Srikant, R.: Mining sequential patterns. In: Proceedings of the 11th International Conference on Data Engineering (ICDE), pp. 3–14 (1995)
3. Srikant, R., Agrawal, R.: Mining sequential patterns: generalizations and performance improvements. In: 5th International Conference on Extending Database Technology Proceedings (EDBT), pp. 3–17 (1996)
4. Zaki, M.J.: Efficient enumeration of frequent sequences. In: Proceedings of ACM CIKM International Conference on Information and Knowledge Management, pp. 68–75 (1998)
5. Han, J., Pei, J., Yin, Y.: Mining frequent patterns without candidate generation. In: Proceedings of the ACM SIGMOD International Conference on Management of Data, pp. 1–12 (2000)
6. Pei, J., Han, J., Mortazavi-Asl, B., Pinto, H., Chen, Q., Dayal, U., Hsu, M.: Prefixspan: mining sequential patterns by prefix-projected growth. In: Proceedings of the 17th International Conference on Data Engineering, pp. 215–224 (2001)
7. Sun, P., Chawla, S., Arunasalam, B.: Mining for outliers in sequential databases. In: Proceedings of the 6th SIAM International Conference on Data Mining, pp. 94–105 (2006)
8. Hemalatha, C.S., Vaidehi, V., Lakshmi, R.: Minimal infrequent pattern based approach for mining outliers in data streams. Expert Syst. Appl. **42**, 1998–2012 (2015)

9. Cheng, H., Yan, X., Han, J.: Seqindex: indexing sequences by sequential pattern analysis. In: Proceedings of SIAM International Conference on Data Mining. SDM, pp. 601–605 (2005)

10. Lin, M.Y., Lee, S.Y.: Fast discovery of sequential patterns through memory indexing and database partitioning. J. Inf. Sci. Eng. **21**, 109–128 (2005)

11. Xin, D., Han, J., Yan, X., Cheng, H.: Mining compressed frequent-pattern sets. In: Proceedings of the 31st International Conference on Very Large DataBases, pp. 709–720 (2005)

12. Lam, H.T., Mörchen, F., Fradkin, D., Calders, T.: Mining compressing sequential patterns. Stat. Anal. Data Min. **7**, 34–52 (2014)

13. Li, H., Homer, N.: A survey of sequence alignment algorithms for next-generation sequencing. Briefings Bioinform. **11**, 473–483 (2010)

14. Rajaraman, A.: More data usually beats better algorithms (2008). http://anand.typepad.com/datawocky/2008/04/data-versus-alg.html

15. Srikant, R.: IBM quest synthetic data generator (1999). http://sourceforge.net/projects/ibmquestdatagen/files/

16. Grid5000: Large-scale and versatile testbed for experiment-driven research: distributed computing-HPC and big data (2015). https://www.grid5000.fr/

17. Kum, H.C., Chang, J.H., Wang, W.: Benchmarking the effectiveness of sequential pattern mining methods. Data Knowl. Eng. **60**, 30–50 (2007)

18. Moussa, R.: Mining big sequence databases (2015). https://sites.google.com/site/rimmoussa/miningbigseqdb

19. Pei, J., Mao, R., Hu, K., Zhu, H.: Towards data mining benchmarking: a testbedfor performance study of frequent pattern mining. In: Proceedings of ACM SIGMOD International Conference on Management of Data, p. 592 (2000)

20. Gray, J.: Sort benchmark home page (2008). http://research.microsoft.com/barc/SortBenchmark/

21. Tilmann, R., Meikel, P.: Parallel data generation for performance analysis of large, complex RDBMS. In: Proceedings of the 4th International Workshop on Testing Database Systems, pp. 5:1–5:6 (2011)

22. Poess, M., Rabl, T., Frank, M., Danisch, M.: A PDGF implementation for TPC-H. In: Nambiar, R., Poess, M. (eds.) TPCTC 2011. LNCS, vol. 7144, pp. 196–212. Springer, Heidelberg (2012)

23. Luo, C., Gao, W., Jia, Z., Han, R., Li, J., Lin, X., Wang, L., Zhu, Y., Zhan, J.: Handbook of BigDataBench: A Big Data Benchmark Suite (2015). http://prof.ict.ac.cn/BigDataBench

24. Jim, G., Prakash, S., Susanne, E., Ken, B., Weinberger, P.J.: Quickly generating billion-record synthetic databases. In: Proceedings of ACM SIGMOD International Conference on Management of Data, pp. 243–252 (1994)

25. Transaction Processing Council: TPC benchmarks (2015). http://www.tpc.org/

26. Karl, H.: The art of building a good benchmark. In: Proceedings of TPC-TC, pp. 18–30 (2009)

27. Raïssi, C., Pei, J.: Towards bounding sequential patterns. In: Proceedings of the 17th ACM SIGKDD International Conference on Knowledge Discovery and Data Mining, pp. 1379–1387 (2011)

28. Dean, J., Ghemawat, S.: Mapreduce: simplified data processing on large clusters. In: 6th Symposium on Operating System Design and Implementation (OSDI), pp. 137–150 (2004)

A Benchmark Framework for Data Compression Techniques

Patrick Damme[✉], Dirk Habich, and Wolfgang Lehner

Database Systems Group, Technische Universität Dresden,
01062 Dresden, Germany
{patrick.damme,dirk.habich,wolfgang.lehner}@tu-dresden.de

Abstract. Lightweight data compression is frequently applied in main memory database systems to improve query performance. The data processed by such systems is highly diverse. Moreover, there is a high number of existing lightweight compression techniques. Therefore, choosing the optimal technique for a given dataset is non-trivial. Existing approaches are based on simple rules, which do not suffice for such a complex decision. In contrast, our vision is a cost-based approach. However, this requires a detailed cost model, which can only be obtained from a systematic benchmarking of many compression algorithms on many different datasets. A naïve benchmark evaluates every algorithm under consideration separately. This yields many redundant steps and is thus inefficient. We propose an efficient and extensible benchmark framework for compression techniques. Given an ensemble of algorithms, it minimizes the overall run time of the evaluation. We experimentally show that our approach outperforms the naïve approach.

Keywords: Lightweight data compression · Main memory database systems · Efficient benchmarking

1 Introduction

Nowadays, main memory-centric column-oriented database management systems are the prevailing technology for data processing [5,7,12]. Many of these systems reduce the amount of data they have to store and process by making use of lossless lightweight compression [1,3]. Owing to its reduced size, compressed data offers several advantages such as less time spent on load and store instructions, a better utilization of the cache hierarchy and less misses in the translation lookaside buffer. Moreover, many plan operators in database systems can be modified to directly process compressed data, which can be faster than processing the original data [1,16]. On the other side, compression and decompression introduce a certain computational overhead. For that reason, it is crucial to implement these algorithms as efficient as possible.

The data being stored and processed by in-memory column stores is as diverse as the application domains of such systems. It is characterized by a multitude of

© Springer International Publishing Switzerland 2016
R. Nambiar and M. Poess (Eds.): TPCTC 2015, LNCS 9508, pp. 77–93, 2016.
DOI: 10.1007/978-3-319-31409-9_6

properties, such as data types, value distributions – including value ranges and the number of distinct values – and correlations between subsequent values – e.g., multiple subsequent occurrences of the same value. All these different kinds of data must be compressed appropriately, since databases are expected to be generic regarding the application area. At the same time, several decades of research in the field of lossless compression yielded a multitude of different compressed formats and compression algorithms to choose from. Some of these use completely different approaches, i.e., address different sources of redundancy in the original data, while others just differ in minor – but perhaps decisive – details of the memory layout of their outputs. Some are tailored to fit certain characteristics of modern hardware, while others are kept more generic.

When integrating compression into a database management system, it is crucial to know which compression technique is suited best for what data. In that respect, *suited best* can have different meanings ranging from *lowest latency* or *highest throughput* over *best compression rate* to *optimal for further processing by plan operator X*. Not leveraging such knowledge during the integration leads to a suboptimal improvement of the database performance, in the best case. It might, however, even cause a degradation of the performance, since most compression techniques increase the size of the data if it does not exhibit appropriate characteristics.

In the literature, several approaches exist attempting to identify a good compression technique for some given data using *rule-based* strategies. One example of these is the decision tree provided by Abadi et al. in [1]. However, rule-based approaches are too coarse-grained and can hardly capture all imaginable data characteristics. In contrast, we believe that a *cost-based* approach should be used instead. For this, an underlying cost model is required, which must be obtained from a *systematic* and *exhaustive* benchmarking and evaluation of numerous compression algorithms on multitudes of different original data and on different hardware. This systematic benchmarking is the scope of this paper. Thus, our contribution is a benchmark framework for data compression techniques with the following key features:

- It minimizes the overall evaluation run time for an ensemble of algorithms by identifying and eliminating redundant steps and making use of today's large main memories.
- It efficiently verifies the correctness of the results of the evaluated algorithms.
- It is highly extensible; in particular, it allows the integration of third-party compression algorithms and data generators, e.g., via a wrapper.

The rest of this paper is organized as follows: In the next section, we give an overview of existing lightweight compression techniques and state more precisely which classes of algorithms are relevant to our benchmarking. After that, Sect. 3 provides a high-level description of our benchmark framework. Section 4 discusses the execution of compression algorithms in detail. Our experimental results are presented in Sect. 5. We discuss related work in Sect. 6. Finally, we conclude our paper in Sect. 7.

2   Compression Techniques

In the context of database-oriented data compression, there are three classes of
algorithms relevant to our benchmark framework. The first two – compression
and decompression – are discussed in Sect. 2.1. The third one – transformation
– is discussed in Sect. 2.2. We only consider lossless techniques. Furthermore, we
only investigate 32-bit integers as the data type of the uncompressed data at
the current status. However, this limitation is not too strict, since integers can
be obtained from values of any data type by applying dictionary coding [1,11],
first. Our framework itself is generic in terms of data types.

2.1   Compression and Decompression

The general idea of compression is to represent some given original data in
another format in which the data has a smaller size. Thereby, the information
necessary to re-obtain the original data must be preserved, in order to allow a
lossless decompression. There are two classes of compression techniques: heavyweight and lightweight. Heavyweight techniques, such as Huffman encoding [6],
arithmetic coding [17], or LZW [10] compress the given data close to its entropy.
However, they require a lot of computation and are, hence, rather suited for disk-
centric DBMS. For main memory-centric systems, there are lightweight compression techniques which require much less computation. As a consequence, they
achieve much higher throughputs, while still yielding good compression rates.

The basic types of lightweight compression are dictionary coding (DICT)
[1,11,18], delta coding (DELTA) [9,13], frame-of-reference (FOR) [4,18], null
suppression (NS) [1,13], and run-length encoding (RLE) [1,13]. DICT maps
each distinct value to a unique key. DELTA and FOR represent each value as
the difference to its predecessor or a certain reference value, respectively. The
aim of these three techniques is to obtain a sequence of small integers from the
original data. After that, a scheme from the family of NS is typically applied
to achieve the actual compression. NS eliminates leading zeros in small integers.
RLE compresses uninterrupted sequences of occurrences of the same value, so-
called *runs*, by representing them by just one occurrence followed by the length.

Recent research in the field of lightweight compression has especially investigated the efficient implementation of these classic schemes on modern hardware.
For instance, Zukowski et al. [18] introduced the paradigm of patched coding,
which especially aims at the exploitation of pipelining in modern CPUs. Another
promising direction is the vectorization of compression techniques by using SIMD
instruction set extensions such as SSE and AVX. Numerous vectorized techniques
have been proposed in recent years, e.g., in [9,14,15].

Besides compression and decompression algorithms for *different* compressed
formats, we explicitly consider different *variants* of the compression to and
decompression from *a single* compressed format. Such variants exist at both,
the algorithmic and the implementation level. Two implementations of the same
compression algorithm could, e.g., differ in whether they use SIMD extensions

or not. We show an example of this case in Sect. 5. Furthermore, when composing two distinct compression algorithms, e.g., DELTA followed by NS, there are several variants regarding the degree of integration. Our benchmark framework especially optimizes the comparison of different variants of one algorithm.

2.2 Transformation

Beyond compression and decompression, we are also concerned with a third class of algorithms: *transformation*, which we recently introduced in [2]. A transformation is a lossless change of the (compressed) format some data is represented in. It expects data of a certain *source format* and outputs the representation of that data in its *destination format*. Thus, transformation is a generalization of compression and decompression. Henceforth, we use the term transformation to refer to those transformations which are neither a compression nor a decompression, i.e., that do not involve uncompressed data as their input or output.

There are two possible ways to transform some data represented in a compressed format A to a compressed format B. A naïve approach, which we call *indirect transformation*, first applies the decompression algorithm of its source format to its entire compressed input data and materializes the result in main memory. After that, it uses the compression algorithm of its destination format. While indirect transformations can easily be implemented for arbitrary pairs of a source and a destination format, they are very inefficient due to their many accesses to main memory. In contrast, there are *direct transformation* techniques which do not materialize any intermediate data in main memory. Instead, intermediate data stays in CPU registers or at worst in the L1 cache. In general, direct transformations can be implemented by interleaving the code of the decompression of the source format with the compression of the destination format. Thereby, the intermediate store and load instructions are omitted. In many cases, even more optimizations are possible, which we described in detail in [2] for some direct transformation techniques. In [2] we also experimentally showed that direct transformations outperform their indirect counterparts in most cases.

Our benchmark framework supports the evaluation of transformation algorithms and makes use of them, in order to minimize the overall evaluation run time. How this is done is described in detail in Sect. 4.

3   Framework Overview

In this section, we provide a high-level view of our benchmark framework[1]. Section 3.1 describes the general workflow of the framework. After that, Sect. 3.2 explicitly explains our design principles.

---

[1] The source code of our framework can be downloaded at https://wwwdb.inf.tu-dresden.de/team/staff/patrick-damme-msc/.

3.1 General Workflow

The general workflow of our benchmark framework is shown in Fig. 1. The applications performing the individual steps are invoked by a script. In the following, we briefly present each step.

Benchmark Specification. Before the framework can start, the user needs to specify a benchmark. She decides which algorithms shall be evaluated and subdivides these into several, possibly overlapping sets. The algorithms in one set will be evaluated on the same data. For each set of algorithms, the user specifies the data characteristics by choosing (1) a data generator, (2) one data property to be varied, including the distinct values to be assigned to it, and (3) the configuration of the remaining, fixed data properties. For instance, the user could specify to generate $100M$ values using generator simpleGen, whereby the values follow a uniform distribution over the interval $[2^8, 2^{16} - 1]$, while the data consists of runs, whose lengths follow a normal distribution with a standard deviation of 5 and a mean that is varied from 20 to 200 in steps of 10. Varying a data property allows to investigate the influence of that property on the performance of the algorithms. If the user wants to vary more than one data property or she wants one data property to be varied in conjunction with multiple configurations of fixed properties, then she must provide multiple specifications of the input data for that set of algorithms, since only one property can be varied at a time. The specification of the benchmark is passed to the framework as a file with a very simple text-based format, an example of which is presented in Fig. 2.

Parsing. The first step of the framework is parsing the benchmark specification. After that, it knows which algorithms the user wants to evaluate on what data.

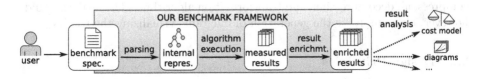

Fig. 1. An overview of our benchmark framework.

```
data generator name   suffixes for orders of magnitude   varying the mean from 20 to 200 in steps of 10
data=simpleGen(count=100M runlength=rndNormal(stddev=5 mean=20..200+10)
               values=rndUniform(min=256 max=0xffff))
algorithms=RleSeq-Co.,RleSimd-Co.,Rle-De.,Rle-2-Dict,Rle-2-4Ns
comma-separated list of algorithm names                   specification of numbers in different formats
```

Fig. 2. Example benchmark specification using our minimalistic specification language. One benchmark may contain several of such pairs of data and algorithm specifications.

Algorithm Execution. This is the core step of the framework. It is invoked once for each specified pair of a set of algorithms and a configuration of data properties. It iterates over all values to be assigned to the varied data property. In each iteration, the data is generated using the specified generator parameterized with the specified data properties. After that, the specified algorithms are run on the generated data. The framework also checks the output buffers of the algorithms for correctness. The approach the evaluation follows is crucial for its efficiency. We describe a naïve as well as our sophisticated approach in detail in Sects. 4.1 and 4.2, respectively. Since performance is crucial in this step, it is implemented in C++. The output is a set of CSV files. Each of these contains some meta data regarding the evaluation and a table containing only actual measurements, i.e., no derived results. For instance, for all algorithms we measure their *run time* and for each format, we measure the *size* of the data in that format.

Result Enrichment. In this step, the measured results output by the previous step are enriched with derived columns. We differentiate between two types of enrichment. The first one provides additional representations of the measurements for a single algorithm or compressed format. Examples include the *execution speed* of all algorithms or *compression rates* for all formats. The second kind of enrichment is concerned with the relation between the measurements of different algorithms or formats. These could, for instance, be *speed ups* of one algorithm compared to another one. Separating the result enrichment from the algorithm execution was an explicit decision. That way we can easily calculate new derived results from *existing measurements without having to re-run the evaluation* at a later point in time *as a part of the framework's workflow*.

Result Analysis. After the benchmark framework is done, the collected results can be analyzed. Our vision is the creation of a cost model for the investigated compression, decompression, and transformation algorithms. The analysis could, however, also simply be the generation of diagrams visualizing the results.

3.2 Design Principles

When designing our benchmark framework, we tried to adhere to three major design principles:

Simplicity. Our framework uses a simple and yet expressive language to specify a benchmark. Instead of describing it in detail, we just provide an example in Fig. 2. Moreover, the steps of the framework are easily repeatable. Once a benchmark has been specified, it can be run arbitrarily often, e.g., on different hardware.

Efficiency. The framework minimizes the overall run time of the evaluation. Our main focus is on the avoidance of redundant steps during the algorithm execution. To achieve this, we utilize today's large main memories by keeping outputs instead of recomputing them. Details are provided in Sect. 4.

Extensibility. The framework can be extended at several crucial points. In particular, it allows the integration of third-party compression, decompression and transformation algorithms. The framework defines a common interface for these. To use an existing algorithm with our framework, the algorithm must implement that interface. Alternatively, a wrapper can be provided which translates our interface to that of the third-party algorithm. In fact, we implemented a wrapper for the compression and decompression algorithms of the FastPFor library by Lemire et al. [8]. In a similar way, third-party data generators can be integrated. One particular extension could be a data generator which does not produce synthetic data, but provides the system with data from a real world dataset.

4   Efficient Execution of Compression Techniques

Since it is the most critical step for the evaluation efficiency, the *algorithm execution* from Sect. 3.1 is explained in detail here. Its input is a specification of the data properties along with a set $\mathcal{A}$ of algorithms to be evaluated on that data. We assume that (1) the original data has a non-trivial size, e.g., several hundreds of megabytes, and (2) the value of one data property is varied within a range of a non-negligible cardinality, e.g., several hundreds or thousands of different values. Otherwise, the evaluation would not take much time and therefore not offer much potential for optimization.

When applying a compression or transformation algorithm to some data, it must be ensured that a sufficiently large output buffer was allocated to prevent buffer overflows. However, in general, it is impossible to know the *exact* size of the output beforehand. Thus, a *pessimistic estimation* of the result size is required. If nothing about the characteristics of the original data is known, such an estimation can only be based on the number of original values. Unfortunately, for most compressed formats, the size of the data increases, in the worst case. For instance, data compressed with RLE is twice as large as the uncompressed data, if it does not contain any run of a length greater than one. As a consequence, the system could end up allocating to much memory. While this might be a problem in a DBMS, we can circumvent it in our framework, since we know the properties of the original data from the user's specifications. Our estimation uses this information to find a tighter fit for the actual result size, while never underestimating it. Note, that this information is not made available to the algorithms under investigation, since this could be considered unfair.

During the evaluation, we also check the result of each algorithm for correctness. Each result is compared to the original data, which might require a decompression, first. Moreover, we place some random bytes after the end of each output buffer, in order to be able to detect buffer overflows. Note that we assume that all algorithms have been designed, implemented, and tested carefully *before* the benchmark. Hence, the purpose of the checks is only the detection of errors, not the generation of detailed information for debugging.

While a certain overhead for the evaluation cannot be avoided, different evaluation approaches differ in the implied amount of overhead. In the following, we

Table 1. The notations used in this section.

Symbol	Meaning
$S, D, X, Y; U$	arbitrary formats; the uncompressed format
$O; O_X$	the original data; the representation of O in the format X
$A; \mathcal{A}$	an algorithm; the set of all algorithms specified by the user

describe a naïve evaluation approach in Sect. 4.1. After that, we present our sophisticated approach in Sect. 4.2. Finally, we compare the two of them in Sect. 4.3. Table 1 presents the notations used in those sections. As a running example, we assume the user wants to benchmark two variants of the compression of RLE (*RleSeq-Co.*, *RleSimd-Co.*), the decompression of a dictionary scheme (*Dict-De.*) as well as the transformation from the format of 4-Wise Null Suppression [14] to that of 4-Gamma Coding [14] and vice versa (*4Ns-2-4G*, *4G-2-4Ns*).

4.1   A Naïve Evaluation Approach

When conducting the benchmark naïvely, every algorithm is evaluated in isolation, i.e., as if it was the only algorithm to be investigated. For each algorithm A in $\mathcal{A}$ with source format S and destination format D, the following steps have to be performed for *every* value to be assigned to the varied data property:

1. Generate the original data O_U using the specified data generator and data characteristics, including the current value of the varied data characteristic.
2. If $S \neq U$: Obtain O_S by applying a compression algorithm for S to O_U.
3. Apply A to O_S. Let the output of A be R_D.
4. If $D \neq U$: Obtain R_U by applying a decompression algorithm for D to R_D.
5. Compare R_U and O_U byte by byte to check whether all involved algorithms worked correctly.

Figure 3 illustrates these steps for the example $\mathcal{A}$ given above. This procedure is very simple and thus easy to implement. However, it is very inefficient in general, since it implies multiple invocations of the same algorithms on the same

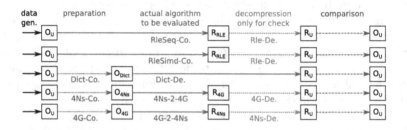

Fig. 3. The steps of a naïve evaluation strategy.

data. In our example, the decompression of RLE is applied twice and the data generation is done five times using the same properties.

4.2   Our Sophisticated Evaluation Approach

The basic idea of our sophisticated approach is the avoidance of redundant steps in the evaluation. That is, no algorithm is invoked twice with the same input. This holds for the algorithms and for the data generation. The key to this is keeping the result buffers of all algorithms, *as long as they are needed* by another algorithm being executed later. These are the high-level steps of our approach:

1. Find out which additional algorithms are needed for preparations and checks.
2. Determine a valid execution order of the algorithms.
3. Run the algorithms one by one and take the measurements.

Step 3 is re-executed for each value to be assigned to the varied data property, step 2 is only re-run if otherwise the memory consumption would be too high and step 1 is done only once in advance for $\mathcal{A}$. In the following, we explain each of these steps in detail. Figure 4 illustrates them for the example given above.

Finding Required Additions for Preparations and Checks. For this step, we formalize the benchmark as a directed graph. The vertices of that graph represent formats, while an edge (X, Y) represents an algorithm with source format X and destination format Y. Since we explicitly consider different variants of a certain algorithm, multiple edges between two nodes are allowed.

First, we build a graph representing the user's benchmark. For each algorithm A in $\mathcal{A}$ with source format S and destination format D, we add the two nodes S and D as well as an edge (S, D) to the graph. That is, we initialize the graph such that it contains only the algorithms in $\mathcal{A}$ as well as the formats involved in them. If the uncompressed format is not already included as a node, we explicitly add it. The result of this step for our example $\mathcal{A}$ is shown in Fig. 4 (a).

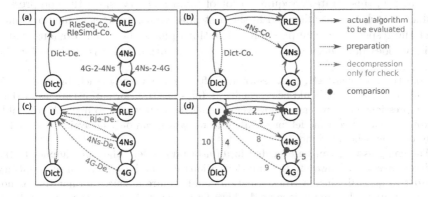

Fig. 4. The steps of our sophisticated evaluation strategy.

Next, we ensure that the source format of each algorithm A in $\mathcal{A}$ can actually be reached from the uncompressed format by a sequence of transformations. This is important, since otherwise the input data for A might not be available. To achieve this, we iterate the following two steps until all nodes are reachable (see Fig. 4 (b) for a possible resulting graph for our example $\mathcal{A}$):

1. *Identify an unreachable node* X. If the graph contains a source, i.e., a node without ingoing edges, we select this one. If there are no sources, there could still be nodes on cycles unreachable from the node of the uncompressed format. To find these, we perform a cycle-aware depth-first search. If the search does not find all nodes, we randomly pick one of the nodes not found.
2. *Make* X *reachable*. For doing so, there could be multiple possibilities. For simplicity, we always connect X by adding a compression from U to X.[2]

Since we also want to check the algorithms in $\mathcal{A}$ for correctness, we need to decompress the representation of the data in each involved format in order to be able to compare it to the original data. Consequently, for each node in the graph we add an edge to the node of the uncompressed format, *if there is not already one*. The result of this step for our example $\mathcal{A}$ is depicted in Fig. 4 (c). We denote the set of algorithms resulting from this step by $\mathcal{A}^+$.

Determining the Execution Order. After it is clear which additional algorithms must be performed, the second step is to determine the order in which the algorithms shall be applied. A valid execution order must fulfil two requirements: (1) it must contain each algorithm in $\mathcal{A}^+$ exactly once, and (2) before an algorithm with a *source* format X other than the uncompressed format is applied, an algorithm with *destination* format X must have been applied. The latter condition ensures that the appropriate input data is available for each algorithm, whereby in the beginning, only the uncompressed data is present.

One strategy to obtain a valid order is the following: First, all compressions in $\mathcal{A}^+$ are executed. Second, all transformations are run. Finally, all decompressions are applied.[3] One possible outcome for our example $\mathcal{A}$ is shown in Fig. 4 (d). For general $\mathcal{A}^+$, this strategy requires a lot of main memory, since the compressed buffers of each format allocated in the first phase must be kept in memory until after the respective decompression in the third phase. Thus it is obvious that – while it does not affect the run time – the execution order is decisive for the

---

[2] Note that, alternatively, a transformation from some already reachable node to X could be added. This could be especially useful, since transformations are faster than compressions in many cases. However, finding the fastest way to make X reachable would require a cost model for the algorithms, which can only be available *after* the systematic benchmarking.

[3] The compressions can be executed in an arbitrary order. The same applies to the decompressions. However, the transformations cannot be applied in an arbitrary order in general, since a transformation could require a source format that is not present after all compressions in $\mathcal{A}^+$ have been executed, as it is the case for 4G-2-4Ns in our example.

maximum memory requirement of the evaluation. There are simple memory-efficient solutions for certain special cases. For instance, if $\mathcal{A}^+$ contains only compressions and decompressions, we simply determine the order the following way: We process the compressed formats involved in $\mathcal{A}^+$ one by one. For each compressed format X, we first execute all compressions to X in $\mathcal{A}^+$, then we perform all decompressions from X in $\mathcal{A}^+$. That way, there is no point in time when O_X and O_Y are both in memory, for any compressed formats X and Y, with $X \neq Y$. If $\mathcal{A}^+$ also contains transformations, finding an optimal order – or a sufficiently good order with respect to some upper bound for the maximum memory consumption – is non-trivial and might itself take considerable time. However, our framework can easily be extended at that point by implementing an appropriate order strategy.

Evaluating the Algorithms. When the order of the algorithms is fixed, the actual evaluation begins. In this step, two auxiliary data structures are maintained: (1) a map m mapping each format X to a buffer containing O_X, and (2) a set of *reference counters*, one for each format involved in $\mathcal{A}^+$. Initially, m is empty and for each format X involved in $\mathcal{A}^+$, the reference counter of X is the number of algorithms in $\mathcal{A}^+$ with source format X plus the number of those with destination format X. Thus, the reference counter of X is the number of times, O_X is needed either as input data or for a comparison. In the beginning, a buffer for the original data is allocated. Then the original data is generated according to the user's specifications and put into m with the key U.

Then, the algorithms are executed. A loop iterates over all A in $\mathcal{A}^+$ with source format S and destination format D using the order determined in the previous step and does the following:

1. A buffer b that fits O_D is allocated.
2. A is executed on O_S, which is looked up in m. Note that O_S is always available if the execution order is valid.
3. It is checked, whether m already contains a buffer for D.
   (a) If this is not the case, i.e., if A is the first algorithm producing a copy of O_D, then b is put in m with key D.
   (b) Otherwise, i.e., if there is already a copy of O_D, the content of b is compared to that copy byte by byte. If they are not the same, this means an error at some point. After the comparison, b is released.
4. The reference counters of both, S and D are decremented. If any of them reaches 0, i.e., if no algorithm executing later will need them any more, then the corresponding buffer is fetched from m and released to free memory.

This procedure guarantees that each required buffer is allocated as late as possible and released as early as possible. Note that all checks are covered by step 3b. If D is a compressed format, the check is performed *in the compressed space*. If D is the uncompressed format, it is not possible that step 3a is executed. This is due to the fact that O_U is in m right from the beginning onwards. It might be released before the end of the evaluation, but not before the last decompression, otherwise the reference counter for U cannot become 0. Thus, a decompression is always followed by a check with the uncompressed data.

4.3 Comparison of the Two Approaches

Our sophisticated approach avoids redundant executions of algorithms at several points. In particular, these are:

- The naïve approach generates the original data anew *for each algorithm* in $\mathcal{A}$. Our approach generates it *only once* for the entire ensemble of algorithms.
- If multiple algorithms in $\mathcal{A}$ share the same compressed source format X, then the naïve approach performs a compression to X *for each of these*, while our approach performs it *just once*. If some compression to X is already included in $\mathcal{A}$, our approach causes *no overhead* for the preparation regarding X.
- If several algorithms in $\mathcal{A}$ share the same compressed destination format Y, then the naïve approach executes a decompression from Y *for each of these*, whereas our approach runs it *just once*. Again, if this decompression is already part of $\mathcal{A}$, our approach causes *no overhead*.
- The naïve approach performs all checks in the uncompressed space, i.e., compares large buffers. In contrast, our approach does as many checks as possible in the compressed space, i.e., compares smaller compressed buffers.

To summarize these points, our approach is especially well-suited if $\mathcal{A}$ contains many algorithms with shared source and/or destination formats. This is, for instance, the case when different variants of the same algorithm are evaluated. Even if none of the algorithms in $\mathcal{A}$ have any formats in common, our approach can still save the time for the redundant data generation. If $\mathcal{A}$ contains only one algorithm, then both approaches do exactly the same. We investigate the quantitative differences between the two approaches in the next section.

5 Experimental Evaluation

We implemented our framework as well as several compression, decompression, and transformation algorithms in C++ and compiled them with g++ 4.8 using the optimization flag -O3. Our experiments are conducted on a machine equipped with an Intel Core i7-4710MQ CPU at 2.5 GHz and 16 GB of RAM. Section 5.1 focuses on the comparison of the naïve and our sophisticated evaluation approach. After that, Sect. 5.2 reports some results output by our framework.

5.1 Naïve Approach vs. Our Sophisticated Approach

We compare the naïve approach as described in Sect. 4.1 (N) to our sophisticated approach as described in Sect. 4.2 (S). Regarding the execution order in S, we use the second idea described in Sect. 4.2 whenever possible and the first idea, otherwise. Additionally, we investigate a variant of the naïve approach that generates the original data only once for the ensemble of algorithms (N^+),

Table 2. The example benchmarks used in this section. **C**, **D**, and **T** stand for compression, decompression, and transformation algorithms, respectively.

Benchmark	Varied property	#variations	Algorithms
B1	avg. run length	1.000	**C**: RleSeq, RleSimd
B2	max. bit width	24	**C**: 4Ns, 4G, Dict; **D**: 4Ns, 4G, Dict
B3	avg. run length	200	**C**: RleSeq, RleSimd; **D**: Dict;
			T: Rle-2-Dict, 4Ns-2-4G, 4G-2-4Ns
B4	max. bit width	24	**C**: 4G; **D**: Dict; **T**: 4Ns-2-Rle
B5	avg. run length	1.000	**C**: RleSimd

since this is an obvious and easy-to-implement improvement of N. We define five different example benchmarks (B1 to B5), representing different cases of sets of algorithms. Their specifications are summarized in Table 2. We consider the compression schemes 4-Wise NS (4Ns) [14], 4-Gamma (4G) [14], dictionary coding (Dict), a sequential and our vectorized variant of RLE (RleSeq and RleSimd) as well as transformations between these. The original data consists of $125M$ uncompressed 32-bit integers, i.e., 500 MB for each benchmark. We ran each of the three evaluation approaches for each of the five example benchmarks.

Figure 5 (a) presents the overall run times of the benchmarks as well as the time spent on the *specified* algorithms, the data generation, and the remaining overhead. Naturally, the execution of the algorithms specified in the benchmark takes equally much time, independent of the evaluation approach. N^+ and S need the same time for the data generation, since they generate it only once for the entire ensemble per value of the varied data property. In contrast, N re-generates the data for each algorithm, which is its major inefficiency. Due to that, it is never faster than any of the other two. The remaining overhead, i.e., preparations, decompressions added by the framework, and checks, is subject to the approach and the ensemble of algorithms. When $\mathcal{A}$ contains many algorithms with formats they have in common (B1 to B3), S can eliminate the redundant steps and thus outperforms the other two approaches. These cases are especially relevant to us. The more algorithms with formats they have in common $\mathcal{A}$ contains, respectively the longer these take, the higher the speed up of S. In B4, the specified algorithms have no compressed formats in common. Additionally, a compressed format is only used as the input of a transformation in $\mathcal{A}$, namely 4Ns. In this special case, S is slightly slower than N^+, because S also performs a check for 4Ns, which N^+ does not. In all other cases, S is not slower than any of the other two approaches. If only one algorithm is evaluated (B5), all three approaches require the same amount of time, since they do exactly the same then.

Figure 5 (b) reports the maximum memory consumption of each of the approaches during each of the benchmarks. It can be seen that the speed up of S in B1 and B3 is bought at the cost of a higher memory demand. However, in B2, S outperforms N and N^+ without requiring more memory. This is due to the execution order used by S in B2. Since $\mathcal{A}$ contains only one compression

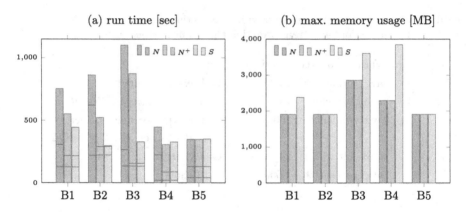

Fig. 5. A comparison of the three evaluation approaches for the different example benchmarks: (a) run times, subdivided into the time consumed by the specified algorithms (bottom), the data generation, and the remaining overhead (top), (b) maximum memory consumptions.

and one decompression algorithm for some formats, S does not need to keep the compressed buffers of any format longer than N and N^+. However, in certain cases (B4) S requires more memory without being faster.

5.2 Example Benchmark

Independent from the evaluation approach, our framework gives us insights into the performance of the investigated algorithms. To show just one example of the outputs of our framework, we choose B3 from the previous section. In B3, the data was generated such that it consists of runs. The individual run lengths were chosen uniformly from the interval $[x - 5, x + 5]$ whereby x was varied from 6 to 404 in steps of 2. The run values are uniformly distributed within the interval $[0, 255]$. In order not to overload the diagrams, we limit the presentation to our two variants of the compression of RLE (RleSeq and RleSimd) as well as the transformations 4Ns-2-4G and 4G-2-4Ns, respectively their involved formats. Figure 6 (a) reports the speeds of the algorithms. It can be seen that the speeds of RleSeq and RleSimd are subject to the run length, while those of the transformations between 4Ns and 4G are not. Furthermore, the vectorized algorithm RleSimd outperforms the sequential one for all run lengths. Figure 6 (b) presents the achieved compression rates of the formats. As expected, the compression rate of RLE decreases, i.e., gets better, as the run length increases. Interestingly, the compression rate of the format of 4-Gamma [14] is also slightly better for longer runs. This is due to the fact that 4G uses a shared bit width for four values at a time. With longer runs, there are more blocks consisting of four equal values, which have the same bit width, and thus waste less bits.

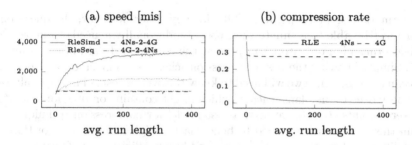

Fig. 6. The processing speeds in million integers per second (mis) (a) and compression rates (b) of some of the algorithms and formats included in B3.

6 Related Work

While we intend to base the decision for a compression technique on a cost model created from the output of our framework, there already exist other approaches to identify an optimal technique in the literature.

Abadi et al. [1] integrate several compression techniques into the column-oriented DBMS C-Store. Their aim is to improve the query performance by compressing every column appropriately. From their experiments, they *manually* derive a decision tree, which is based on certain data characteristics and on the access patterns of a column. However, they consider only a small number of compression schemes. We intend to consider a high number of techniques and *automatically* create a cost model.

Another interesting approach was proposed by Paradies et al. [11]. They intend to decrease the space requirement of the column-oriented SAP BW Accelerator. Being committed to dictionary coding, their goal is not to decide *how*, but *what* to compress. They observe that correlated columns can be stored more efficiently if their corresponding values are coded in pairs. To identify the most promising pairs of correlated columns, they propose an efficient algorithm, which employs sampling and pruning and is aware of additional compression techniques already applied to the data.

7 Conclusions and Future Work

We described our highly extensible benchmark framework for compression, decompression, and transformation algorithms. Based on a benchmark specification by a user, it generates synthetic data with certain characteristics and automatically runs the specified algorithms on it. We proposed a highly efficient evaluation approach, which is based on the elimination of redundant steps during the benchmark execution and thus minimizes the overall benchmark run time. Our experiments proved the superiority of our approach over a naïve approach.

Our ultimate research goal is to employ lightweight compression for the intermediate results in an in-memory DBMS and to make compression subject to query optimization. We intend to implement compression, decompression, and transformation as plan operators. Like for any other operator, the query optimizer must be able to estimate their costs (additionally, it needs to know, how efficient other plan operators can process the compressed data of a certain format). Simply knowing the best compression scheme for a given dataset does not suffice in our case, since we will need to know the overall costs of multiple alternative query executions plans, each of which might contain compression operators at several points. Hence, we need a cost model for compression techniques. To obtain this cost model, we need to benchmark a high number of algorithms on many different datasets in a structured and highly efficient way. Our framework enables us to do precisely that. Besides the execution of a single compression algorithm, we also intend to consider compositions of such algorithms as well as direct transformations between two formats. Both of these further increase the size of the benchmark space and thus stress the importance of our framework.

Acknowledgments. This work was funded by the German Research Foundation (DFG) in the context of the project "Lightweight Compression Techniques for the Optimization of Complex Database Queries" (LE-1416/26-1).

References

1. Abadi, D., Madden, S., Ferreira, M.: Integrating compression and execution in column-oriented database systems. In: SIGMOD, pp. 671–682 (2006)
2. Damme, P., Habich, D., Lehner, W.: Direct transformation techniques for compressed data: general approach and application scenarios. In: Morzy, T., Valduriez, P., Ladjel, B. (eds.) ADBIS 2015. LNCS, vol. 9282, pp. 151–165. Springer, Heidelberg (2015)
3. Färber, F., May, N., Lehner, W., Große, P., Müller, I., Rauhe, H., Dees, J.: The SAP HANA database - an architecture overview. IEEE Data Eng. Bull. **35**(1), 28–33 (2012)
4. Goldstein, J., Ramakrishnan, R., Shaft, U.: Compressing relations and indexes. In: ICDE, pp. 370–379 (1998)
5. Große, P., Lehner, W., May, N.: Advanced analytics with the SAP HANA database. In: DATA, pp. 61–71 (2013)
6. Huffman, D.: A method for the construction of minimum-redundancy codes. Proc. IRE **40**(9), 1098–1101 (1952)
7. Lee, J., Kwon, Y.S., Färber, F., Muehle, M., Lee, C., Bensberg, C., Lee, J., Lee, A.H., Lehner, W.: SAP HANA distributed in-memory database system: transaction, session, and metadata management. In: ICDE, pp. 1165–1173 (2013)
8. Lemire, D., Boytsov, L., Kaser, O., Caron, M., Dionne, L., Lemay, M., Kruus, E., Bedini, A., Petri, M.: The FastPFOR c++ library: Fast integer compression. https://github.com/lemire/FastPFOR
9. Lemire, D., Boytsov, L.: Decoding billions of integers per second through vectorization (2012). CoRR abs/1209.2137
10. Lempel, A., Ziv, J.: On the complexity of finite sequences. IEEE Trans. Inf. Theory **22**, 75–81 (1976)
11. Paradies, M., Lemke, C., Plattner, H., Lehner, W., Sattler, K.U., Zeier, A., Krueger, J.: How to juggle columns: an entropy-based approach for table compression. In: IDEAS, pp. 205–215 (2010)

12. Plattner, H.: A common database approach for OLTP and OLAP using an in-memory column database. In: SIGMOD, pp. 1–2 (2009)
13. Roth, M.A., Van Horn, S.J.: Database compression. SIGMOD Rec. **22**(3), 31–39 (1993)
14. Schlegel, B., Gemulla, R., Lehner, W.: Fast integer compression using SIMD instructions. In: DaMoN Workshop, pp. 34–40 (2010)
15. Stepanov, A.A., Gangolli, A.R., Rose, D.E., Ernst, R.J., Oberoi, P.S.: SIMD-based decoding of posting lists. In: CIKM, pp. 317–326 (2011)
16. Willhalm, T., Popovici, N., Boshmaf, Y., Plattner, H., Zeier, A., Schaffner, J.: SIMD-scan: ultra fast in-memory table scan using on-chip vector processing units. Proc. VLDB Endow. **2**(1), 385–394 (2009)
17. Witten, I.H., Neal, R.M., Cleary, J.G.: Arithmetic coding for data compression. Commun. ACM **30**(6), 520–540 (1987)
18. Zukowski, M., Heman, S., Nes, N., Boncz, P.: Super-scalar RAM-CPU cache compression. In: ICDE, pp. 59–70 (2006)

Enhancing Data Generation in TPCx-HS with a Non-uniform Random Distribution

Raghunath Nambiar[1]([⊠]), Tilmann Rabl[2], Karthik Kulkarni[1], and Michael Frank[3]

[1] Cisco Systems, Inc.,
275 East Tasman Drive, San Jose, CA 95134, USA
{rnambiar,kakulkar}@cisco.com
[2] University of Toronto,
27 King's College Circle, Toronto, ON M5S, Canada
tilmann.rabl@utoronto.ca
[3] Bankmark, Bahnhofstrasse 10, 94032 Passau, Germany
michael.frank@bankmark.de

Abstract. Developed by the Transaction Processing Performance Council, the TPC Express Benchmark™ HS (TPCx-HS) is the industry's first standard for benchmarking big data systems. It is designed to provide an objective measure of hardware, operating system and commercial Apache Hadoop File System API compatible software distributions, and to provide the industry with verifiable performance, price-performance and availability metrics [1, 2]. It can be used to compare a broad range of system topologies and implementation methodologies of big data systems in a technically rigorous and directly comparable and vendor-neutral manner. The modeled application is simple and the results are highly relevant to hardware and software dealing with Big Data systems in general. The data generation is derived from TeraGen [3] which uses uniform distribution of data. In this paper the authors propose normal distribution (Gaussian distribution) which may be more representative of real life datasets. The modified TeraGen and complete changes required to the TPCx-HS kit are included as part of this paper.

Keywords: TPC · Big data · Industry standard · Benchmark

1 TPCx-HS Current State

As Big Data technologies like Hadoop have become an integral part of enterprise IT ecosystem across all major industry verticals, industry standard benchmarks that can fairly compare technologies and products are critical [4]. Big Data was identified as critical area for benchmarking at conferences such as TPCTC 2013 [5]. Keep this in mind the Transaction Processing Performance Council (TPC) developed TPC Express Benchmark™HS (TPCx-HS) that provides an objective measure of hardware, operating

© Springer International Publishing Switzerland 2016
R. Nambiar and M. Poess (Eds.): TPCTC 2015, LNCS 9508, pp. 94–129, 2016.
DOI: 10.1007/978-3-319-31409-9_7

system and commercial Apache Hadoop File System API compatible software distributions. TPCx-HS provides the industry with verifiable performance, price-performance and availability metrics. The benchmark models a continuous system availability of 24 h a day, 7 days a week [1, 6, 7].

Even though the modeled application is simple, the results are highly relevant to hardware and software dealing with Big Data systems in general. The TPCx-HS stresses both hardware and software including Hadoop runtime, Hadoop File System API compatible systems and MapReduce layers. This workload can be used to asses a broad range of system topologies and implementation of Hadoop clusters. The TPCx-HS can be used to assess a broad range of system topologies and implementation methodologies in a technically rigorous and directly comparable, in a vendor-neutral manner [4–6].

TPCx-HS workload is based on TeraSort [1] designed to evaluate the sorting performance of a system-under-test (SUT) [2]. This is highly relevant for every big data system because sorting is a basic operation required in many high level abstractions like ordering, grouping, and joining. The dataset of TPCx-HS consists of records of 100 Byte length where the first 10 Bytes of each record is the sorting key. The keys are distributed uniformly and randomly over the key space. Because of the large key space (2^{80} possible keys), duplicate keys are very unlikely and the key space is sparsely populated. In most real world data sets keys are either of sequential type indexing the row of a table or they are referencing other tuples. In both cases, keys are almost never uniformly distributed over the key space. Depending on the data set properties, keys are dense in some areas (e.g., a sequence with some missing keys) and sparse in others or some keys occur more often than others (e.g., in a purchase table one product ID will be bought more frequently than others). The underlying system often is not aware of the nature of data, but its properties like ordering, density, sparsity, and duplication are important to perform efficient sorting.

2   Extending TPCx-HS

TPCx-HS uses 100 Byte records, where the first 10 Bytes are the keys on which the data is sorted and the remaining 90 Bytes are random payload. TPCx-HS has two implementations –for MapReduce 1 (MR1) and for MapReduce 2 (MR2). They differ in the way random numbers are generated and in the key layout.

2.1   MR1 Implementation

The MR1 version uses a 64 Bit linear congruential generator (LCG) based random number generator. To generate each key, three random numbers are drawn. Each 64 Bit random number is split into four bytes. The last random number only populates two bytes, resulting in a total of 10 bytes per key. During the split the byte value is mapped to the range of the 95 printable ASCII characters. Because of this reduction the total number of distinct keys is only $10^{95} \cong 2^{66}$.

2.2   MR2 Implementation

The MR2 version uses a 128 Bit LCG random number generator. To generate a key, a single 128 Bit random number is drawn. From that 128 Bit random number the highest 80 Bits are used for the key. Unlike the MR1 version, the keys remain in the binary format and cover the whole 2^{80} key range.

Both versions split the random number sequence based on the current mapper row for parallelization. The sequence is pre-split and the pre-calculated seeds for these splits are stored inside TPCx-HS' random number generator. This splitting schema only works if the same amount of random numbers is generated for each row. The MR1 version requires exactly three 64 Bit random numbers and the MR2 version exactly one 128 Bit random number to generate a key.

2.3   Proposed Changes

Main change proposed is the key distribution from uniform distribution to normal distribution (Gaussian distribution). The normal distribution is typically used to describe independent random processes such as growth, income, and measurement errors. A typical example for a uniformly distributed random event is a single fair roll of a die, each side of the die has the same probability and, thus, the results will be uniformly distributed. However, the probability distribution of the sum of multiple rolls converges to a normal distribution. As few natural observations consist of a single random event but rather of a process of random events, the normal distribution is more frequently found than a uniform distribution in real and is the most important distribution in statistics[1].

In order to change the key distribution in TeraGen, an interface was introduced that enables plugging in and parametrizing different ways of generating the key. This was done in the following classes and functions, `HsGen.SortGenMapper.addKey()` in the MR1 version and `HsGen.SortGenMapper.map()` and `GenSort.GenerateRe-cord()` in the MR2 version.

The code of the existing uniform key-generation implementation was copied into a separate plugin. The uniform key generation plugin is used as default, if no other key generation strategy is specified. Additional changes were made to enable the specification and configuration of the key generation strategy via command line. An example

---

[1] Cf., http://www.itl.nist.gov/div898/handbook/pmc/section5/pmc51.htm.

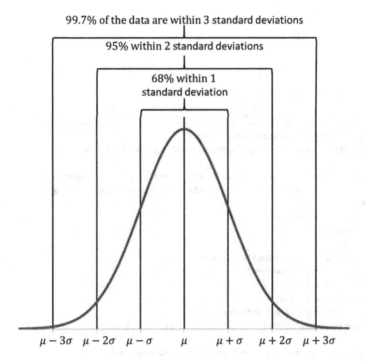

Fig. 1. Normal distribution, its parameters and their implications (Based on Dan Kernler, http://en.wikipedia.org/wiki/File:Empirical_Rule.PNG)

will be given below. Besides the existing default implementation for uniform key generation, an implementation to produce normal distributed keys (Gaussian distribution) was added for both the MR1 and MR2 version of TPCx-HS HsGen:

- `org.tpc.hs.hsgen.mr1.dist.NormalDistributionBigInt`
- `org.tpc.hs.hsgen.mr2.dist.NormalDistributionBigInt`

A normal distribution is parametrized by two values. A mean value μ (mu) and the standard deviation σ (sigma). A visual representation of the normal distribution and the meaning of its parameters can be seen in Fig. 1. The implementation uses a standard polar Box-Muller algorithm for generating normally distributed values using two values sampled from a uniform random number source. Modifications had to be made to scale the algorithm producing 64 Bit double values to the required 80 Bit BigInteger values.

```
01 double SCALE_D = Long.MAX_VALUE / 10;
02 BigInteger SCALE_BI = BigInteger.valueOf(Long.MAX_VALUE / 10);
03
04 public static BigInteger normalDistributedBigInteger(BigInteger mu_bi,
05                 BigInteger sd_bi,BigInteger maxValue, HelperPRNG rng) {
06 do {
07  // Polar box-muller
08  double x, y, r, z;
09  do {
10   x = 2.0 * rng.nextDouble() - 1.0;
11   y = 2.0 * rng.nextDouble() - 1.0;
12   r = x * x + y * y;
13  } while (r >= 1.0);
14  z = Math.sqrt(-2.0 * Math.log(r) / r);
15  double normalDistNumber = y * z; // range: ~ -5.0/+5.0
16
17  // scale "normalDistNumber" with specified mean (mu)
18  //and standard deviation (sd) values
19
20  // naive version, using BigDecimal
21  // Formula: res = mu + sd * normalDistNumber
22  // Range of mu and sd is [0, 2^80]
23  // res = new BigDecimal(mu_bi).add(new BigDecimal(sd_bi)
24  //        .multiply(BigDecimal.valueOf(normalDistNumber))).toBigInteger();
25
26  // we can convert the number to long by scaling up
27  // to Long.MaxValue. As the value range of normalDistNumber is
28  // ~ -5.0/+5.0 we can optimistically multiply normalDistNumber with:
29  // Long.MaxValue/10. After the calculation we have to revert the
30  // scaling by dividing by Long.MaxValue/10.
31  BigInteger normScaled = BigInteger.valueOf((long)(normalDistNumber * SCALE_D));
32  res = mu_bi.add(sd_bi.multiply(normScaled).divide(SCALE_BI));
33 } while (res.compareTo(KEY_RANGE) > 0 || res.compareTo(BigInteger.ZERO) < 0);
34 return res;
35 }
```

Listing 1 NormalDistribution – Polar box-muller method

```
01 long s0, s1; //internal state of HelperPRNG
02 public void seed(long... seeds) {
03   s0 = seeds[0];
04   s1 = seeds[1];
05     nextLong();
06 }
07 /*
08  * Xor-shift PRNG with a period of 2^128
09  * (c) by Sebastiano Vigna (vigna@acm.org)
10  * To the extent possible under law, the author has dedicated all copyright
11  * and related and neighboring rights to this software to the public domain
12  * worldwide. This software is distributed without any warranty.
13  * See <http://creativecommons.org/publicdomain/zero/1.0/>.
14  * source: http://xorshift.di.unimi.it/xorshift128plus.c
15  */
16 public long nextLong() {
17     final long s0 = this.s0;
18     long s1 = this.s1;
19     this.s0 = s1;
20     s1 ^= s1 << 23;
21     return (this.s1 = (s1 ^ s0 ^ (s1 >>> 17) ^ (s0 >>> 26))) + s0;
22 }
23 double TWO_POW_64_INV = (1.0 / Math.pow(2, 64));
24 public double nextDouble() {
25     return nextLong() * TWO_POW_64_INV + 0.5:
26 }
```

Listing 2 HelperPRNG – xorShift128

The nature of this algorithm is to randomly require more the two random values, if certain conditions are not met (see Listing 1 NormalDistribution – Polar box-muller method). Because of this requirement, the default random number generators of TPCx-HS cannot be used, as they only work for if a predefined amount of random numbers is drawn per row as described earlier. Because of this issue, a helper random number generator is used (see Listing 2 HelperPRNG – xorShift128), which is seeded with the random number for each row, obtained from the main random number generator. This allows to draw an arbitrary amount of random samples in each row, as required by the normal distribution algorithm. The implementation was verified to work correctly and the verification results can be seen in Fig. 2. The plot shows the accumulated density distribution of $\sim 6*10^7$ samples, drawn from the implemented normal distribution with parameters mu: 2^{79} and sigma: 2^{76}. To be able to count and plot the values, they were quantized to the range [0, 65536] by using the highest 16 Bit of the full 80 Bit value, resulting in mu: 32768 and sd: 4096. Additionally a wrapper was added for all the tools in the tpcx-hs.jar to comfortably run the TPCx-HS benchmark end to end. Available are the following modules, where 1 stands for the MR1 version and 2 for the MR2 version:

- hsgen1
- hsgen2

- hssort1
- hssort2
- hsvalidate1
- hsvalidate2

An example on how to start and parametrize the generation of normally distributed keys can be seen in the following listing:

```
hadoop jar tpcx-hs.jar hsgen1
   -D Hssort.distribution=org.tpc.hs.hsgen.mr1.dist.NormalDistributionBigInt
   -D Hssort.distribution.mu=29936846961918945312
   -D Hssort.distribution.sd=1000000000 100000000000 tpcxhs/terasort-input
```

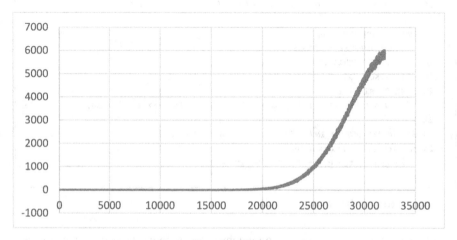

Fig. 2. Accumulated density with mu: 2^{79} sigma: 2^{76} quantized from highest 16 bit of the full 80 bit value to mu: 32768 and sigma: 4096

3 Test Results

We compared the impact on data generation and sorting performance using uniformly and normally distributed keys. The tests where done both for the MR1 and MR2 version of TPCx-HS. We ran a test with a data set size of 9,09 TB (100.000.000.000 records).

For the test runs using the new normal distributed key schema we used the following parameters:

Mu	29.936.846.961.918.900.000
Sigma	1.000.000.000

SD is chosen to be 1/100 of the number of records, to ensure a high number of duplicates within the generated keys. All tests were performed on the same 16 node cluster with the following specification:

Servers: 16 Cisco UCS C240M3 Rack Server
CPU: 2 × Intel® Xeon® Processor E5-2650 v2 (20 M Cache, 2.60 GHz)
Memory: 256 GB
Storage Controller: LSI MegaRAID SAS 9271-8i
Disk: 12 × 3 TB Large Form Factor HDD
Network: Cisco UCS VIC 1225 2 10GE SFP+

Software configuration:

- Disabled SElinux on all the nodes
- Disabled iptables on all the nodes
- NTP configured
- Ulimit set to 64000

A default Hadoop installation using Yarn was used. Looking at the CPU resources, it is obvious that generating non-uniform values is more CPU intensive than generating uniform random values, as shown in Fig. 4. The MapReduce 1 version is more expensive to generate than the MapReduce 2 version because of the additional step of converting the binary key into an ASCII representation. However, there was not much difference in real clock time as shown in Fig. 3, because the cluster was I/O bound the entire time.

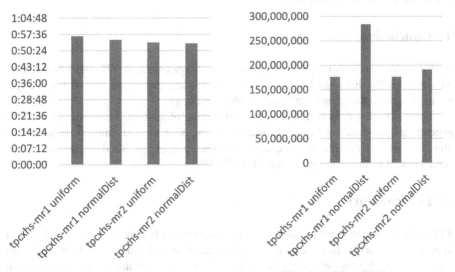

Fig. 3. HSGen wall clock time   **Fig. 4.** HSGen CPU time

The interesting result is the impact of the non-uniform data on the sort performance of TeraSort (Fig. 5). It shows that for both the MR1 and MR2 versions, the skewed dataset takes more time to sort than the uniformly distributed dataset. The difference is most notable when comparing the CPU times in Fig. 6. The impact was not as severe as initially expected. TPCx-HS employs techniques to mitigate skewed datasets. It does so by employing a custom split format and partitioning logic. This logic draws random

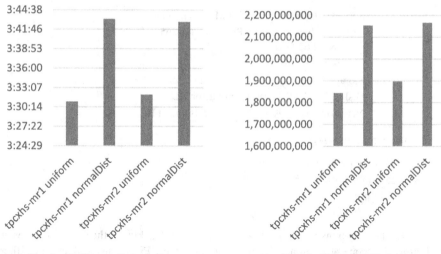

Fig. 5. HSSort wall clock time   **Fig. 6.** HSSort CPU time

samples from the generated data and sorts the samples locally to get an estimate of the key distribution. Based on this sample, TPCx-HS' sorting logic pre-partitions the data and distributes it to the mappers.

4   Conclusion

In this paper, the authors propose a potential enhancement to TPCx-HS benchmark with a normally distributed keys. The impact on data generation and sorting performance is compared against uniformly distributed keys.

The test results demonstrate that the distribution of keys has an impact on the data generation and data sorting performance of the system. The authors believe that non-uniform data distributions are more representative of real life datasets and a good enhancement to the next generation of TPCx-HS.

5   Future Work

TTPCx-HS can further extend with more distributions that fit data skew commonly found in production workloads. An example might be the Zipfian distribution, which models an access pattern where some few keys are accessed very often and most of the keys rarely to almost never. Another interesting addition would be the simulation of "null" values or more generally a single key that accounts for a high percentage of the total keys. Null values impose a great scaling problem, for example, in Hive queries, if not addressed properly because many parallel algorithms rely on distributing the values by key. If a single key occurs in, for example, 25 % of all data sets, a single mapper/reducer ends up processing 25 % of the dataset by itself, greatly reducing speedup in a large cluster.

Acknowledgements. The authors thank the contributors of the original TPCx-HS development committee, Andrew Bond (Red Hat), Andrew Masland (NEC), Avik Dey (Intel), Brian Caufield (IBM), Chaitanya Baru (SDSC), Da Qi Ren (Huawei), Dileep Kumar (Cloudera), Jamie Reding

(Microsoft), John Fowler (Oracle), John Poelman (IBM), Karthik Kulkarni (Cisco), Meikel Poess (Oracle), Mike Brey (Oracle), Mike Crocker (SAP), Paul Cao (HP), Reza Taheri (VMware), Simon Harris (IBM), Tariq Magdon-Ismail (VMware), Wayne Smith (Intel), Yanpei Chen (Cloudera), Michael Majdalany (L&M), Forrest Carman (Owen Media), and Andreas Hotea (Hotea Solutions). Thanks to Manankumar Trivedi for his support with benchmark testing and analysis.

Authors also thank Satinder Sethi for his guidance and support with this effort.

Appendix

Command lines used to conduct the experiments
Hsgen MR1 normal distribution
```hadoop jar /root/tpcx-hs/tpcx-hs.jar hsgen1 -D mapreduce.map.speculative=false -D mapreduce.reduce.speculative=false -D dfs.client.block.write.replace-datanode-on-failure.policy=NEVER -D mapred.job.name=hsgen__tpcxhs_mr1_NormalDistributionBigInt_2993684696 1918945312_1000000000 -D mapred.map.tasks=512 -D Hssort.distribution=org.tpc.hs.hsgen.mr1.dist.NormalDistributionBigInt -D Hssort.distribution.mu=29936846961918945312 -D Hssort.distribution.sd=1000000000 100000000000 tpcxhs/terasort-input```
Hsgen MR1 uniform distribution
```hadoop jar /root/tpcx-hs/tpcx-hs.jar hsgen1 -D mapreduce.map.speculative=false -D mapreduce.reduce.speculative=false -D dfs.client.block.write.replace-datanode-on-failure.policy=NEVER -D mapred.job.name=hsgen__tpcxhs_mr1_UniformDistribution -D mapred.map.tasks=512 -D Hssort.distribution=org.tpc.hs.hsgen.mr1.dist.UniformDistribution -D Hssort.distribution.mu=29936846961918945312 -D Hssort.distribution.sd=1000000000 100000000000 tpcxhs/terasort-input```
Hsgen MR2 normal distribution
```hadoop jar /root/tpcx-hs/tpcx-hs.jar hsgen2 -D mapreduce.map.speculative=false -D mapreduce.reduce.speculative=false -D dfs.client.block.write.replace-datanode-on-failure.policy=NEVER -D mapred.job.name=hsgen__tpcxhs_mr2_NormalDistributionBigInt_2993684696 1918945312_1000000000 -D mapred.map.tasks=512 -D Hssort.distribution=org.tpc.hs.hsgen.mr2.dist.NormalDistributionBigInt -D Hssort.distribution.mu=29936846961918945312 -D Hssort.distribution.sd=1000000000 100000000000 tpcxhs/terasort-input```
Hsgen MR1 uniform distribution
```hadoop jar /root/tpcx-hs/tpcx-hs.jar hsgen2 -D mapreduce.map.speculative=false -D mapreduce.reduce.speculative=false -D dfs.client.block.write.replace-datanode-on-failure.policy=NEVER -D mapred.job.name=hsgen__tpcxhs_mr2_UniformDistribution -D mapred.map.tasks=512 -D Hssort.distribution=org.tpc.hs.hsgen.mr2.dist.UniformDistribution -D Hssort.distribution.mu=29936846961918945312 -D```

`Hssort.distribution.sd=1000000000 100000000000 tpcxhs/terasort-input`
Hssort MR1 normal distribution

`hadoop jar /root/tpcx-hs/tpcx-hs.jar hssort1 -D`
`mapreduce.map.speculative=false -D mapreduce.reduce.speculative=false`
`-D dfs.client.block.write.replace-datanode-on-failure.policy=NEVER -D`
`mapred.job.name=hssort__tpcxhs_mr1_NormalDistributionBigInt_299368469`
`61918945312_1000000000 -D mapred.reduce.tasks=512 tpcxhs/terasort-`
`input/ tpcxhs/terasort-sorted/`

Hssort MR1 uniform distribution

`hadoop jar /root/tpcx-hs/tpcx-hs.jar hssort1 -D`
`mapreduce.map.speculative=false -D mapreduce.reduce.speculative=false`
`-D dfs.client.block.write.replace-datanode-on-failure.policy=NEVER -D`
`mapred.job.name=hssort__tpcxhs_mr1_UniformDistribution -D`
`mapred.reduce.tasks=512 tpcxhs/terasort-input/ tpcxhs/terasort-`
`sorted/`

Hssort MR2 normal distribution

`hadoop jar /root/tpcx-hs/tpcx-hs.jar hssort2 -D`
`mapreduce.map.speculative=false -D mapreduce.reduce.speculative=false`
`-D dfs.client.block.write.replace-datanode-on-failure.policy=NEVER -D`
`mapred.job.name=hssort__tpcxhs_mr2_NormalDistributionBigInt_299368469`
`61918945312_1000000000 -D mapred.reduce.tasks=512 tpcxhs/terasort-`
`input/ tpcxhs/terasort-sorted/`

Hssort MR1 uniform distribution

`hadoop jar /root/tpcx-hs/tpcx-hs.jar hssort2 -D`
`mapreduce.map.speculative=false -D mapreduce.reduce.speculative=false`
`-D dfs.client.block.write.replace-datanode-on-failure.policy=NEVER -D`
`mapred.job.name=hssort__tpcxhs_mr2_UniformDistribution -D`
`mapred.reduce.tasks=512 tpcxhs/terasort-input/ tpcxhs/terasort-`
`sorted/`

```
package org.tpc.hs.hsgen;

import org.apache.hadoop.util.ProgramDriver;

/**
 * @author Michael Frank (Michael.Frank@bankmark.de)
 * @version 1.0 27.02.2015
 */
public class Driver {

 public static void main(String argv[]) {
  int exitCode = -1;
  ProgramDriver pgd = new ProgramDriver();
  try {
   pgd.addClass("hsgen1",
     org.tpc.hs.hsgen.util.mr1.HSGen.class,
     "Generate data for the hssort using mr1");
   pgd.addClass("hssort1",
     org.tpc.hs.hsgen.util.mr1.HSSort.class,
     "Run the hssort using mr1");
   pgd.addClass("hsvalidate1",
     org.tpc.hs.hsgen.util.mr1.HSValidate.class,
     "Checking results of hssort using mr1");
   pgd.addClass("hsgen2",
     org.tpc.hs.hsgen.util.mr2.HSGen.class,
     "Generate data for the hssort using mr2");
   pgd.addClass("hssort2",
     org.tpc.hs.hsgen.util.mr2.HSSort.class,
     "Run the hssort using mr2");
   pgd.addClass("hsvalidate2",
     org.tpc.hs.hsgen.util.mr2.HSValidate.class,
     "Checking results of hssort using mr2");
   exitCode = pgd.run(argv);
  } catch (Throwable e) {
   e.printStackTrace();
  }
  System.exit(exitCode);
 }
}
```

```
package org.tpc.hs.hsgen.util;
/**
 * TeraGen random number system does not allow to sample
 * arbitrary numbers of random values for a single record. Because of
this we
```

```
  * use the limited available random number as a seed for this helper
PRNG
  *
  * @author Michael Frank (Michael.Frank@bankmark.de)
  * @version 1.0 27.02.2015
  */
public class HelperPRNG {

 private static final double TWO_POW_64_INV = (1.0 / Math.pow(2,
 64));

 private long s0, s1; // internal state

 /**
  * seed array, arbitrary length but only first 2 bytes are used
  *
  * @param seeds
  * @return this
  */
 public HelperPRNG seed(long... seeds) {
  // seed =seeds[0];
  s0 = seeds[0];
  s1 = seeds[1];
  // apply one round of mixing
  // in case of bad input seed entropy (e.g. never negative), first
  // rand128() result would also be never negative
  rand128();
  return this;
 }

 public long nextLong() {
  return rand128();
 }

 /*--
  * Xor-shift PRNG with a period of 2^128
  * (c) by Sebastiano Vigna (vigna@acm.org)
  * To the extent possible under law, the author has dedicated all
copyright
  * and related and neighboring rights to this software to the public
domain
  * worldwide. This software is distributed without any warranty.
  * See <http://creativecommons.org/publicdomain/zero/1.0/>
  * http://xorshift.di.unimi.it/xorshift128plus.c
  */
 private long rand128() {
  final long s0 = this.s0;
  long s1 = this.s1;
  this.s0 = s1;
  s1 ^= s1 << 23;
  return (this.s1 = (s1 ^ s0 ^ (s1 >>> 17) ^ (s0 >>> 26))) + s0;
```

```
}

 public static final double randLongToDouble(long r) {
  return r * TWO_POW_64_INV + 0.5;
 }

 public double nextDouble() {
  return randLongToDouble(nextLong());
 }
}
```

```
package org.tpc.hs.hsgen.util;
import java.math.BigInteger;

/**
 * <DISTRIBUTION> Helper for HSGen to do BigInteger conversion
 *
 * @author Michael Frank (Michael.Frank@bankmark.de)
 * @version 1.0 02.03.2015
 */
public class HsgenHelper {
 public static final BigInteger LONG_MAX_BI =
BigInteger.valueOf(Long.MAX_VALUE);
 public static final int KEY_SIZE_IN_BYTES = 10;
 public static final BigInteger KEY_RANGE_BINARY_BI =
BigInteger.ONE.shiftLeft(
    KEY_SIZE_IN_BYTES * 8).subtract(BigInteger.ONE);

 public static final int KEY_TO_STRING_RADIX = 95;
 public static final BigInteger KEY_TO_STRING_RADIX_BI =
BigInteger.valueOf(KEY_TO_STRING_RADIX);
 public static final BigInteger KEY_RANGE_ASCII_BI =
KEY_TO_STRING_RADIX_BI.pow(
    HsgenHelper.KEY_SIZE_IN_BYTES).subtract(BigInteger.ONE);
 /**
  * Convert a BigInteger value to bytes in radix 95 and + offset ' '
Storage
  * of the 10 key bytes in Little endian format. e.g.
  *
  * <pre>
  * <code>
  * value =
  *          95^9 * keyBytes[9]
  *        + 95^8 * keyBytes[8]
  *        + 95^7 * keyBytes[7]
  *        + 95^6 * keyBytes[6]
  *        + 95^5 * keyBytes[5]
  *        + 95^4 * keyBytes[4]
```

```
 *              + 95^3 * keyBytes[3]
 *              + 95^2 * keyBytes[2]
 *              + 95^1 * keyBytes[1]
 *              + 95^0 * keyBytes[0]
 * </code>
 * </pre>
 *
 * @param key
 * @param res
 */
public static void toRadix_LE(BigInteger res, byte[] keyBytes) {
  BigInteger tmp = res;

  for (int i = 0; i < HsgenHelper.KEY_SIZE_IN_BYTES; i++) {
    BigInteger[] qrem =
tmp.divideAndRemainder(HsgenHelper.KEY_TO_STRING_RADIX_BI);
    // System.out.println(i + ": "+res+" divmod " + RADIX_BI +
    // " = "
    // + qrem[0] + " rem: "
    // + qrem[1] + " asint: " + qrem[1].intValue() + " val: "
    // + (char) (' ' + qrem[1].intValue())));
    tmp = qrem[0];
    int rem = qrem[1].intValue();

    keyBytes[i] = (byte) (' ' + rem);
  }
}

/**
 * Convert a BigInteger value to bytes in radix 95 and + offset ' '
Storage
 * of the 10 key bytes in BigEndian format. e.g.
 *
 * <pre>
 * <code>
 * value =
 *            95^9 * keyBytes[0]
 *          + 95^8 * keyBytes[1]
 *          + 95^7 * keyBytes[2]
 *          + 95^6 * keyBytes[3]
 *          + 95^5 * keyBytes[4]
 *          + 95^4 * keyBytes[5]
 *          + 95^3 * keyBytes[6]
 *          + 95^2 * keyBytes[7]
 *          + 95^1 * keyBytes[8]
 *          + 95^0 * keyBytes[9]
 * </code>
 * </pre>
 *
 * @param res
 * @param key
```

```
 */
 public static void toRadix_BE(BigInteger res, BigInteger radix,
byte[] resultBuffer,
   int maxLen, char addToRadixOffset) {
  int KEY_TO_STRING_RADIX = radix.intValue();
  BigInteger tmp_BI = res;

  long tmp_l;
  int i = maxLen - 1;

  // convert radix 10 value to radix 95 bytes
  // use BigInteger arithmetic only as long as needed
  // if tmp value can fit into a long, switch to faster native
  // algorithm
  for (; i >= 0 && tmp_BI.compareTo(LONG_MAX_BI) > 0; i--) {
   BigInteger[] qrem = tmp_BI.divideAndRemainder(radix);
   tmp_BI = qrem[0];
   int rem = qrem[1].intValue();

   resultBuffer[i] = (byte) (addToRadixOffset + rem);
  }

  if (i >= 0) {
   tmp_l = tmp_BI.longValue();
   for (; i >= 0; i--) {
    long rem = tmp_l % KEY_TO_STRING_RADIX;
    tmp_l = tmp_l / KEY_TO_STRING_RADIX;
    resultBuffer[i] = (byte) (addToRadixOffset + rem);
   }
  }
 }
}
```

```
package org.tpc.hs.hsgen.distribution;

import java.math.BigInteger;

import org.tpc.hs.hsgen.util.HelperPRNG;

/**
 * @author Michael
 * @version 1.0 01.11.2015
 */
public class Normal {

 // static helper values for normal distribution
 private static final long SCALE_L = Long.MAX_VALUE / 10;
 private static final double SCALE_D = SCALE_L;
```

```
 private static final BigInteger SCALE_BI =
BigInteger.valueOf(SCALE_L);
 private static final BigInteger LONG_MAX_BI =
BigInteger.valueOf(Long.MAX_VALUE);

 public static BigInteger normalDistributedBigInteger(BigInteger
mu_bi, BigInteger sd_bi,
   BigInteger maxValue, HelperPRNG rng) {

  BigInteger res;
  do {
   /*
    * assumption is: 64 Precision for calculating the standard
    * deviation should still be sufficient
    */
   // Polar box-muller
   double x, y, r, z;
   do {

    x = 2.0 * rng.nextDouble() - 1.0;
    y = 2.0 * rng.nextDouble() - 1.0;
    r = x * x + y * y;
   } while (r >= 1.0);
   z = Math.sqrt(-2.0 * Math.log(r) / r);
   // res = mean + sd * y * z;
   double normalDistNumber = y * z; // range: -5.0/+5.0

   // ################################################
   // scale normalDistNumber with specified mean (mu) and
   // standard deviation (sd) values
   // ################################################

   // Variant one: naive version
   // Formula: res = mu + sd * normalDistNumber
   // Range of mu and sd is [0, 2^80] -> use BigDecimal
   // res = new BigDecimal(mu_bi).add(new
   //
BigDecimal(sd_bi).multiply(BigDecimal.valueOf(normalDistNumber))).toB
igInteger();

   /*
    * Optimization: As the range of mu and sd is [0, 2^80] we would
    * need to use BigDecimal to calculate:
    *
    * res=mu + sd * normalDistNumber
    *
    * But we can convert the number to long by scaling up (normalize)
    * to Long.MaxValue. As the value range of normalDistNumber is ~
    * -5.0/+5.0 we can optimistically multiply normalDistNumber with:
    * Long.MaxValue/10. After the calculation we have to revert the
    * scaling (de-normalize) by dividing by Long.MaxValue/10.
```

```
    *
    * Hint: Implementing and using a UInt128 Datatype (or usage of
the
    * Unsigned16 class from the hsgen.mr2 package) did not show
    * performance gains, as BigIntegers algorithms are very well
    * optimized
    */
   BigInteger normScaled = BigInteger.valueOf(((long)
(normalDistNumber * SCALE_D)));

   // scale to mu and sd values
   res = mu_bi.add(sd_bi.multiply(normScaled).divide(SCALE_BI));
   } while (res.compareTo(maxValue) > 0 ||
res.compareTo(BigInteger.ZERO) < 0);
   return res;

 }
}
```

```
package org.tpc.hs.hsgen.mr1.dist;

import java.util.Arrays;
import java.util.List;

import org.apache.hadoop.mapred.JobConf;

/**
 *
 * @author Michael Frank (Michael.Frank@bankmark.de)
 * @version 1.0 27.02.2015
 */
public class DistributionFactory {

 public static class DistributionException extends Exception {
  public DistributionException(String msg, Throwable cause) {
   super(msg, cause);
  }
 }

 // CMD_LINE/JobConf key
 public static final String HSSORT_DISTRIBUTION =
"Hssort.distribution";

 // ##########################################################
 // Add statically know distributions here:
 // you can always load any distribution class via reflection
 // ##########################################################
 public static final List<Class<? extends Distribution>> dists = Ar-
rays.asList(
```

```
  UniformDistribution.class, NormalDistributionBigInt.class);

 public static Distribution getDistribution(JobConf job) throws
DistributionException {
  String distributionClassName = Distribu-
tion.getStringFromConf(HSSORT_DISTRIBUTION,
    NormalDistributionBigInt.class.getName(), job);

  System.out.println("getConf(\"" + HSSORT_DISTRIBUTION + "\", " +
dists.get(0).getName()
    + ")=" + distributionClassName);
  System.out.println("loading distribution: " + distributionClassName
+ " ...");

  Distribution dist;
  try {
   dist = (Distribution)
Class.forName(distributionClassName).newInstance();
  } catch (Exception e) {
   throw new DistributionException("Could not load distribution
class. Cause:  "
    + e.getClass().getName() + ": " + e.getMessage() + "\nAvailable
distributions:"
    + dists, e);
  }

  dist.initialize(job);
  System.out.println("loaded distribution " + dist.toString());
  return dist;
 }
}
```

```
package org.tpc.hs.hsgen.mr1.dist;

import java.math.BigInteger;

import org.apache.hadoop.io.Text;
import org.apache.hadoop.mapred.JobConf;
import org.tpc.hs.hsgen.mr1.HSGen;

/**
 *
 * @author Michael Frank (Michael.Frank@bankmark.de)
 * @version 1.0 27.02.2015
 */
public abstract class Distribution {
```

```java
  public static BigInteger getBigIntegerFromConf(String name,
BigInteger defaultValue, JobConf job) {
    String option = job.get(name, defaultValue.toString());
    System.out.println("getConf(\"" + name + "\", " + defaultValue +
")=" + option);
    return new BigInteger(option);
  }

  public static double getDoubleFromConf(String name, double
defaultValue, JobConf job) {
    double option = job.getDouble(name, defaultValue);
    System.out.println("getConf(\"" + name + "\", " + defaultValue +
")=" + option);
    return option;
  }

  public static boolean getBooleanFromConf(String name, boolean
defaultValue, JobConf job) {
    boolean option = job.getBoolean(name, defaultValue);
    System.out.println("getConf(\"" + name + "\", " + defaultValue +
")=" + option);
    return option;
  }

  public static String getStringFromConf(String name, String
defaultValue, JobConf job) {
    String option = job.get(name, defaultValue.toString());
    System.out.println("getConf(\"" + name + "\", " + defaultValue +
")=" + option);
    return option;
  }

  public abstract void initialize(JobConf c);

  /**
   * Contract of HSGen.RandomGenerator rand is: make exactly! 3 calls
to
   * rand.next(). If you require more random numers, use a helper PRNG
e.g.:
   *
   * <pre>
   * HelperPRNG helperRNG;
   * helperRNG.seed(rand.next(), rand.next(), rand.next()); </ore>
   *
   * @param key
   * @param rand
   */
  public abstract void generateKey(Text key, HSGen.RandomGenerator
rand);
}
```

```java
package org.tpc.hs.hsgen.mr1.dist;

import org.apache.hadoop.io.Text;
import org.apache.hadoop.mapred.JobConf;
import org.tpc.hs.hsgen.mr1.HSGen;
import org.tpc.hs.hsgen.util.HsgenHelper;

/**
 * @author Michael Frank (Michael.Frank@bankmark.de)
 * @version 1.0 27.02.2015
 */
public class UniformDistribution extends Distribution {

 public UniformDistribution() {
 }

 // reuseable buffer
 private byte[] keyBytes = new byte[HsgenHelper.KEY_SIZE_IN_BYTES +
2];

 @Override
 public void generateKey(Text key, HSGen.RandomGenerator rand) {
  // generates 12 bytes, later truncate to 10
  for (int i = 0; i < 3; i++) {
   long temp = rand.next() / 52;
   keyBytes[3 + 4 * i] = (byte) (' ' + (temp %
HsgenHelper.KEY_TO_STRING_RADIX));
    temp /= HsgenHelper.KEY_TO_STRING_RADIX;
   keyBytes[2 + 4 * i] = (byte) (' ' + (temp %
HsgenHelper.KEY_TO_STRING_RADIX));
    temp /= HsgenHelper.KEY_TO_STRING_RADIX;
   keyBytes[1 + 4 * i] = (byte) (' ' + (temp %
HsgenHelper.KEY_TO_STRING_RADIX));
    temp /= HsgenHelper.KEY_TO_STRING_RADIX;
   keyBytes[4 * i] = (byte) (' ' + (temp %
HsgenHelper.KEY_TO_STRING_RADIX));
  }
  key.set(keyBytes, 0, HsgenHelper.KEY_SIZE_IN_BYTES);
 }

 @Override
 public void initialize(JobConf c) {
  // nothing to do
 }

 @Override
 public String toString() {
  return this.getClass().getSimpleName() + " []";
 }
```

```
}
```

```java
package org.tpc.hs.hsgen.mr1.dist;

import java.math.BigInteger;

import org.apache.hadoop.io.Text;
import org.apache.hadoop.mapred.JobConf;
import org.tpc.hs.hsgen.distribution.Normal;
import org.tpc.hs.hsgen.mr1.HSGen;
import org.tpc.hs.hsgen.util.HelperPRNG;
import org.tpc.hs.hsgen.util.HsgenHelper;

/**
 * NormalDistribution or GussianDistribution
 * http://en.wikipedia.org/wiki/Normal_distribution
 *
 * @author Michael Frank (Michael.Frank@bankmark.de)
 * @version 1.0 27.02.2015
 */
public class NormalDistributionBigInt extends Distribution {
  public static final String HSSORT_DISTRIBUTION_mu =
"Hssort.distribution.mu";
  public static final String HSSORT_DISTRIBUTION_sd =
"Hssort.distribution.sd";

  /*
   * mean value (the most common key / the position of tip of the bell
shaped
   * distribution curve in the keyspace)
   */
  private BigInteger mu_bi;
  public static final BigInteger DEFAULT_MU =
HsgenHelper.KEY_RANGE_ASCII_BI.divide(BigInteger
    .valueOf(2));

  /*-
   * standard deviation
   * about 68% of values drawn from a normal distribution are within
one standard deviation σ away from the mean
   * about 95% of the values lie within two standard deviations and
   * about 99.7% are within three standard deviations.
   *
http://en.wikipedia.org/wiki/Normal_distribution#Standard_deviation_a
nd_tolerance_intervals
   */
  /*
```

```
 * The default value of KEY_RANGE/8 was chosen because the distribu-
tion will
 * still spread over the whole key range. Every key is possible to
be
 * generated. However you may want to significantly decrease the SD
value to
 * achieve a narrower bell shaped curve. You should consider choos-
ing the SD
 * parameter based on the number of keys/records (aka. data size).
E.g. a sd
 * of 1/100 of the number of records will give you 5% unique keys
and 95%
 * dupplicates of keys.
 */
 private BigInteger sd_bi;
 public static final BigInteger DEFAULT_SD =
HsgenHelper.KEY_RANGE_ASCII_BI.divide(BigInteger
    .valueOf(8));

 private byte[] keyBytes = new byte[HsgenHelper.KEY_SIZE_IN_BYTES];

 private HelperPRNG helperRNG = new HelperPRNG();
 private Normal normalDist = new Normal();

 public NormalDistributionBigInt() {
  this(DEFAULT_MU, DEFAULT_SD);
 }

 public NormalDistributionBigInt(BigInteger mu2, BigInteger sd2) {
  set(mu2, sd2);
 }

 private void set(BigInteger mu2, BigInteger sd2) {
  validate(mu2, sd2);
  this.mu_bi = mu2;
  this.sd_bi = sd2;
 }

 private void validate(BigInteger mu2, BigInteger sd2) {
  if (mu2.add(sd2).compareTo(HsgenHelper.KEY_RANGE_ASCII_BI) > 0) {
   throw new IllegalArgumentException("mu(" + mu2 + ") + sd(" + sd2 +
") = "
     + mu2.add(sd2) + " > KEY_SIZE = " +
HsgenHelper.KEY_RANGE_ASCII_BI);
  }
 }

 @Override
 public void initialize(JobConf c) {
  set(getBigIntegerFromConf(HSSORT_DISTRIBUTION_mu, DEFAULT_MU, c),
    getBigIntegerFromConf(HSSORT_DISTRIBUTION_sd, DEFAULT_SD, c));
```

```java
  }

  @Override
  public void generateKey(Text key, HSGen.RandomGenerator rand) {
    /*
     * key consists of 10 bytes from ' ' to ' '+95. 95^12 == 2^78 val-
ues =>
     * requiring ~78 bits
     */

    /*
     * Contract of HSGen.RandomGenerator is: call next() 3 times per
key.
     * Unfortunately most distribution algorithms require n*2 random
numbers
     * with an unknown number of n (in case the conditional while loops
of
     * e.g. a NormalDistribution doesn't get results meeting the condi-
tions)
     * Because of this, the 3 random numbers are used as a seed for a
custom
     * helper PRNG.
     */
    helperRNG.seed(rand.next(), rand.next(), rand.next());

    BigInteger normalDistValue =
normalDist.normalDistributedBigInteger(mu_bi, sd_bi,
      HsgenHelper.KEY_RANGE_ASCII_BI, helperRNG);

    // convert normal distributed value to radix 95 using BigInteger
    // arithmetic, because mr1 expects
    // ASCII keys in range [' ', ' '+95]
    HsgenHelper.toRadix_BE(normalDistValue,
HsgenHelper.KEY_TO_STRING_RADIX_BI, keyBytes,
      HsgenHelper.KEY_SIZE_IN_BYTES, ' ');
    key.set(keyBytes, 0, HsgenHelper.KEY_SIZE_IN_BYTES);

  }

  @Override
  public String toString() {
    return this.getClass().getSimpleName() + " [mu=" + mu_bi + ", sd="
+ sd_bi + "]";
  }
}
```

```java
package org.tpc.hs.hsgen.mr1;
```

```
// [..] imports
import org.tpc.hs.hsgen.mr1.dist.Distribution;
import org.tpc.hs.hsgen.mr1.dist.DistributionFactory;

// [..]
public class HSGen extends Configured implements Tool {

// [..]

  /**
   * The Mapper class that given a row number, will generate the ap-
propriate
   * output line.
   */
  public static class SortGenMapper extends MapReduceBase implements
    Mapper<LongWritable, NullWritable, Text, Text> {

    private Distribution keyDistribution;
    private Text key = new Text();
    private Text value = new Text();
    private RandomGenerator rand;

    private byte[] spaces = "            ".getBytes();
    private byte[][] filler = new byte[26][];
    {
     for (int i = 0; i < 26; ++i) {
      filler[i] = new byte[10];
      for (int j = 0; j < 10; ++j) {
       filler[i][j] = (byte) ('A' + i);
      }
     }
    }

    /**
     * <DISTRIBUTION> added to load and instantiate chosen distribution
on
     * mappers
     */
    @Override
    public void configure(JobConf job) {
     super.configure(job);
     try {
      keyDistribution = DistributionFactory.getDistribution(job);
     } catch (Exception e) {
      // should not happen! pre-checked in HSGen.run() method
      e.printStackTrace();
     }
    }

    /**
     * Add a random key to the text
```

```
     *
     * @param key
     * @param rand
     *
     * @param rowId
     */
    private void addKey(Text key, RandomGenerator rand) {
     // <DISTRIBUTION> original code for uniform key generation relo-
cated
      // to org.tpc.hs.hsgen.mr1.dist.UniformDistribution
      keyDistribution.generateKey(key, rand);
    }

    /**
     * Add the rowid to the row.
     *
     * @param rowId
     * @param value
     * @param value
     */
    private void addRowId(long rowId, Text value) {
     byte[] rowid = Integer.toString((int) rowId).getBytes();
     int padSpace = 10 - rowid.length;
     if (padSpace > 0) {
      value.append(spaces, 0, 10 - rowid.length);
     }
     value.append(rowid, 0, Math.min(rowid.length, 10));
    }

    /**
     * Add the required filler bytes. Each row consists of 7 blocks of
10
     * characters and 1 block of 8 characters.
     *
     * @param rowId
     *                the current row number
     */
    private void addFiller(long rowId, Text value) {
     int base = (int) ((rowId * 8) % 26);
     for (int i = 0; i < 7; ++i) {
      value.append(filler[(base + i) % 26], 0, 10);
     }
     value.append(filler[(base + 7) % 26], 0, 8);
    }

    public void map(LongWritable row, NullWritable ignored,
OutputCollector<Text, Text> output,
      Reporter reporter) throws IOException {
     long rowId = row.get();
     if (rand == null) {
      // we use 3 random numbers per a row
```

```
  rand = new RandomGenerator(rowId * 3);
  }
  addKey(key, rand);
  value.clear();
  addRowId(rowId, value);
  addFiller(rowId, value);
  output.collect(key, value);
 }


}

private static void usage() throws IOException {
 System.err.println("HSGen <num rows> <output dir>");
}

/**
 * @param args
 *             the cli arguments
 * @throws ParseException
 */
public int run(String[] args) throws Exception {
 if (args.length < 2) {
  usage();
  return 1;
 }
 JobConf job = (JobConf) getConf();

 /*
  * <DISTRIBUTION> Test if chosen distribution exists and parameters
are
  * correct. Eagerly testing this here prevents later exceptions in
  * mappers
  */
 DistributionFactory.getDistribution(job);

 setNumberOfRows(job, Long.parseLong(args[0]));
 FileOutputFormat.setOutputPath(job, new Path(args[1]));
 // if job name not overridden by cmd line
 if (job.getJobName() == null || job.getJobName().isEmpty())
  job.setJobName("HSGen");
 job.setJarByClass(HSGen.class);
 job.setMapperClass(SortGenMapper.class);
 job.setNumReduceTasks(0);
 job.setOutputKeyClass(Text.class);
 job.setOutputValueClass(Text.class);
 job.setInputFormat(RangeInputFormat.class);
 job.setOutputFormat(HSOutputFormat.class);
 JobClient.runJob(job);
 return 0;
 }
```

```java
 public static void main(String[] args) throws Exception {
   int res = ToolRunner.run(new JobConf(), new HSGen(), args);
   System.exit(res);
 }
}
```

```java
package org.tpc.hs.hsgen.mr2.dist;

import java.util.Arrays;
import java.util.List;

import org.apache.hadoop.conf.Configuration;

/**
 * @author Michael Frank (Michael.Frank@bankmark.de)
 * @version 1.0 27.02.2015
 */
public class DistributionFactory {

 public static class DistributionException extends Exception {
  public DistributionException(String msg, Throwable cause) {
   super(msg, cause);
  }
 }

 // CMD_LINE/JobConf key
 public static final String HSSORT_DISTRIBUTION =
"Hssort.distribution";

 // ############################################################
 // Add statically know distributions here:
 // you can allways load any distribution class via reflection
 // ############################################################
 public static final List<Class<? extends Distribution>> dists = Ar-
rays.asList(
   UniformDistribution.class, NormalDistributionBigInt.class);

 public static Distribution getDistribution(Configuration configura-
tion)
   throws DistributionException {

  String distributionClassName = Distribu-
tion.getStringFromConf(HSSORT_DISTRIBUTION, dists
   .get(0).getName(), configuration);

  System.out.println("loading distribution: " + distributionClassName
+ " ...");
```

```
  Distribution dist;
  try {
    dist = (Distribution)
Class.forName(distributionClassName).newInstance();
  } catch (Exception e) {
    throw new DistributionException("Could not load distribution
class. Cause:  "
        + e.getClass().getName() + ": " + e.getMessage() + "\nAvailable
distributions:"
        + dists, e);
  }

  dist.initialize(configuration);
  System.out.println("loaded distribution " + dist.toString());
  return dist;


 }
}
```

```
package org.tpc.hs.hsgen.mr2.dist;

import java.math.BigInteger;

import org.apache.hadoop.conf.Configuration;
import org.tpc.hs.hsgen.mr2.Unsigned16;

/**
 * @author Michael Frank (Michael.Frank@bankmark.de)
 * @version 1.0 02.03.2015
 */
public abstract class Distribution {

  public static BigInteger getBigIntegerFromConf(String name,
BigInteger defaultValue,
    Configuration job) {
    String option = job.get(name, defaultValue.toString());
    System.out.println("getConf(\"" + name + "\", " + defaultValue +
")=" + option);
    return new BigInteger(option);
  }

  public static double getDoubleFromConf(String name, double
defaultValue, Configuration job) {
    double option = job.getDouble(name, defaultValue);
    System.out.println("getConf(\"" + name + "\", " + defaultValue +
")=" + option);
    return option;
```

```
    }

    public static boolean getBooleanFromConf(String name, boolean
    defaultValue, Configuration job) {
      boolean option = job.getBoolean(name, defaultValue);
      System.out.println("getConf(\"" + name + "\", " + defaultValue +
    ")=" + option);
      return option;
    }

    public static String getStringFromConf(String name, String
    defaultValue, Configuration job) {
      String option = job.get(name, defaultValue.toString());
      System.out.println("getConf(\"" + name + "\", " + defaultValue +
    ")=" + option);
      return option;
    }

    public abstract void initialize(Configuration configuration);

    public abstract void generateKey(byte[] recBuffer, Unsigned16 rand);

    public abstract BigInteger generateKey(Unsigned16 rand);

}
```

```
package org.tpc.hs.hsgen.mr2.dist;

import java.math.BigInteger;

import org.apache.hadoop.conf.Configuration;
import org.tpc.hs.hsgen.mr2.Unsigned16;
import org.tpc.hs.hsgen.util.HsgenHelper;

/**
 * @author Michael Frank (Michael.Frank@bankmark.de)
 * @version 1.0 02.03.2015
 */
public class UniformDistribution extends Distribution {

  @Override
  public void generateKey(byte[] recBuffer, Unsigned16 rand) {
    for (int i = 0; i < HsgenHelper.KEY_SIZE_IN_BYTES; ++i) {
      recBuffer[i] = rand.getByte(i);
    }
  }

  @Override
```

```
  public void initialize(Configuration configuration) {
   // nothing to do
  }

  @Override
  public String toString() {
   return this.getClass().getSimpleName() + " []";
  }

  @Override
  public BigInteger generateKey(Unsigned16 rand) {
   return rand.toBigInteger();
  }
 }
```

```
package org.tpc.hs.hsgen.mr2.dist;

import java.math.BigInteger;

import org.apache.hadoop.conf.Configuration;
import org.tpc.hs.hsgen.distribution.Normal;
import org.tpc.hs.hsgen.mr2.Unsigned16;
import org.tpc.hs.hsgen.util.HelperPRNG;
import org.tpc.hs.hsgen.util.HsgenHelper;

/**
 * NormalDistribution or GussianDistribution
 * http://en.wikipedia.org/wiki/Normal_distribution
 *
 * @author Michael Frank (Michael.Frank@bankmark.de)
 * @version 1.0 02.03.2015
 */
public class NormalDistributionBigInt extends Distribution {

 public static final String HSSORT_DISTRIBUTION_mu =
"Hssort.distribution.mu";
 public static final String HSSORT_DISTRIBUTION_sd =
"Hssort.distribution.sd";

 /*
  * mean value (the most common key / the position of tip of the bell
shaped
  * distribution curve in the keyspace)
  */
 private BigInteger mu_bi;
 public static final BigInteger DEFAULT_MU =
HsgenHelper.KEY_RANGE_BINARY_BI.divide(BigInteger
```

```
  .valueOf(2));

/*-
 * standard deviation
 * about 68% of values drawn from a normal distribution are within
one standard deviation σ away from the mean
 * about 95% of the values lie within two standard deviations and
 * about 99.7% are within three standard deviations.
 *
http://en.wikipedia.org/wiki/Normal_distribution#Standard_deviation_a
nd_tolerance_intervals
 */
/*
 * The default value of KEY_RANGE/8 was chosen because the distribu-
tion will
 * still spread over the whole key range. Every key is possible to
be
 * generated. However you may want to significantly decrease the SD
value to
 * achieve a narrower bell shaped curve. You should consider choos-
ing the SD
 * parameter based on the number of keys/records (aka. data size).
E.g. a sd
 * of 1/100 of the number of records will give you 5% unique keys
and 95%
 * dupplicates of keys.
 */
private BigInteger sd_bi;
public static final BigInteger DEFAULT_SD =
HsgenHelper.KEY_RANGE_BINARY_BI.divide(BigInteger
  .valueOf(8));

private HelperPRNG helperRNG = new HelperPRNG();
private Normal normalDist = new Normal();

public NormalDistributionBigInt() {
  this(DEFAULT_MU, DEFAULT_SD);
}

public NormalDistributionBigInt(BigInteger mu2, BigInteger sd2) {
  set(mu2, sd2);
}

private void set(BigInteger mu2, BigInteger sd2) {
  validate(mu2, sd2);
  this.mu_bi = mu2;
  this.sd_bi = sd2;
}

private void validate(BigInteger mu2, BigInteger sd2) {
  if (mu2.add(sd2).compareTo(HsgenHelper.KEY_RANGE_BINARY_BI) > 0) {
```

```
    throw new IllegalArgumentException("mu(" + mu2 + ") + sd(" + sd2 +
") = "
      + mu2.add(sd2) + " > KEY_SIZE = " +
HsgenHelper.KEY_RANGE_BINARY_BI);
  }
 }

 @Override
 public void initialize(Configuration c) {
  set(getBigIntegerFromConf(HSSORT_DISTRIBUTION_mu, DEFAULT_MU, c),
    getBigIntegerFromConf(HSSORT_DISTRIBUTION_sd, DEFAULT_SD, c));
 }

 @Override
 public BigInteger generateKey(Unsigned16 rand) {
  /*
   * Contract of Unsigned16 rand is: we have a single 128bit random
number
   * to randomly calculate a distributed key. Unfortunately most
   * distribution algorithms require n*2 random numbers with an un-
known
   * number of n (in case the conditional while loops of e.g. a
   * NormalDistribution doesn't get results meeting the conditions)
   * Because of this, the random number 'rand' is used as a seed for
a
   * custom helper PRNG.
   */
  helperRNG.seed(rand.getHigh8(), rand.getLow8());
  BigInteger normalDistValue =
normalDist.normalDistributedBigInteger(mu_bi, sd_bi,
    HsgenHelper.KEY_RANGE_BINARY_BI, helperRNG);
  return normalDistValue;
 }

 @Override
 public void generateKey(byte[] recBuf, Unsigned16 rand) {
  BigInteger normalDist = generateKey(rand);
  copyToResult(recBuf, normalDist, HsgenHelper.KEY_SIZE_IN_BYTES);
 }

 private static void copyToResult(byte[] recBuf, BigInteger res, int
KEY_SIZE_BYTES) {
  byte[] keyBytes = res.toByteArray();
  for (int i = 0; i < 10 - keyBytes.length; i++) {
   recBuf[i] = 0;
  }
  int start = Math.max(0, keyBytes.length - KEY_SIZE_BYTES);
  int startRec = KEY_SIZE_BYTES - Math.min(KEY_SIZE_BYTES,
keyBytes.length);
  int copyLen = Math.min(KEY_SIZE_BYTES, keyBytes.length);
  System.arraycopy(keyBytes, start, recBuf, startRec, copyLen);
```

```
    }

    @Override
    public String toString() {
      return this.getClass().getSimpleName() + " [mu=" + mu_bi + ", sd="
+ sd_bi + "]";
    }
}
```

```java
package org.tpc.hs.hsgen.mr2;

//[..]import
import org.apache.hadoop.util.Tool;
import org.apache.hadoop.util.ToolRunner;
import org.tpc.hs.hsgen.mr2.dist.Distribution;
import org.tpc.hs.hsgen.mr2.dist.DistributionFactory;
import
org.tpc.hs.hsgen.mr2.dist.DistributionFactory.DistributionException;
import org.tpc.hs.hsgen.util.HsgenHelper;

//[..]
public class HSGen extends Configured implements Tool {

//[..]

/**
   * The Mapper class that given a row number, will generate the ap-
propriate
   * output line.
   */
  public static class SortGenMapper extends Mapper<LongWritable,
NullWritable, Text, Text> {

    private Text key = new Text();
    private Text value = new Text();
    private Unsigned16 rand = null;
    private Unsigned16 rowId = null;
    private Unsigned16 checksum = new Unsigned16();
    private Checksum crc32 = new PureJavaCrc32();
    private Unsigned16 total = new Unsigned16();
    private static final Unsigned16 ONE = new Unsigned16(1);
    private byte[] buffer = new byte[HSInputFormat.KEY_LENGTH +
HSInputFormat.VALUE_LENGTH];
    private Counter checksumCounter;

    private Distribution keyDistribution;

    /**
```

```
     * <DISTRIBUTION> added to load and instantiate chosen distribution
on
     * mappers
     */
    @Override
    protected void setup(Mapper<LongWritable, NullWritable, Text,
Text>.Context context)
        throws IOException, InterruptedException {
        super.setup(context);
        try {
         keyDistribution =
DistributionFactory.getDistribution(context.getConfiguration());
         } catch (Exception e) {
         // should not happen! pre-checked in HSGen.run()
         e.printStackTrace();
         }
    }


    public void map(LongWritable row, NullWritable ignored, Context
context)
        throws IOException, InterruptedException {
        if (rand == null) {
         rowId = new Unsigned16(row.get());
         rand = Random16.skipAhead(rowId);
         checksumCounter = context.getCounter(Counters.CHECKSUM);
        }

        Random16.nextRand(rand);

        // <DISTRIBUTION> pass key distribution instance to record
        // generation
        // logic
        GenSort.generateRecord(buffer, rand, rowId, keyDistribution);
        key.set(buffer, 0, HSInputFormat.KEY_LENGTH);
        value.set(buffer, HSInputFormat.KEY_LENGTH,
HSInputFormat.VALUE_LENGTH);
        context.write(key, value);
        crc32.reset();
        crc32.update(buffer, 0, HSInputFormat.KEY_LENGTH +
HSInputFormat.VALUE_LENGTH);
        checksum.set(crc32.getValue());
        total.add(checksum);
        rowId.add(ONE);
    }

    @Override
    public void cleanup(Context context) {
        if (checksumCounter != null) {
         checksumCounter.increment(total.getLow8());
        }
    }
```

```
}

//[..]
}
```

References

1. Nambiar, R., Poess, M., Dey, A., Cao, P., Magdon-Ismail, T., Qi Ren, D., Bond, A.: Introducing TPCx-HS: The First Industry Standard for Benchmarking Big Data Systems. In: Nambiar, R., Poess, M. (eds.) TPCTC 2014. LNCS, vol. 8904, pp. 1–12. Springer, Heidelberg (2015)
2. TPCx-HS Specification. www.tpc.org
3. O'Malley, O.: TeraByte sort on apache hadoop (2008)
4. Nambiar, R., Poess, M.: Keeping the TPC relevant! PVLDB 6(11), 1186–1187 (2013)
5. Nambiar, Raghunath, Poess, Meikel (eds.): TPCTC 2013. LNCS, vol. 8391. Springer, Heidelberg (2014)
6. Nambiar, R.: A standard for benchmarking big data systems. In: BigData Conference 2014, pp. 18–20 (2014)
7. Nambiar, R.: Benchmarking big data systems: introducing TPC express benchmark HS. In: Rabl, T., Sachs, K., Poess, M., Baru, C., Jacobson, H.-A. (eds.) WBDB 2014. LNCS, vol. 8991, pp. 24–28. Springer, Heidelberg (2015)

Rethinking Benchmarking for Data

Jignesh M. Patel[✉]

Pivotal Software Inc., Palo Alto, USA
jmpatel@pivotal.io

Benchmarking has been critical in making progress in the field of data, as it has provided a crucial mechanism to accelerate the progress in the data community. Early benchmarks have been responsible for spurring innovation and serving as a quantitative way to get past marketing salvos. Prime examples of this observation are the Anon et al. benchmark and the Wisconsin benchmark that spurred rapid advances in database transaction and analytic query processing. These dual technologies are now crucial to running our "digital planet[1]" today.

However, data benchmarking has changed considerably over the past four decades. In the early days, pioneers like Jim Gray and David DeWitt, were crucial in creating benchmarks that were genuinely designed to move the community forward. Back then the data industry was in its "Wild West" days. A few good-meaning cowboys is all that it took to set the industry in the right direction.

Sadly, those halcyon days are long gone. The digital planet is simply too dependent on data. In fact, as has been noted before, data in the new currency. Thus, there are deeply-vested interests in modern benchmarks that simply do not achieve the goals that benchmarks claim to achieve. To address these issues, this article proposes a radical rethinking of data benchmarks. This article makes three concrete suggestions: First, data benchmarks should have no optional components, forcing the vendors to make "hard" choices when reporting benchmark results (e.g. reporting on energy consumption in TPC benchmarks, and reporting results on newer benchmarks that subsume older ones). Second, benchmarking in the cloud-era implies that each customer will have their own measures that are important to them. Thus, a service that offers automated benchmarking (and associated tuning) of customer workload in the cloud is far more important than actual benchmarks. Finally, we should dramatically rethink how our benchmark councils (including TPC) work. We should reverse the stewardship of these councils by replacing vendors from the council by the actual customers of data products, and let customers directly drive the definition of new benchmarks.

1 Benchmarking Today: Issues and Root Causes

The art of benchmarking is nearly as old as the field of Computer Sciences. In the field of data, which is the focus of this article, benchmarking has played a crucial role is

---

[1] *"Digital Planet" is a descriptive phrase used here to capture the notion that our world is increasingly viewed by the data that describes the physical world, and operated by analytics on this data.*

© Springer International Publishing Switzerland 2016
R. Nambiar and M. Poess (Eds.): TPCTC 2015, LNCS 9508, pp. 130–134, 2016.
DOI: 10.1007/978-3-319-31409-9_8

spurring big advances in data processing technologies. From early benchmarks such as the Anon et al. benchmark [1] and the Wisconsin benchmark [2] to modern day benchmarks like those published by the TPC council, we as a community of developers and users of data products gravitate to the results of benchmarks. A well-defined benchmark allows a neutral and objective perspective of competing technologies, and forces vendors to fix gaps in their products. Thus, the entire industry moves forward, and we all win. This is exactly what happen with early data benchmark that accelerated the pace of product development and maturity in data [3].

But, the crucial nature of benchmarks has also unleashed an ugly side. Vested interests focused on short-terms gains endlessly aim to make benchmarks skewed towards specific points-of-view. The financial and perception implication of under-performing on a widely-publicized industry benchmark encourages vendors to maintain a tight control over the benchmark creation process. Most benchmark are created by consortiums like the Transaction Processing Council (TPC). Such consortiums are also funded by vendors, who naturally need to protect their companies' best interests.

At the same time, it is far harder for independent researchers to develop a benchmark that is widely-adopted. There is simply too much more noise in the ecosystem today than many decades ago, and it often takes (lots of) real dollars to drive adoption of a new benchmark. Admittedly, independent researchers may also not have a broader perspective on actual customer needs, and thus may be in the dark when proposing benchmarks that end-users actually care about.

The result of this unfortunate set of forces is that we now live with benchmarks that are prescribed by consortiums, which in turn is made up of participants who have vested interests. Even if a representative at a benchmarks council has the best intention, it is hard to imagine anyone representing a company supporting features in a new benchmark that would put their companies' products at a disadvantage.

Consequently, benchmarks are moving further and further away from their original goal – namely to help move the industry forward by providing an objective and neutral view of performance characteristics that matter to actual customers. It is time to rethink how we as a community (of developer and consumers of data products) spend our time, energy, and money in creating future benchmarks. This paper proposes three concrete measures (as described below) to radically rethinking benchmarks for data.

#1: Remove Ambiguity from Benchmarks

Benchmark councils often have robust arguments when designing a benchmark. Such arguments result in positions that are hard to reconcile. Such situations are "easier" to resolve by creating optional reporting components in benchmarks. Optional components are meaningless and weaken benchmarks.

For example, the TPC adopted energy as a measurement requirement in 2010, and made it an optional feature. Nearly everyone ignores this measure when reporting benchmark results, although it is hard to find a vendor who does not think energy consumption is important. Energy consumption is especially crucial when moving to cloud-hosted data services, as the service provider now has a big incentive to reduce the deployment and operational costs, of which energy consumption is a big component.

Thus, if some measure is deemed important to be part of the benchmark specification, then it must be a mandatory part in reporting the benchmark results.

Another source of ambiguity in benchmarks is multiple benchmarks from the same benchmark council in the same target application area. TPC is the dominant benchmark council in data. It has two benchmarks for OLTP, namely TPC-C and TPC-E. It also has two benchmarks for data warehousing, namely TPC-H and TPC-DS. Multiple benchmarks that target the same domain allows for manipulation by those vendors who are at a disadvantage. For example, it is hard to argue that TPC-C is a relevant OLTP benchmark compared to TPC-E, but only one vendor reports TPC-E results. Other OLTP vendors have conveniently "chosen" to ignore it. Similarly, TPC-H is often used (especially by the new data warehousing companies), while any data expert would find it hard to argue that it is a better benchmark than TPC-DS today. To address this problem, councils should immediately deprecate an old benchmark as soon as a newer replacement benchmark is created. Thus, reducing the benefits for vendors that choose to continue reporting results on "dead" benchmarks.

The first proposal is: ***Remove opportunities for confusion by having zero optional reporting measures in benchmarks, and deprecate benchmarks immediately when new replacement benchmarks are created.***

#2: Focus on Benchmark Measurement Methodology

Benchmarks are fascinating since they allow one to compare systems in precise quantitative ways. However, for most major customers of data products (i.e. the folks who actually write the checks for data products) generic benchmarks are of limited use. Every big customer typically has her own benchmark, and any big sale requires that vendors go through a proof-of-concept (PoC) process that often requires running the customer's specific benchmark.

Here is where the benchmark councils and other professional benchmark developers can really help move the industry forward. A crucial aspect of benchmarking is developing a well thought-out methodology to measure complex deployments, such as measuring the query throughput of a data service running in a cluster, or measuring energy consumption in a meaningful way. The benchmark developers in organizations like the TPC have done an amazing job of developing measurement frameworks and methodologies that can be used across different vendors. A key contribution that these benchmark developers could continue making is to proposed industry-wide standard measurement frameworks, making it easy for custom benchmarks to be run.

Such a move is crucial for the current move towards cloud-hosted databases as the metric that is of interest to a customer changes from one customer to the other. For example, in a cloud-hosted database an important metric for a specific customer may be the lowest price that meets a certain response time latency for queries – no current benchmark in data incorporates such SLAs.

One can go even further and think of extending this idea of a measurement framework to developing "Benchmarking-as-a-Service (BaaS)." With BaaS a customer simply provides a sample (perhaps synthetic) dataset, a workload and an SLA, and the service determines the best configuration to deploy that meets precisely defined SLAs. (A more detailed argument for BaaS was presented earlier [4].)

Finally, we note that today many benchmarks are audited, and for good reasons including ensuring that vendors stay honest. With BaaS there is not need to audit – a customer is not going to complain if the vendor has techniques to speed up their workload. Furthermore, with BaaS when the workload changes, the customer simply runs that BaaS service again to determine the "right" configuration or the "right" cloud provider. (We acknowledge that switching vendors requires many more considerations rather than just performance, but with BaaS at least the customer has an answer to the performance aspect, which is what benchmarks target.)

The second proposal is: *Benchmark developers should consider abstracting the measurement component of existing benchmarks (such as the TPC benchmarks) and develop them as independent frameworks to use with any benchmark. A step further is for cloud data providers to provide a Benchmark-as-a-Service function.*

#3: Rethinking the Composition of Benchmark Councils

The crux of the problem at hand with benchmarking is that benchmarks are designed by vendors who (naturally) also aim to "win" on the benchmarks. This situation is obviously rife with conflict of interest. Benchmarks aim to compute precise and reproducible measure(s) of how well products perform on customer workloads. Who understands these workloads the best? The actual customers!

Thus, the last suggestion is simple: Flip the composition of benchmark councils (such as the TPC), so that the benchmark specification is driven by key customers. Thus, the customers become the drivers, and vendors can be passive participants in the benchmark councils that help with aspects such as measurement frameworks and industry-wide methodology for reporting benchmark results.

Some may be alarmed by the notion of handing over the running of benchmark councils to customers. It could be argued that customers may not have the incentives to do the work of creating a benchmark. But, it is clear to anyone who has dealt with large customers of data products that the customers have the biggest incentives to drive changes across the industry. The reason is simple: in the end the customer wins when product innovation moves at a faster pace, and relevant benchmarks helps catalyze innovations.

In fact, such a flipping of the benchmark council composition would also help the vendors. Rather than spend endless energy in crafting marketing messages around product shortcomings, it levels the playing field and allows the best technology to shine. This approach also allows more resources to be dedicated to actually improving and fixing shortcomings in data products. In fact, the early benchmarks in data were created in such "conflict-free" ways, and allowed the industry to innovate at a rapid pace.

The final proposal is: *Let's flip the composition of benchmark and have customers drive the benchmark creation. Vendors can help with operational aspects of the benchmark such as industry-wide methodology to run the benchmark, but should be silent observers in the creation of the actual benchmark definitions.*

Disclaimers: The author is currently employed at Pivotal Inc. and is also a Professor (on leave) from the University of Wisconsin. All opinions expressed in the document are those of the author, and do not necessarily reflect that of the organizations the author is affiliated with.

References

1. Anon, et al.: A measure of transaction processing power. Datamation **31**, 112–118 (1985)
2. Bitton, D., DeWitt, D.J., Turbyfil, C.: Benchmarking database systems: a systematic approach. In: Proceedings of the 1983 Very Large Database Conference, October 1983
3. Gray, J.: A measure of transaction processing 20 years later. IEEE Data Eng. Bull. **28**(2), 3–4 (2005)
4. Floratou, A., Patel, J.M., Lang, W., Halverson, A.: When free is not really free: what does it cost to run a database workload in the cloud? In: Nambiar, R., Poess, M. (eds.) TPCTC 2011. LNCS, vol. 7144, pp. 163–179. Springer, Heidelberg (2012)

Big Data Benchmark Compendium

Todor Ivanov[1]([⊠]), Tilmann Rabl[2], Meikel Poess[3], Anna Queralt[4],
John Poelman[5], Nicolas Poggi[4], and Jeffrey Buell[6]

[1] Goethe University Frankfurt, Frankfurt, Germany
todor@dbis.cs.uni-frankfurt.de
[2] bankmark, Passau, Germany
tilmann.rabl@bankmark.de
[3] Oracle Corporation, Redwood Shores, USA
meikel.poess@oracle.com
[4] Barcelona Supercomputing Center (BSC), Barcelona, Spain
{anna.queralt,nicolas.poggi}@bsc.es
[5] IBM, San Jose, USA
poelman@us.ibm.com
[6] VMware, Palo Alto, USA
jbuell@vmware.com

Abstract. The field of Big Data and related technologies is rapidly
evolving. Consequently, many benchmarks are emerging, driven by academia and industry alike. As these benchmarks are emphasizing different
aspects of Big Data and, in many cases, covering different technical platforms and uses cases, it is extremely difficult to keep up with the pace
of benchmark creation. Also with the combinations of large volumes of
data, heterogeneous data formats and the changing processing velocity,
it becomes complex to specify an architecture which best suits all application requirements. This makes the investigation and standardization of
such systems very difficult. Therefore, the traditional way of specifying
a standardized benchmark with pre-defined workloads, which have been
in use for years in the transaction and analytical processing systems,
is not trivial to employ for Big Data systems. This document provides
a summary of existing benchmarks and those that are in development,
gives a side-by-side comparison of their characteristics and discusses their
pros and cons. The goal is to understand the current state in Big Data
benchmarking and guide practitioners in their approaches and use cases.

1 Introduction

Big Data is a new and rapidly evolving discipline in computer science utilizing a
diverse spectrum of technical platforms and serving a wide range of applications.
This is because, with the combinations of large volumes of data, heterogeneous
data formats and the rapidly improving performance of both hardware and Big
Data systems, it is hard to generalize architectural aspects that best suit all
application requirements, making the investigation and standardization of such
systems very difficult.

© Springer International Publishing Switzerland 2016
R. Nambiar and M. Poess (Eds.): TPCTC 2015, LNCS 9508, pp. 135–155, 2016.
DOI: 10.1007/978-3-319-31409-9_9

As these systems are evolving, there is an inherent need to evaluate and quantify their performance with the ultimate goal of comparing these systems. Comparisons are desirable in different dimensions, such as software stack, hardware, use case, and tuning parameters. That is, one might want to compare a particular software stack on different hardware systems, a particular hardware setting on different software stacks, or one software stack on a particular hardware with different tunings.

With the rapid increase in Big Data solutions, both academia and industry alike are developing new benchmarks at a rapid pace. Driven by the "velocity of change" many performance benchmark developers "cut corners" by customizing their benchmarks too closely to the architectural characteristic of the system they want to benchmark, instead of abstracting its core performance attributes. These benchmarks become "island solutions" that only fit the systems they targeted in the first place. This approach works well if the goal is to compare the performance of a particular software stack on a particular hardware setting. However, this does not work well to compare the performance of different software stacks on the same hardware platforms or vice versa.

Many standard performance organizations, such as TPC, SPEC, and SPC follow similar approaches when developing benchmarks. One of their approaches, which is targeted at increasing the acceptance of benchmarks across many hardware and software vendors, is developing technology agnostic benchmarks for general use cases. The goal is to define a set of functional requirements that can be applied to any system that claims to be able to solve the use case, regardless of hardware, database management software or operating system. It is the responsibility of those measuring the performance of systems using the benchmarks to implement the specification and to submit proof that the implementation meets all benchmark requirements, i.e., that the implementation complies with the specification. The proof is generally captured in a document, e.g., Full Disclosure Report (FDR), whose intent is to enable other parties to reproduce the performance measurement. This approach allows any vendor, using "proprietary" or "open" systems, to implement the benchmarks while still guaranteeing end-users that the resulting measurements are comparable. A second approach is to provide executable versions of benchmarks that are targeted on a small number of hardware and software solutions. While these benchmarks can only be used to compare a small number of systems, they are generally easier to develop and deploy. Both approaches can be modeled after actual production applications and environments or be synthetic. The former allows for benchmark analysts to better understand and interpret benchmark results, while the latter is generally better for engineering, e.g., in product development and product improvement.

Employing these traditional ways of specifying standardized benchmarks with predefined workloads is not trivial for Big Data systems, because of the combinations of large volumes of data, heterogeneous data formats, and velocity of changes in the processing technology used in Big Data solutions. As a consequence, many companies and research institutions are developing their own "island solutions" that only fit systems they target. It is a challenge for both industry and academia to keep track of the large number of emerging benchmarks.

This document serves as a compendium of Big Data benchmarks that are currently available and that are under development. The contributions of this paper are a detailed summary of these benchmarks as well as a detailed discussion of the commonalities and differences of them, which can guide academia and industry in choosing the most appropriate benchmark to suit their needs. The paper concludes by proposing a simplified Big Data benchmarks classification, which can be used to come up with a more generalized Big Data benchmark in the future.

2   Existing Big Data Benchmarks

This section presents, in alphabetical order, Big Data benchmarks that are most frequently referenced in current literature. They were developed to stress test and evaluate Big Data systems such as the Hadoop framework and its extensions into the open source ecosystem.

2.1   AMP Lab Big Data Benchmark

AMP Lab Benchmark [2] measures the analytical capabilities of data warehousing solutions. This benchmark currently provides quantitative and qualitative comparisons of five data warehouse systems: RedShift, Hive, Stinger/Tez, Shark, and Impala. Based on Pavlo's Benchmark [44,53] and HiBench [28,32], it consists of four queries involving scans, aggregations, joins, and UDFs. It supports different data sizes and scaling to thousands of nodes.

2.2   BigBench

BigBench [13,15,27] is an end-to-end Big Data benchmark that represents a data model simulating the volume, velocity, and variety characteristics of a Big Data system, together with a synthetic data generator for structured, semi-structured, and unstructured data. The structured part of the retail data model is adopted from the TPC-DS benchmark and further extended with semi-structured (registered and guest user clicks) and unstructured data (product reviews). The BigBench raw data volumes can be dynamically changed based on a scale factor. The simulated workload is based on a set of 30 queries covering the different aspects of Big Data analytics proposed by McKinsey [37]. The benchmark consists of four key steps: (i) System setup; (ii) Data generation; (iii) Data load; and (iv) Execute application workload. A reference implementation [15] for the Hadoop ecosystem is available. Currently the TPC committee is working towards standardizing it as a TPC Big Data benchmark [14].

2.3   BigDataBench

BigDataBench [57] is an open source Big Data benchmark suite [31] consisting of 14 data sets and 33 workloads. Six of the 14 data sets are real-world based, generated using the BDGS [39] data generator. The generated data types include text, graph, and table data, and are fully scalable. According to the literature it is unclear of what the upper bound of the data set sizes are. The remaining eight data sets are generated from a small seed of real data and are not scalable yet. The 33 workloads are divided into five common application domains: search engine, social networks, electronic commerce, multimedia analytics, and bioinformatics. BigDataBench has many similarities with the DCBench [30], a benchmark suite developed to test data center workloads. This is a rapidly evolving benchmark. Please check the official website for current updates.

2.4   BigFrame

BigFrame [34] is a benchmark generator offering a benchmarking-as-a-service solution for Big Data analytics. While the latest version together with documentation is available on GitHub [16], changes are still being made to the benchmark generator. The benchmark distinguishes between two different analytics workload, (1) offline-analytics and (2) real-time analytics. It consists of structured data (Sales, Item, Customer and Promotion tables) adapted from the TPC-DS benchmark and semi-structured JSON data types containing unstructured text. The current version of the benchmark provides data models for two types of workloads: historical and continuous query. The data in the historical workflow is processed at typical data warehouse rates, e.g., week, whereas the continuous workflow is processed in real-time. It enables real-time decision making based on instant sales and user feedback updates. The development of mixed workloads combining relational, text and graph data is also in progress.

2.5   CloudRank-D

CloudRank-D [29,36] is a benchmark suite for evaluating the performance of cloud computing systems running Big Data applications. The suite consists of 13 representative data analysis tools, which are designed to address a diverse set of workload data and computation characteristics (i.e., data semantics, data models, and data sizes, the ratio of the size of data input to that of data output). Table 1 depicts the representative applications along with its workload type. The benchmark suite reports two complimentary metrics: *data processed per second* (DPS) and *data processed per Joule* (DPJ). DPS is defined as the total amount of data inputs of all jobs divided by the total running time from the submission time of the first job to the end time of the last job. The DPJ is defined as the total amount of data inputs of all jobs divided by the total energy consumed during the duration from the submission time of the first job to the end time of the last job.

2.6   CloudSuite

CloudSuite [25] is a benchmark suite consisting of both emerging scale-out workloads and traditional benchmarks. The goal of the benchmark suite is to analyze and identify key inefficiencies in the processor's core micro-architecture and

Table 1. Representative applications in CloudRank-D; Adopted from [36]

Category	No	Workload
Basic Operations	1	Sort
	2	WordCount
	3	Grep
Classification	4	Naive bayes
	5	Support vector machine
Clustering	6	K-means
Recommendation	7	Item based collaborative filtering
Association rule mining	8	Frequent pattern growth
Sequence learning	9	Hidden Markov
Data warehouse operations	10	Grep select
	11	Ranking select
	12	User-visits aggregation
	13	User-visits ranking join

Table 2. Applications in CloudSuite; Adopted from [25]

Category	Application
Data Serving	Cassandra 0.7.3 with YCSB 0.1.3
MapReduce	Bayesian classification from Mahout 0.4 lib
Media Streaming	Darwin Streaming Server 6.0.3 with Faban Driver
SAT Solver	Klee SAT Solver
Web Frontend	Olio, Nginx and CloudStone
Web Search	Nutch 1.2/Lucene 3.0.1
Web Backend	MySQL 5.5.9
Traditional Benchmarks	PARSEC 2.1, SPEC CINT2006, SPECweb09, TPC-C, TPC-E

memory system organization when running today's cloud workloads. Table 2 summarizes the workload categories as well as the applications that were actually benchmarked.

2.7   GridMix

GridMix [9] is a benchmark suite for Hadoop clusters, which consists of a mix of synthetic jobs. The benchmark suite emulates different users sharing the same cluster resources and submitting different types and number of jobs. This includes also the emulation of distributed cache loads, compression, decompression, and job configuration in terms of resource usage. In order to run the

GridMix benchmark a trace describing the mix of all running MapReduce jobs in the given cluster has to be recorded.

2.8 Hadoop Workload Examples

Since its first version the Hadoop framework has included several ready to use MapReduce sample applications. They are located in the *hadoop-examples-version.jar* jar file. These applications are commonly used to both learn and benchmark Hadoop. The most popular ones include: WordCount, Grep, Pi, and Terasort. The Hibench suite, which is briefly described in the next sub-section, also includes these example workloads.

Grep Task. Grep [6] is a standard MapReduce program that is included in the major Hadoop distributions. The program extracts strings from text input files, matches regular expressions against those strings and counts their number of occurrences. More precisely it consists of two MapReduce jobs running in sequence. The first job counts how many times a matching string occurred, and the second job sorts the matching strings by their frequency and stores the output in a single output file.

Pi. Pi [4] is a MapReduce program computing the exact binary digits of the mathematical constant Pi. It uses multiple map tasks to do the computation and a single reducer to gather the results of the mappers. Therefore, the application is more CPU bound and produces very little network and storage I/O.

2.9 HiBench

HiBench [28,32] is a comprehensive benchmark suite for Hadoop consisting of ten workloads including both synthetic micro-benchmarks and real-world applications. HiBench features several ready-to-use benchmarks from 4 categories: micro benchmarks, web search, machine learning, and HDFS benchmarks. Table 3 depicts the category and the exact workload included in HiBench.

The HiBench suite evaluates and characterizes the MapReduce framework in terms of speed (*job running time*) and throughput (*the number of tasks completed per minute*) and the HDFS in terms of bandwidth, system resource utilization and data access patterns.

The following list briefly describes the benchmarks currently implemented. For a complete description please refer to [28,32].

- *Sort*, uses the MapReduce framework to sort the input directory into the output directory, being predominately I/O intensive.
- *WordCount*, counts number of word occurrences in a large text files. It is distributed with Hadoop and used in many MapReduce learning books. It is CPU bound.

Table 3. HiBench Workloads

Category	No	Workload
Micro Benchmarks	1	Sort
	2	WordCount
	3	TeraSort
	4	EnhancedDFSIO
Web Search	5	Nutch Indexing
	6	PageRank
Machine Learning	7	Bayesian Classification
	8	K-means Clustering
Analytical Query	9	Hive Join
	10	Hive Aggregation

- *TeraSort*, sorts data generated by the *TeraGen* program distributed with Hadoop. *TeraSort* is widely used as reference in research papers as well as in Big Data competitions. *TeraSort* is I/O and CPU intensive.
- *EnhancedDFSIO* or DFSIOE,is an I/O intensive benchmark that measures throughput in HDFS using MapReduce. It features separate read and write workloads.
- *Nutch Indexing*, tests the search indexing sub-system in Nutch, a popular open source (Apache project) search engine.
- *PageRank*, an implementation of Google's Web page ranking algorithm. It crawls Wikipedia sample pages.
- *Bayes*, Bayesian Machine Learning classification using the Mahout library. The input of this benchmark is extracted from a subset of the Wikipedia dump.
- *K-means*, Mahout's implementation of the k-means clustering algorithm for knowledge discovery and data mining.
- *HiveBench*, the OLAP-style Join and Aggregation queries, are adapted from the Pavlo's Benchmark [44] and have the goal to test the Hive performance.

Since version 4.0, HiBench contains 12 Spark workloads implemented in Java, Scala and Python.

2.10 MRBench

MRBench [33] is a benchmark evaluating the processing of business oriented queries and concurrent data modifications on MapReduce systems. It implements the 22 queries of the TPC-H decision support system benchmark directly in map and reduce operations. The MRBench supports three configuration options: database size and number of map and reduce tasks.

2.11   MapReduce Benchmark Suite (MRBS)

MRBS [40,50,51] is a comprehensive benchmark suite for evaluating the performance of MapReduce systems. It covers five application domains listed in Table 4. The high-level metrics reported by the benchmark are client request latency, throughput and cost. Additionally, low-level metrics like size of read/written data, throughput of MR jobs, and tasks are also reported. The MRBS implements a service that provides different types of operations, which can be requested by clients. Two execution modes are supported: interactive mode and batch mode. The benchmark run consists of three phases dynamically configurable by the end-user: warm-up phase, run-time phase, and slow-down phase. The user can specify the number of runs and the different aspects of load: dataload and workload. The dataload is characterized by the size and the nature of the data sets used as inputs for a benchmark, and the workload is characterized by the number of concurrent clients and the distribution of the request type.

Table 4. Representative Applications in MRBS

Domain	Application
Recommendation	Benchmark based on real movie database
Business Intelligence	TPC-H
Bioinformatics	DNA sequencing
Text Processing	Search patterns, word occurrence and sorting on randomly generated text files
Data Mining	Classifying newsgroup documents into categories, canopy clustering operations

2.12   Pavlo's Benchmark (CALDA)

Pavlo's Benchmark [3,44,53] consists of five tasks defined as SQL queries among which is the original MapReduce Grep task, which is a representative of most real user MapReduce programs. The benchmark was developed to specifically compare the capabilities of Hadoop with those of commercial parallel Relational Database Management Systems (RDBMS). Although the reported results do not favor the Hadoop platform, the authors remain optimistic that MapReduce systems will coexist with traditional database systems. Table 5 summarizes all types of tasks in Pavlo's Benchmark and their complimentary SQL statements.

2.13   PigMix

PigMix/PigMix2 [11] is a set of 17 queries specifically created to test the performance of Pig systems. Specifically, it tests the latency and scalability of Pig

Table 5. Pavlo's Benchmark Queries

Category	No	Workload/SQL Query
General task	1	SELECT * FROM Data WHERE field LIKE '%XYZ%';
PageRank/Selection Task	2	SELECT pageURL, pageRank FROM Rankings WHERE pageRank >X;
Web Log/Aggregation Task	3	SELECT sourceIP, SUM(adRevenue) FROM UserVisits GROUP BY sourceIP;
		SELECT SUBSTR(sourceIP,1,7), SUM(adRevenue) FROM UserVisits GROUP BY SUBSTR(sourceIP, 1, 7);
Join Task	4	SELECT INTO Temp sourceIP, AVG(pageRank) as avgPageRank, SUM(adRevenue) as totalRevenue FROM Rankings AS R, UserVisits AS UV WHERE R.pageURL = UV.destURL AND UV.visitDate BETWEEN Date('2000-01-15') AND Date('2000-01-22') GROUP BY UV.sourceIP; SELECT sourceIP, totalRevenue, avgPageRank FROM Temp ORDER BY totalRevenue DESC LIMIT 1;
UDF Aggregation Task	5	SELECT INTO Temp F(contents) FROM Documents; SELECT url, SUM(value) FROM Temp GROUP BY url;

systems. The queries, written in Pig Latin [42], test different operations like data loading, different types of joins, group by clauses, sort clauses, as well as aggregation operations. The benchmark includes eight data sets, with varying schema attributes and sizes, generated using the DataGeneratorHadoop [7] tool. PigMix/PigMix2 are not considered true benchmarks as they lack some of the main benchmark elements, such as metrics.

2.14   PRIMEBALL

PRIMEBALL [26] is a novel and unified benchmark specification for comparing the parallel processing frameworks in the context of Big Data applications hosted in the cloud. It is implementation- and technology-agnostic, using a fictional news hub called New Pork Times, based on a popular real-life news site.

Included are various use-case scenarios made of both queries and data-intensive batch processing. The raw data set is fetched by a crawler and consists of both structured XML and binary audio and video files, which can be scaled by a pre-defined scale factor (SF) to 1 PB.

The benchmark specifies two main metrics: throughput and price performance. The throughput metric reports the total time required to execute a particular scenario. The price performance metric is equal to the throughput divided by the price, where the price is defined by the specific cloud provider and depends on multiple factors. Additionally, the benchmark specifies several relevant properties characterizing cloud platforms, such as (1) scale-up; (2) elastic speedup; (3) horizontal scalability; (4) latency; (5) durability; (6) consistency and version handling; (7) availability; (8) concurrency and other data and information retrieval properties.

2.15 SparkBench

SparkBench [35,38], developed by IBM, is a comprehensive Spark specific benchmark suite. It comprises of four main workload categories: machine learning, graph processing, streaming, and SQL queries. Currently ten workloads are implemented, listed in Table 6. The purpose of the benchmark suite is to help users evaluate and analyze the tradeoffs between different system designs, guide the optimization of workload configurations and cluster provisioning for Spark deployments. SparkBench reports two metrics: *job execution time* (seconds) and *data process rate* (MB/second). The job execution time measures the execution time of each workload, whereas the data process rate is defined as the input data size divided by the job execution time.

Table 6. SparkBench Workloads

Application Type	Workload
Machine Learning	Logistic Regression
	Support Vector Machine
	Matrix Factorization
Graph Computation	PageRank
	SVD++
	TriangleCount
SQL Queries	Hive
	RDDRelation
Streaming Application	Twitter
	PageView

2.16   Statistical Workload Injector for MapReduce (SWIM)

SWIM [20,21,60] is a benchmark, which takes a different approach in the testing process. It consists of a framework, which is able to synthesize representative workload from real MapReduce traces taking into account the job submit time, input data size, and shuffle/input and output/shuffle data ratio. The result is a synthetic workload, which has the exact characteristics of the original workload. Similarly, the benchmark generates artificial data. Then the workload executor runs a script which takes the input data and executes the synthetically generated workload (jobs with specified data size, data ratios, and simulating gabs between the job executions). Additionally, the reproduced workload includes a mix of job submission rates and sequences and a mix of common job types. Currently, the benchmark includes multiple real Facebook traces and the goal is to further extend the repository by including new real workload traces.

2.17   TPC-H

TPC-H [54] is the de facto benchmark standard for testing data warehouse capability of a system. Instead of representing the activity of any particular business segment, TPC-H models any industry that manages, sells, or distributes products worldwide (e.g., car rental, food distribution, parts, suppliers, etc.). The benchmark is technology-agnostic. The purpose of TPC-H is to reduce the diversity of operations found in a typical data warehouse application, while retaining the application's essential performance characteristics, namely: the level of system utilization and the complexity of operations. The core of the benchmark is comprised of a set of 22 business queries designed to exercise system functionalities in a manner representative of complex decision support applications. These queries have been given a realistic context, portraying the activity of a wholesale supplier to help the audience relate intuitively to the components of the benchmarks. It also contains two refresh functions (RF1, RF2) modeling the loading of new sales information (RF1) and the purging of stale or obsolete sales information (RF2) from the database. The exact definition of the workload can be found in the latest specification [54]. It was adapted very early in the development of Hive [10,12] and Pig [8], and implementations of the benchmark are available for both. In order to publish a TPC-H compliant performance result the system needs to support full ACID (Atomicity, Consistency, Isolation, and Durability).

2.18   TPC-DS

TPC-DS [55] is a decision support benchmark that models several generally applicable aspects of a decision support system, including queries and data maintenance. It takes the marvels of TPC-H and, now obsolete TPC-R, and fuses them into a modern DSS benchmark. The main focus areas:

- Multiple snowflake schemas with shared dimensions
- 24 tables with an average of 18 columns
- 99 distinct SQL 99 queries with random substitutions
- More representative skewed database content
- Sub-linear scaling of non-fact tables
- Ad-hoc, reporting, iterative and extraction queries
- ETL-like data maintenance

While TPC-DS may be applied to any industry that must transform operational and external data into business intelligence, the workload has been granted a realistic context. It models the decision support tasks of a typical retail product supplier. The goal of selecting a retail business model is to assist the reader in relating intuitively to the components of the benchmark, without tracking that industry segment so tightly as to minimize the relevance of the benchmark. The schema, an aggregate of multiple star schemas, contains essential business information, such as detailed customer, order, and product data for the classic sales channels: store, catalog, and Internet. Wherever possible, real world data are used to populate each table with common data skews, such as seasonal sales and frequent names. In order to realistically scale the benchmark from small to large datasets, fact tables scale linearly while dimensions scale sub linearly. The benchmark abstracts the diversity of operations found in an information analysis application, while retaining essential performance characteristics. As it is necessary to execute a great number of queries and data transformations to completely manage any business analysis environment, TPC-DS defines 99 distinct SQL-99 (with OLAP amendment) queries and twelve data maintenance operations covering typical DSS like query types such as ad-hoc, reporting, iterative (drill down/up), and extraction queries and periodic refresh of the database. The metric is constructed in a way that favors systems that can overlap query execution with updates (trickle updates). As with TPC-H full ACID characteristics are required. Implementation with more than 50 sample queries is available for Hive [12].

2.19   TPCx-HS

This section presents the TPCx-HS benchmark, its methodology and some of its major features as described in the current specification (version 1.3.0 from February 19, 2015) [56].

The TPCx-HS was released in July 2014 as the first industry's standard benchmark for Big Data systems [41]. It stresses both the hardware and software components including the Hadoop run-time stack, Hadoop File System, and MapReduce layers. The benchmark is based on the TeraSort workload [5], which is part of the Apache Hadoop distribution. Similarly, it consists of four modules: HSGen, HSDataCkeck, HSSort, and HSValidate. The HSGen is a program that generates the data for a particular Scale Factor (see Clause 4.1 from the TPCx-HS specification) and is based on the TeraGen, which uses a random data generator. The HSDataCheck is a program that checks the compliance of

Table 7. TPCx-HS Phases

Phase	Description as provided in TPCx-HS specification [56]
1	Generation of input data via HSGen. The data generated must be replicated 3-ways and written on a durable medium
2	Dataset (See Clause 4) verification via HSDataCheck. The program is to verify the cardinality, size, and replication factor of the generated data. If the HSDataCheck program reports failure then the run is considered invalid
3	Running the sort using HSSort on the input data. This phase samples the input data and sorts the data. The sorted data must be replicated 3-ways and written on a durable medium
4	Dataset (See Clause 4) verification via HSDataCheck. The program is to verify the cardinality, size and replication factor of the sorted data. If the HSDataCheck program reports failure then the run is considered invalid
5	Validating the sorted output data via HSValidate. HSValidate validates the sorted data. If the HSValidate program reports that the HSSort did not generate the correct sort order, then the run is considered invalid

the dataset and replication. The HSSort is a program, based on TeraSort, which sorts the data into a total order. Finally, HSValidate is a program, based on TeraValidate, that validates the output is sorted.

A valid benchmark execution consists of five separate phases which have to be run sequentially to avoid any phase overlapping. Additionally, Table 7 provides the exact description of each of the execution phases. The benchmark is started by the <TPCx-HS-master> script and consists of two consecutive runs, Run1 and Run2. No activities except file system cleanup are allowed between Run1 and Run2. The completion times of each phase/module (HSGen, HSSort and HSValidate) except HSDataCheck are currently reported.

An important requirement of the benchmark is to maintain 3-way data replication throughout the entire experiment.

The benchmark reports the total elapsed time (T) in seconds for both runs. This time is used for the calculation of the TPCx-HS performance metric also abbreviated with HSph@SF. The run that takes more time and results in lower TPCx-HS performance metric is defined as the performance run. On the contrary, the run that takes less time and results in TPCx-HS performance metric is defined as the repeatability run. The benchmark reported performance metric is the TPCx-HS performance metric for the performance run.

The scale factor defines the size of the dataset, which is generated by HSGen and used for the benchmark experiments. In TPCx-HS, it follows a stepped size model. Table 8 summarizes the supported scale factors, together with the corresponding data sizes and number of records. The last column indicates the argument with which to start the TPCx-HS-master script.

Table 8. TPCx-HS Phases

Dataset Size	Scale Factor (SF)	Number of Records	Option to Start Run
100 GB	N/A	1 Billion	./TPCx-HS-master.sh -g 1
300 GB	N/A	3 Billion	./TPCx-HS-master.sh -g 2
1 TB	1	10 Billion	./TPCx-HS-master.sh -g 3
3 TB	3	30 Billion	./TPCx-HS-master.sh -g 4
10 TB	10	100 Billion	./TPCx-HS-master.sh -g 5
30 TB	30	300 Billion	./TPCx-HS-master.sh -g 6
100 TB	100	1000 Billion	./TPCx-HS-master.sh -g 7
300 TB	300	3000 Billion	./TPCx-HS-master.sh -g 8
1 PB	1000	10000 Billion	./TPCx-HS-master.sh -g 9

2.20   Yahoo! Cloud Serving Benchmark (YCSB)

YCSB [23,43] is a benchmark designed to compare emerging cloud serving systems like Cassandra, HBase, MongoDB, Riak, and many more, which do not support ACID. The benchmark consists of a workload generator and a generic database interface, which can be easily extended to support other relational or NoSQL databases. YCSB provides a core package of six pre-defined workloads A-F, which simulate a cloud OLTP application (read and update operations). The reported metrics are execution time and throughput (operations per second). The benchmark is open source and available on GitHub [59].

3   Discussion

There is a great number of existing benchmarks focused on testing certain features of data intensive systems, but they are all developed with different goals in mind and for different platforms. With the steady growth of Big Data, the need for a specific benchmark testing the Big Data characteristics of current platforms becomes more important. At the same time, the platforms are becoming more complex as the number of requirements they should address also grows. This makes the creation of an objective Big Data benchmark, that covers all relevant characteristics, a complex task.

The workload diversity is one such important characteristics in a Big Data benchmark, as outlined in related papers [13,18–20,22,27,36,57]. The benchmark should include a wide range of workloads, based on real world applications, and offer the ability to easily integrate new ones. At the same time these workloads should not be redundant or test similar data and component characteristics [58]. The different workload types should be seen as complementary to each other in a benchmark suite, with the overall goal to test a bigger range of functionalities. Tightly coupled with the workload type is the data generator used to synthesize the test data, based on real data samples, for a specifically set scale factor and size. The generated data varies between structured, semi-structured, unstructured, or mixed. Because of this data heterogeneity, there are various different approaches to generate the data discussed in research papers [1,20,39,46,47]. Similarly, existing benchmarks differ in how they define accurate and representative benchmark metrics, which incorporate all the necessary information to independently compare the systems under test. Motivated by the platform and benchmark complexity, data heterogeneity, size, and scalability, there is an urgent need of new metrics. They can be workload specific like in HiBench [28] or more complex based on multiple workloads in an end-to-end benchmark suite [27]. Others, like the SWIM benchmark [20,21], define job specific metrics like number of jobs for each job type and job submission patterns, which are limited only to MapReduce platforms. On the contrary, more general metrics, independent of workload type, based on processor micro-architecture characteristics are reported. Such examples, presented in [24,58], are Cycles per Instructions (CPI), first level data cache misses per 1000 instructions (L1 MPKI), and last level cache (LLC) miss ratio. Finally, new types of metrics like data processed per second and data processed per Joule implemented in CloudRank-D [36], improve the measurement of data processing and energy consumption.

4   Benchmarking Platforms

Benchmarking platforms are systems and tools that facilitate the different phases of executing and evaluating benchmark results. These include: benchmark planning, server deployment and configuration, execution and queuing, metrics collection, data and results management, data transformation, error detection, and evaluation of results. The evaluation of results can be either by individual benchmarks or by group of benchmarks.

4.1   ALOJA Benchmarking Platform

The ALOJA research project [45] is an initiative from the Barcelona Supercomputing Center (BSC) to produce a systematic study of Hadoop configuration and deployment options. The project provides an open source platform for executing Big Data frameworks in an integrated manner facilitating benchmark execution and evaluation of results. ALOJA currently provides tools to deploy, provision, configure, and benchmark Hadoop, as well as providing different evaluations for the analysis of results covering both software and hardware configurations of executions.

The project also hosts the largest public Hadoop benchmark repository with over 42,000 executions from HiBench (See Sect. 2.9). The online repository can be used as a first step to understand and select benchmarks to execute in the selected deployment and reduce benchmarking efforts by sharing results from different systems. The repository and the tools can be found online [17].

Table 9. Big Data Benchmarks - Data Types: Structured(S), Semi-structured(SS), Unstructured(U); Hadoop = MapReduce and HDFS

Benchmark	Workloads	Metrics	S	SS	U	Current Implementations	Available
AMP Lab Big Data Benchmark	Micro Benchmark	Query time	Yes	No	No	Hive, Tez, Shark, Impala, Redshift	Yes [2]
BigBench	30 Queries	Query time and BBQpH	Yes	Yes	Yes	Teradata Aster, Hadoop, Spark	Yes [15]
BigDataBench	Multiple (See [31])	Multiple metrics	Yes	Yes	Yes	Multiple technologies	Yes [31]
BigFrame	Multiple	Execution time	Yes	Yes	Yes	Multiple	Yes [16]
CloudRank-D	Multiple (See Table 1)	Data processed per second and Data processed per Joule	Yes	Yes	Yes	Hadoop	Yes [29]
CloudSuite	Multiple (See Table 2)	No	Yes	Yes	Yes	Multiple technologies	No
GridMix	Synthetic and Basic Operations	Number of completed jobs and elapsed time	Yes	No	No	Hadoop	Yes [9]
Hadoop Workload Examples	Micro Benchmarks	No	No	No	Yes	Hadoop	Yes [4,6]
HiBench	Micro Benchmarks (See Table 3)	Execution time and throughput	Yes	Yes	Yes	Hadoop, Spark	Yes [32]
MRBench	Data warehouse operations: TPC-H	Query time	Yes	No	No	Hadoop	No
MRBS	Multiple (See Table 4)	Client request latency, throughput and cost	Yes	Yes	Yes	Hadoop	Yes [40]
Pavlo's Benchmark (CALDA)	Micro Benchmark (See Table 5)	Query time	Yes	No	No	Hive	Yes [3]
PigMix	Pig Specific Queries	Execution time	Yes	No	No	Pig, Hadoop	Yes [11]
PRIMEBALL	Multiple (See Subsection 2.14)	Price performance and other property specific	Yes	Yes	Yes	Hadoop	No
SparkBench	Multiple (See Table 6)	Job execution time and data process rate	Yes	Yes	Yes	Spark	Yes [38]
SWIM	Synthetically User-generated	Multiple metrics	No	No	No	Hadoop	Yes [60]
TPC-H	Data warehouse operations	Query time and throughput: QphH@Size, $/QphH@Size	Yes	No	No	Hive, Pig, Impala, IBM Big SQL	Yes [8,10]
TPC-DS	Data warehouse operations	Query time and throughput: QphDS@SF, $/QphDS@SF	Yes	No	No	Hive, Pig, Impala, IBM Big SQL	Yes [12]
TPCx-HS	HSGen, HSData Ckeck, HSSort and HSValidate	Performance, price and energy: HSph@SF, $/HSph@SF, Watts/HSph@SF	No	No	Yes	Hadoop	Yes [56]
YCSB	Cloud OLTP	Execution time and throughput	Yes	No	No	NoSQL databases	Yes [59]

4.2   Liquid Benchmarking Platform

Liquid Benchmarking [48, 49, 52] is an online cloud-based platform for democratizing the performance evaluation and benchmarking processes. The goals of the project are to:

- Dramatically reduce the time and effort for conducting performance evaluation processes by facilitating the process of sharing the experimental artifacts (software implementations, datasets, computing resources, and benchmarking tasks) and enabling the users to easily create, mashup, and run the experiments with zero installation or configuration efforts.
- Support for searching, comparing, analyzing, and visualizing (using different built-in visualization tools) the results of previous experiments.
- Enable the users to subscribe for notifications about the results of any new running experiments for the domains/benchmarks of their interest.
- Enable social and collaborative features that can turn the performance evaluation and benchmarking process into a living process where different users can run different experiments and share the results of their experiments with other users.

5   Conclusion

This document presented a review of existing Big Data benchmarks, as well as a discussion about their major characteristics. Table 9 summarizes the Big Data benchmarks described in our survey.

5.1   Future Work

This benchmark survey is the beginning of a mid-term project to perform an in-depth analysis of Big Data benchmarks. This project not only aims to cover more benchmarks, but also to provide a performance characterization that can be used as a reference for the results one should expect from each benchmark type. There is also the intention to compare different data compression and storage formats i.e., avro, parquet, ORC, as well as testing different implementations of reference benchmarks such as BigBench and TCP-H.

Acknowledgment. This research has been supported by the Research Group of the Standard Performance Evaluation Corporation (SPEC).

References

1. Alexandrov, A., Brücke, C., Markl, V.: Issues in big data testing and benchmarking. In: Proceedings of the Sixth International Workshop on Testing Database Systems, DBTest 2013, New York, NY, USA, June 24, pp. 1: 1–1: 5 (2013)
2. AMP Lab: AMP Lab Big Data Benchmark (2013). https://amplab.cs.berkeley.edu/benchmark/

3. Pavlo, A.: Benchmark (2011). http://database.cs.brown.edu/projects/mapreduce-vs-dbms/

4. Hadoop, A.: Package org.apache.hadoop.examples.pi (2015). http://hadoop.apache.org/docs/r0.23.11/api/org/apache/hadoop/examples/pi/package-summary.html

5. Hadoop, A.: TPC Express Benchmark HS - Standard Specification (2015). http://hadoop.apache.org/docs/current/api/org/apache/hadoop/examples/terasort/package-summary.html

6. Apache Software Foundation: Grep (2009). http://wiki.apache.org/hadoop/Grep

7. Apache Software Foundation: DataGeneratorHadoop (2010). http://wiki.apache.org/pig/DataGeneratorHadoop

8. Apache Software Foundation: Running TPC-H Benchmark on Pig (2012). https://issues.apache.org/jira/browse/PIG-2397

9. Apache Software Foundation: GridMix (2013). https://hadoop.apache.org/docs/stable1/gridmix.html

10. Apache Software Foundation: Hive performance benchmarks (2013). https://issues.apache.org/jira/browse/HIVE-396

11. Apache Software Foundation: PigMix (2013).https://cwiki.apache.org/confluence/display/PIG/PigMix

12. Apache Software Foundation: TPC-H and TPC-DS for Hive (2015). https://github.com/hortonworks/hive-testbench/tree/hive14

13. Baru, C., Bhandarkar, M., Nambiar, R., Poess, M., Rabl, T.: Setting the direction for big data benchmark standards. In: Nambiar, R., Poess, M. (eds.) TPCTC 2012. LNCS, vol. 7755, pp. 197–208. Springer, Heidelberg (2013)

14. Baru, C., et al.: Discussion of BigBench: a proposed industry standard performance benchmark for big data. In: Nambiar, R., Poess, M. (eds.) TPCTC 2014. LNCS, vol. 8904, pp. 44–63. Springer, Heidelberg (2015)

15. BigBench: BigBench (2015). https://github.com/intel-hadoop/Big-Data-Benchmark-for-Big-Bench

16. Team, B.: BigFrame (2013). https://github.com/bigframeteam/BigFrame/wiki

17. BSC: Aloja home page (2014). http://aloja.bsc.es/

18. Chang, J., Lim, K.T., Byrne, J., Ramirez, L., Ranganathan, P.: Workload diversity and dynamics in big data analytics: implications to system designers. In: Proceedings of the 2nd Workshop on Architectures and Systems for Big Data. ASBD 2012, pp. 21–26. ACM, NY (2012)

19. Chen, Y.: We dont know enough to make a big data benchmark suite-an academia-industry view. Technical report No. UCB/EECS-2012-71 (2012)

20. Chen, Y., Alspaugh, S., Katz, R.H.: Interactive analytical processing in big data systems: a cross-industry study of mapreduce workloads. PVLDB 5(12), 1802–1813 (2012)

21. Chen, Y., Ganapathi, A., Griffith, R., Katz, R.H.: The case for evaluating mapreduce performance using workload suites. In: 19th Annual IEEE/ACM International Symposium on Modeling, Analysis and Simulation of Computer and Telecommunication Systems. MASCOTS 2011, Singapore, 25–27 July 2011, pp. 390–399 (2011)

22. Chen, Y., Raab, F., Katz, R.: From TPC-C to big data benchmarks: a functional workload model. In: Rabl, T., Poess, M., Baru, C., Jacobsen, H.-A. (eds.) WBDB 2012. LNCS, vol. 8163, pp. 28–43. Springer, Heidelberg (2014)

23. Cooper, B.F., Silberstein, A., Tam, E., Ramakrishnan, R., Sears, R.: Benchmarking cloud serving systems with YCSB. In: Proceedings of the 1st ACM Symposium on Cloud Computing. SoCC 2010, Indianapolis, Indiana, USA, 10–11 June 2010, pp. 143–154 (2010)

24. Dimitrov, M., Kumar, K., Lu, P., Viswanathan, V., Willhalm, T.: Memory system characterization of big data workloads. In: Proceedings of the 2013 IEEE International Conference on Big Data, 6–9 October 2013, Santa Clara, CA, US, pp. 15–22 (2013)
25. Ferdman, M., Adileh, A., Koçberber, Y.O., Volos, S., Alisafaee, M., Jevdjic, D., Kaynak, C., Popescu, A.D., Ailamaki, A., Falsafi, B.: Clearing the clouds: a study of emerging scale-out workloads on modern hardware. In: Proceedings of the 17th International Conference on Architectural Support for Programming Languages and Operating Systems, ASPLOS 2012, London, UK, 3–7 March 2012, pp. 37–48 (2012)
26. Ferrarons, J., Adhana, M., Colmenares, C., Pietrowska, S., Bentayeb, F., Darmont,J.: PRIMEBALL: A parallel processing framework benchmark for big dataapplications in the cloud. In: Performance Characterization and Benchmarking -5th TPC Technology Conference. TPCTC 2013, Trento, Italy, 26 August 2013, pp. 109–124 (2013)
27. Ghazal, A., Rabl, T., Hu, M., Raab, F., Poess, M., Crolotte, A., Jacobsen., H.A.: BigBench: towards an industry standard benchmark for big data analytics. In: SIGMOD (2013)
28. Huang, S., Huang, J., Dai, J., Xie, T., Huang, B.: The hibench benchmark suite: characterization of the mapreduce-based data analysis. In: Workshops Proceedings of the 26th International Conference on Data Engineering, ICDE 2010, 1–6 March 2010, Long Beach, California, USA, pp. 41–51 (2010)
29. ICT, Chinese Academy of Sciences: CloudRank-D (2013). http://prof.ict.ac.cn/CloudRank/
30. ICT, Chinese Academy of Sciences: DCBench (2013). http://prof.ict.ac.cn/DCBench/
31. ICT, Chinese Academy of Sciences: BigDataBench 3.1 (2015). http://prof.ict.ac.cn/BigDataBench/
32. Intel: HiBench Suite (2015). https://github.com/intel-hadoop/HiBench
33. Kim, K., Jeon, K., Han, H., Kim, S.G., Jung, H., Yeom, H.Y.: Mrbench: a benchmark for mapreduce framework. In: 14th International Conference on Parallel and Distributed Systems, ICPADS 2008, Melbourne, Victoria, Australia, 8–10 December 2008, pp. 11–18 (2008)
34. Kunjir, M., Kalmegh, P., Babu, S.: Thoth: towards managing a multi-system cluster. PVLDB 7(13), 1689–1692 (2014)
35. Li, M., Tan, J., Wang, Y., Zhang, L., Salapura, V.: Sparkbench: a comprehensive benchmarking suite for in memory data analytic platform spark. In: Proceedings of the 12th ACM International Conference on Computing Frontiers. CF 2015, pp. 53:1–53:8. ACM, New York, NY, USA (2015)
36. Luo, C., Zhan, J., Jia, Z., Wang, L., Lu, G., Zhang, L., Xu, C., Sun, N.: Cloudrank-d: benchmarking and ranking cloud computing systems for data processing applications. Front. Comput. Sci. 6(4), 347–362 (2012)
37. Manyika, J., Chui, M., Brown, B., Bughin, J., Dobbs, R., Roxburgh, C., Byers, A.H.: Big data: The Next Frontier for Innovation, Competition, and Productivity. Technical report, McKinsey Global Institute (2011). http://www.mckinsey.com/insights/mgi/research/technology_and_innovation/big_data_the_next_frontier_for_innovation
38. Li, M.: SparkBench (2015). https://bitbucket.org/lm0926/sparkbench

39. Ming, Z., Luo, C., Gao, W., Han, R., Yang, Q., Wang, L., Zhan, J.: BDGS: a scalable big data generator suite in big data benchmarking. In: Rabl, T., Raghunath, N., Poess, M., Bhandarkar, M., Jacobsen, H.-A., Baru, C. (eds.) Advancing Big Data Benchmarks. LNCS, vol. 8585, pp. 138–154. Springer, Heidelberg (2013)
40. MRBS: MRBS (2013). http://sardes.inrialpes.fr/research/mrbs/index.html
41. Nambiar, R., Poess, M., Dey, A., Cao, P., Magdon-Ismail, T., Qi Ren, D., Bond, A.: Introducing TPCx-HS: the first industry standard for benchmarking big data systems. In: Nambiar, R., Poess, M. (eds.) TPCTC 2014. LNCS, vol. 8904, pp. 1–12. Springer, Heidelberg (2015)
42. Olston, C., Reed, B., Srivastava, U., Kumar, R., Tomkins, A.: Pig latin: a not-so-foreign language for data processing. In: Proceedings of the ACM SIGMOD International Conference on Management of Data. SIGMOD 2008, Vancouver, BC, Canada, 10–12 June 2008, pp. 1099–1110 (2008)
43. Patil, S., Polte, M., Ren, K., Tantisiriroj, W., Xiao, L., López, J., Gibson, G., Fuchs, A., Rinaldi, B.: YCSB++: benchmarking and performance debugging advanced features in scalable table stores. In: ACM Symposium on Cloud Computing in conjunction with SOSP 2011, SOCC 2011, Cascais, Portugal, 26–28 October 2011, p. 9 (2011)
44. Pavlo, A., Paulson, E., Rasin, A., Abadi, D.J., DeWitt, D.J., Madden, S., Stonebraker, M.: A comparison of approaches to large-scale data analysis. In: SIGMOD, pp. 165–178 (2009)
45. Poggi, N., Carrera, D., Call, A., Mendoza, S., Becerra, Y., Torres, J., Ayguadé, E., Gagliardi, F., Labarta, J., Reinauer, R., Vujic, N., Green, D., Blakeley, J.: ALOJA: a systematic study of hadoop deployment variables to enable automated characterization of cost-effectiveness. In: 2014 IEEE International Conference on Big Data, Big Data 2014, Washington, DC, USA, 27–30 October 2014, pp. 905–913 (2014)
46. Rabl, T., Frank, M., Sergieh, H.M., Kosch, H.: A data generator for cloud-scale benchmarking. In: Nambiar, R., Poess, M. (eds.) TPCTC 2010. LNCS, vol. 6417, pp. 41–56. Springer, Heidelberg (2011)
47. Rabl, T., Poess, M.: Parallel data generation for performance analysis of large, complex RDBMS. In: DBTest 2011, p. 5 (2011)
48. Sakr, S., Casati, F.: Liquid benchmarks: towards an online platform for collaborative assessment of computer science research results. In: Nambiar, R., Poess, M. (eds.) TPCTC 2010. LNCS, vol. 6417, pp. 10–24. Springer, Heidelberg (2011)
49. Sakr, S., Shafaat, A., Bajaber, F., Barnawi, A., Batarfi, O., Altalhi, A.H.: Liquid benchmarking: a platform for democratizing the performance evaluation process. In: Proceedings of the 18th International Conference on Extending Database Technology, EDBT 2015, Brussels, Belgium, 23–27 March 2015, pp. 537–540 (2015)
50. Sangroya, A., Serrano, D., Bouchenak, S.: MRBS: A Comprehensive MapReduce Benchmark Suite. Technical report, LIG Grenoble Fr (2012)
51. Sangroya, A., Serrano, D., Bouchenak, S.: MRBS: towards dependability benchmarking for hadoop MapReduce. In: Caragiannis, I., Alexander, M., Badia, R.M., Cannataro, M., Costan, A., Danelutto, M., Desprez, F., Krammer, B., Sahuquillo, J., Scott, S.L., Weidendorfer, J. (eds.) Euro-Par Workshops 2012. LNCS, vol. 7640, pp. 3–12. Springer, Heidelberg (2013)
52. Sakr, S.: Liquid benchmarking (2015). http://wiki.liquidbenchmark.net/doku.php/home
53. Stonebraker, M., Abadi, D.J., DeWitt, D.J., Madden, S., Paulson, E., Pavlo, A., Rasin, A.: Mapreduce and parallel dbmss: friends or foes? Commun. ACM **53**(1), 64–71 (2010)

54. Transaction Processing Performance Council: TPC Benchmark H - Standard Specification, version 2.17.1 (2014)
55. Transaction Processing Performance Council: TPC Benchmark DS - Standard Specification, version 1.3.1 (2015)
56. Transaction Processing Performance Council: TPC Express Benchmark HS - Standard Specification, version 1.3.0 (2015)
57. Wang, L., Zhan, J., Luo, C., Zhu, Y., Yang, Q., He, Y., Gao, W., Jia, Z., Shi, Y., Zhang, S., Zhen, C., Lu, G., Zhan, K., Li, X., Qiu, B.: BigDataBench: a Big Data Benchmark Suite from Internet Services. In: HPCA (2014)
58. Xiong, W., Yu, Z., Bei, Z., Zhao, J., Zhang, F., Zou, Y., Bai, X., Li, Y., Xu, C.: A characterization of big data benchmarks. In: Proceedings of the 2013 IEEE International Conference on Big Data, 6–9 October 2013, Santa Clara, CA, USA, pp. 118–125 (2013)
59. Yahoo: YCSB (2015). https://github.com/brianfrankcooper/YCSB
60. Chen, Y.: Statistical Workload Injector for MapReduce (SWIM) (2013). https://github.com/SWIMProjectUCB/SWIM/wiki

Profiling the Performance of Virtualized Databases with the TPCx-V Benchmark

Andrew Bond[1], Doug Johnson[2], Greg Kopczynski[3], and H. Reza Taheri[3(✉)]

[1] Red Hat, Inc., Raleigh, USA
abond@redhat.com
[2] InfoSizing, Inc., Manitou Springs, USA
doug@sizing.com
[3] VMware, Inc., Palo Alto, USA
{gregwk,rtaheri}@vmware.com

Abstract. The proliferation of virtualized servers in data centers has conquered the last frontier of bare-iron servers: back-end databases. The multi-tenancy issues of elasticity, capacity planning, and load variation in cloud data centers now coincide with the heavy demands of database workloads; which in turn creates a call for a benchmark specifically intended for this environment.

The TPC–V benchmark will fill this need with a publicly-available, end-to-end benchmark kit. Using a prototype of the kit, we profiled the performance of a server running 60 virtual machines with 48 databases of different sizes, load levels, and workloads. We will show that virtualized servers can indeed handle the elasticity and multi-tenancy requirements of the cloud, but only after careful tuning of the system configuration to avoid bottlenecks.

In this paper, we will provide a brief description of the benchmark, discuss the results and the conclusions drawn from the experiments, and propose future directions for analyzing the performance of cloud data centers by augmenting the capabilities of the TPCx-V benchmark kit.

Keywords: Database performance · Virtualization · SQL server · Workload consolidation · Performance tuning · Cloud computing

1 Introduction

Server virtualization is ubiquitous in data centers, whether in the cloud or on users' premises. 32 % of the new servers shipped in 2014 were deployed as virtualized servers [13]. In the early days of virtualization, database applications were deemed too demanding to be virtualized, but today's virtualized servers routinely run database applications.

Benchmarking database applications has always been a challenge due to the complexity and demanding nature of the applications. Virtualization adds an additional level of complexity, making it harder to both design and use such a benchmark. The Transaction Processing Performance Council (TPC) has been working on developing the TPCx-V benchmark to fill this need.

© Springer International Publishing Switzerland 2016
R. Nambiar and M. Poess (Eds.): TPCTC 2015, LNCS 9508, pp. 156–172, 2016.
DOI: 10.1007/978-3-319-31409-9_10

Prior publications [1, 2, 8] have reported on the TPCx–V's design philosophy, detailed architecture, and specific properties. We will not repeat those details in this paper. Instead, we will provide a status update on the more recent changes, and show how the benchmark was used to measure and optimize performance on a large server.

2 Other Virtualization Benchmarks

Prior to TPCx–V, there have been 3 other industry-standard, virtualization-specific benchmarks: VMmark 2.x, SPECvirt_sc2013, and TPC–VMS.

The earliest virtualization-specific benchmark was VMware's VMmark [17]. In its latest version, VMmark 2.x has evolved into a multi-host data center virtualization benchmark that includes both application-level workloads and platform-level operations, such as guest VM deployment, dynamic virtual machine relocation (vMotion) and dynamic datastore relocation (storage vMotion). VMmark has a *tile* architecture. Each tile includes 6 workloads of set workload levels. The user is expected to keep adding tiles until the system reaches peak throughput.

SPEC's SPECvirt_sc2013 [11] is another server consolidation benchmark with a tile-based architecture. Each tile includes workloads from earlier SPEC benchmarks SPECweb2005, SPECjAppServer2004, SPECmail2008 and SPECINT2006.

Neither VMmark 2.x nor SPECvirt_sc2013 addressed database workloads, and had lightly-loaded VMs with little storage I/O demands. The first virtualization benchmark with a database workload was TPC's TPC–VMS benchmark [3]. Although TPC–VMS was adequate in emulating a simple server consolidation scenario, its shortcomings included having a single DBMS workload, a constant count of 3 VMs, and no variation in the level of the loads of VMs.

3 TPCx-V Benchmark

A TPC Subcommittee has been working on the development of the TPCx-V benchmark since 2010. The benchmark specification and the Express benchmark kit are nearly complete, and the development subcommittee is planning to submit the benchmark to the TPC General Council for final review and approval in August or November 2015.

3.1 Genesis of TPCx-V

The goal of TPCx–V is to measure how a virtualized server runs database workloads. It uses a database workload to measure the performance of virtualized platforms, notably the hypervisor, the server hardware, storage, and networking. To save development time, it relies on a prior TPC benchmark, in the same manner that SPECvirt_sc2013 used prior SPEC benchmarks as its workloads. The goal for TPCx–V was not to introduce a new database workload. The Subcommittee started out with the TPC–E [14] benchmark as the foundational workload for TPCx–V. However, the TPCx–V workload has evolved to be different from TPC–E in many ways. So comparing TPC–E results and TPCx–V results would be erroneous, as well as against the TPC policies.

Consult [1,2] for details of the TPCx–V architecture. The full functional specification of TPCx-V will be available when the benchmark is officially released.

3.2 TPCx-V Properties

The original design goals of TPCx–V were:

- Simulate cloud computing with:
  - A mix of On Line Transaction Processing (*OLTP*) and Decision Support Systems (*DSS*) workloads
  - Use databases of different sizes and load levels
  - Vary load levels to each VM to represent the elastic nature of load levels on cloud computing servers
- Devise a workload that stresses the virtualization layer and drives the state of the art for future hypervisor designs
- A Tiled architecture that requires more Tiles on larger servers
- But unlike earlier virtualization benchmarks, the load of TPCx–V Tiles is not constant: as in real world, larger servers run larger VMs, not just more VMs
- Improved ease of benchmarking compared to TPC–E. For example, the TPC–E schema makes it impossible to initially populate the database for one performance level, but run against a subset of the loaded data. TPCx–V schema has been updated to allow a benchmark sponsor to initially populate L_1 Load Units[1], but run against L_2 Load Unit, $L_2 < L_1$.
- Currently, the TPCx V kit is written to run on PostgreSQL. Future kit revisions may add the ability to use other databases.

3.2.1 Performance Metric
TPCx–V has a predefined mix of transactions that are used to simulate the business activity of processing a trade. The Trade-Result transactions make up 10 % of this mix. The Performance Metric reported by TPCx–V is *tpsV*, which is a "business throughput" measure of the number of completed Trade-Result transactions per second.

3.3 TPCx-V Architecture

3.3.1 Tiles, Groups, and VMs
The System Under Test (*SUT*) is divided into multiple Tiles. *Tile* is the unit of replication of TPCx–V configuration and load distribution. Each Tile consists of 4 *Groups*. A valid TPCx–V configuration may have between 1 and 6 Tiles, with all Tiles contributing identical proportions of the total load. The number of Tiles and the number of Load Units configured in the initial populations of the databases in each Group depend on the throughput, and are determined by a formula defined in the TPCx-V specification.

---

[1] A Load Unit represents 1,000 rows in the Customers table. The cardinalities of the other 32 tables are either fixed, or are proportional to the number of Customers.

Each Tile has four **Groups**, with Groups 1, 2, 3, and 4 contributing an *average* of 10 %, 20 %, 30 %, and 40 % of the total throughput of the Tile, respectively.

Each Group consists of one **Tier A Virtual Machine** and two transaction-specific **Tier B Virtual Machines**. So there are a total of 12 VMs in each Tile as seen in Fig. 1.

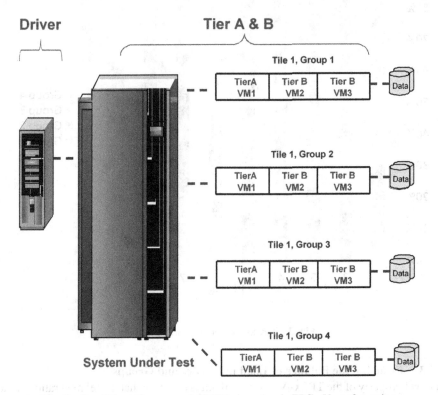

Fig. 1. One Tile, 4 Groups, and 12 VMs in a simple TPCx-V configuration

VM1 of each Group contains that Group's Tier A, which runs the business logic application, and has the *frames* code functions that issue the database transactions. VM1 does not contain a database. VM2 is the Tier B VM that holds the DSS database, and accepts the 2 storage load-heavy DSS transactions. VM3 is the Tier B VM that holds the OLTP database, and accepts the 9 CPU load-heavy OLTP transactions.

3.3.2   Elasticity

Each of the 4 Groups in a Tile contributes a different amount of that Tile's overall load. Although the total load offered by a Tile remains constant over the 10 12-minute **Phases** of a benchmark run, the distribution of that load over the 4 Groups varies greatly, as depicted in Fig. 2. This is done to better emulate the elasticity of the load offered by different tenants of a server in a data center in the cloud.

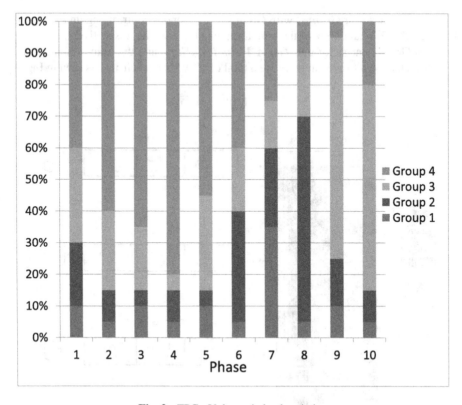

Fig. 2. TPCx-V dynamic load variation

3.3.3   Ensuring the Balance of Load over Tiles and Groups

A novel property of the TPCx–V benchmark kit is ensuring that the relative ratios of the loads offered to the Tiles and Groups conform to the specification requirements. Benchmarks typically vary the number of threads of execution in the benchmark driver to match the load level on the SUT. For example, if there are three Tiles, 1/3 of the driver threads would direct transactions to each of the three Tiles. The fundamental problem with this approach is that if one of the Tiles is too slow, it will fall behind the other two, and we won't have equal performance levels. Rebalancing the load offered to the Tiles is a complex, error-prone task. The TPCx–V benchmark avoids that complexity by having each driver thread distribute its transactions over all Tiles and Groups according to the specification requirements, implemented via a deck of cards algorithm. If three Tiles should receive equal loads, each thread uses a deck of cards with equal numbers of cards for all Tiles. If one Tile slows down, the driver thread will automatically issue transactions more slowly to *all* Tiles. Similarly, a deck of cards method is used to ensure each Group in a Tile receives the proper portion of that Tile's load. The Groups deck is changed at every Phase change. As a result, the benchmark kit is faithful to the ratios specified in the test configuration file to a very high level of precision.

4   TPC Express Benchmarks

The TPC has operated for many years with the same benchmark development and results submission process (TPC Enterprise). TPC Express represents a shift in aspects of the development process and the benchmark execution process. A central component of this shift is the TPC-provided benchmark kit.

4.1   Role of the Benchmarking Kit in the Express Benchmark

In the TPC Enterprise model, the TPC would develop a benchmark specification and it was up to the test sponsor to develop a compliant implementation. This is a non-trivial task. It requires expertise in a variety of areas including software development and performance tuning and optimization. Additionally, it requires a deep understanding of the benchmark specification and the complex subtleties of its many constraints. The net effect can be a prohibitively high bar for otherwise-would-be test sponsors.

TPC Express looks to minimize the cost of entry by utilizing a TPC-provided benchmark kit. With a TPC-provided kit there is no longer a need to carefully craft language to express all of the implementation requirements. There is no longer a need for the test sponsor to have an intimate knowledge of all of the benchmark constraints and their interrelationships. All of this can be captured and expressed cleanly and concisely in the form of code.

In addition to avoiding these complexities, a TPC-provided kit saves development time and costs on the test sponsor's part. This allows a test sponsor to get an environment up and running with less up-front investment. TPCx–HS [16] was the first Express benchmark released by the TPC, with 4 official results published so far.

4.1.1   Software Components of TPCx-V Benchmark Kit

The TPCx-V benchmark specification will be published when the TPC General Council approves the benchmark for official release, and will have a detailed description of the architecture and components of the TPCx-V benchmark kit. We will provide a brief description here.

There are five software components to the TPCx-V benchmark driver; four that are used to drive the workload and one to provide reporting functionality:

- **Prime client**: The prime client (vdriver.jar) is the benchmark execution controller. It coordinates and controls the behavior of the CE client(s), MEE clients(s) and Tier A SUT connectors through RMI connections to each.
- **CE client**: The client emulator (vce.jar) is responsible for emulating customers, requesting a service of the brokerage house, providing the necessary input for the requested service, etc.
- **MEE client**: The market exchange emulator (vmee.jar) is responsible for emulating the stock exchanges by providing services to the brokerage house, performing requested trades, providing market activity updates, etc.

- **Tier A SUT connector**: The Tier A SUT connector (vconnector.jar) receives the transaction requests from the CE and MEE clients and sends queries to its Tier B databases.
- **Reporter**: The reporter (reporter.jar) performs the self-validation checks against the transaction log data and (optionally) creates an executive summary report.

Figure 3 illustrates the four benchmark driver components and the communication paths between them. The RMI communication is used to control and coordinate benchmark runtime behavior while the actual benchmark transactions occur on separate network ports and/or hosts.

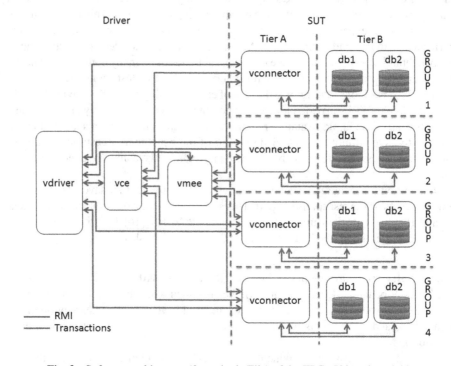

Fig. 3. Software architecture (for a single Tile) of the TPCx-V benchmark kit

4.2 Self-validation

In order to minimize the auditing requirements for this benchmark as well as to help the benchmark user more readily identify run validation errors prior to engaging in a benchmark result audit, the TPCx-V benchmark includes self-validation code in the reporter that checks as many of the validation requirements as possible. These validation checks include:

- **Sampling interval data**: The tpsV sampling data required to create the test run graph referenced in clause 6.8.2 of the benchmark specification

- **Input mix checks**: The input value mix requirements specified in clause 6.5.1 of the benchmark specification
- **Transaction mix checks**: The transaction mix requirements specified in clause 6.4.1 of the benchmark specification
- **Average response time checks**: Checks that the average response time for each type of transaction is not greater than the corresponding 90th % response time per clause 6.6.1.4 of the benchmark specification
- **Group measured throughput checks**: Checks that the Group measured throughput for each phase is between 98 % and 102 % of the expected throughput for that group per clause 6.8.1.3 of the benchmark specification

The reporter writes out a list of each of the validation checks performed and whether the benchmark result passed or failed that check.

4.3 Self-audit

One of the longstanding positive characteristics of all TPC benchmarks is the rigor that is applied in validating each implementation. Traditionally this is accomplished via independent third party review performed by TPC-Certified auditors.

The TPC Express model requires the use of a TPC-provided kit. As a result, all implementations now have much more in common. Thus it is feasible to include a set of tools with the kit that automate, or at least facilitate, some of the required audit tasks. Since the TPC-provided kit limits which DBMS may be used, tools have be written to facilitate many audit tasks related to the database.

- The database schema tool captures details of all user-defined types in every database.
- The cardinality tool captures the current cardinality of all TPCx-V tables in each database in the testbed. This data is used to validate the state of an initially populated database, the state of a database prior to any given test run, and it can be used as the basis for space calculations. Cardinality tests are run in parallel, and the outcomes are hierarchically rolled up from the individual database level up to the SUT level.
- The *atomicity* tool is used to validate that commit and rollback control operations are handled correctly by the DBMS.
- The database population rules and transaction profiles create a set of conditions that should always be true. The specification defines 3 separate conditions that are to be evaluated. The *consistency* tool is used to validate that these three conditions are met in all databases in the testbed.
- The TPCx-V specification defines *isolation* levels that must be maintained for each of the transactions in the workload. Furthermore, it defines three tests that must be performed to ensure that these required isolation levels are met. The tests purposely create conflicts between concurrently executing transactions and thereby show the ability to handle the conflicts correctly. The isolation tool implements the required tests, captures the necessary data, and reports whether the conditions were met.

5   Experimental Results with TPCx-V

To illustrate tuning with TPCx-V, we will use two examples: one that compares a non-varying load with TPCx-V's elastic load, and one that was run on an untuned configurations. First, let us briefly consider the configuration used for testing.

5.1   Testbed Configuration

5.1.1   Benchmark

For this set of experiments, we wanted to create as difficult a challenge for the virtualization platform as we could. So although the server would have normally had 1 or 2 Tiles based on its performance, we built a 5-Tile configuration with 60 VMs. We also loaded as many LUs as the disk drives had space for, which gave us a total of 800 LUs, divided into 5 Tiles of 160 LUs each, with each Group 1/2/3/4 having 16/32/48/64 LUs.

5.1.2   Hardware

- HP ProLiant DL580 G7
  - 4 Intel(R) Xeon(R) CPU E7- 4870 @ 2.40 GHz processors
  - 40 cores/80 threads
  - 512 GB of memory
- Two EMC VNX.5700 disk arrays:
  - Storage Processors with Intel Xeon Dual Core 5600 CPUs and 18 GB of memory
  - 72 SSDs for the tables of DSS VM2s, which have high IOPS requirements
  - 112 spinning 15K RPM drives for the tables of OLTP VM3s
  - 10 spinning 15K RPM drives for PostgreSQL redo logs

As we will see in Sect. 5.2, the key to optimizing performance for TPCx–V (and indeed, for a multi-tenant server in the cloud) is to spread the entire load equally across all the resources. When one tenant is hitting a peak, another one might be experiencing a low-load period, allowing the system resources to keep up with the demand. Following this policy, all the data from all the VMs were striped across all the disk drives.

5.1.3   Software

One of the benefits of virtualization is that a virtual computer can be abstracted as a *file*, and be moved or copied. A common use of this property is to package and distribute applications as self-contained virtual appliances. The TPCx–V subcommittee has created a downloadable VM template in the OVF [4] format with all the necessary software for the benchmark pre-loaded and pre-configured. Although the use of this template is not mandatory, using it greatly reduces the benchmark installation time.

The tests were run on VMware vSphere version 6.0, plus the following software stack required by the benchmark specification:

- Red Hat Enterprise Linux 7.1 (3.10.0-123)
- PostgreSQL 9.3

- unixODBC-2.3.1-10
- Java jdk1.7.0_71
- TPCx-V source code version 242 from the TPC subversion server

5.1.4   Virtual Machines

The 60 VMs were cloned from the OVF file described in Sect. 5.1.3. We used PowerCLI [17] scripts to customize each VM to have a different number of virtual CPUs and a different memory size. *vmdk* virtual disks were created in advance, and were added to Tier B database VMs using PowerCLI scripts.

5.2   Results

Valid TPCx–V test runs are 10-Phase, 2-hours runs. But we also ran 2 h without any Phase changes to have a baseline for investigating the effects of load elasticity.

To aid in locating the plotted graphs (Excel *series*) in the figures, the legend for each figure lists the series in the order that they appear at the leftmost portion of the figure.

5.2.1   Grouping VMs by Group or by Tile

To study the profile of individual components of the System Under test (SUT), throughput values can be calculated and plotted for each VM of each Group of each Tile. In our configuration, that would mean 60 such graphs. However, that is unnecessary. Recall from Sect. 3.3.3 that the benchmark kit guarantees that all 5 Tiles have the same throughput using a deck of cards method. The same is true for the 4 Groups of a Tile: the kit ensures that their offered loads and resulting throughputs conform exactly to the specified ratios. Similarly, the DSS and OLTP VMs will receive the proper ratio of transactions. So, if we have the overall throughput plot, adding the per-Tile throughput plots is not *interesting*: each is receiving exactly $1/5^{th}$ of the overall load. But grouping the results on a per-Group basis presents interesting results since each Group receives a different proportion of the load, which varies for the group from Phase to Phase.

5.2.2   Single Phase Results

For the single-Phase tests, the load contribution of Groups 1/2/3/4 remained constant at 10 % / 20 % / 30 % / 40 % as seen in Fig. 4. Although this avoids elasticity and is clearly not acceptable for publishing TPCx–V results, we ran this test to create a *baseline* to study the effects of elasticity. For Fig. 4, we have added the contributions from Group 1 s of all 5 Tiles together. We can see that these 5 Groups together contribute 10 % of the overall throughput. Groups 2, 3, and 4 similarly contribute 20 %, 30 %, and 40 %, respectively. Figure 5 shows that the sum of CPU utilizations of all 60 VMs, which averages to 5,777 %. The server has 40 cores/80 hyperthreads, and reports an average utilization of 73 % for each thread for a total of 5840 %. The small difference is due to some processing inside the hypervisor that is not recorded by the VMs. The overall I/O rate is 47K IOPS. When we add the CPU utilizations of all Group 1 VMs together, they amount to 550 %, around $1/10^{th}$ of the total as expected from these Groups contributing $1/10^{th}$ of the total throughput. Figure 7 shows a similar behavior for Groups 2–4.

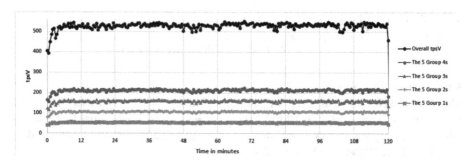

Fig. 4. Run without elasticity: throughputs of 5 Groups 1/2/3/4, summed over the 5 Tiles

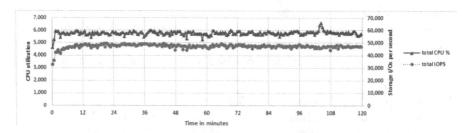

Fig. 5. Total CPU usages and I/O rates for run without elasticity

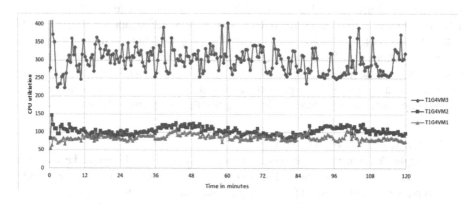

Fig. 6. CPU usage for 3 VMs of Tile 1 Group 1 for run without elasticity

Figure 6 shows the CPU utilizations of the 3 VMs of Tile 1, Group 1. Tier A VM1 has the lowest CPU utilization as expected. Tier B VM2 is also low in CPU utilization at around 20 % average. Tier B VM3 comes in at around 69 %. The situation is reversed for I/O where VM2 has 608 reads/sec and 84 writes/sec, whereas VM3 sees only 97 reads/sec and 140 writes/sec.

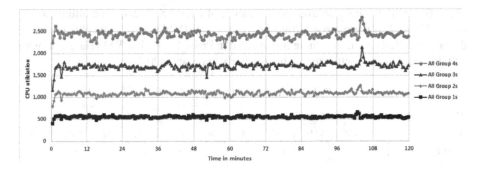

Fig. 7. CPU usage summed by Group for run without elasticity

5.3 10-Phase Results

For these runs, we allowed the kit to vary the load offered to each Group based on the elasticity requirements of the TPCx–V specification. We will study the effects of elasticity on performance by first reporting the result from runs on an early, unoptimized configuration. We will show how TPCx–V identified the source of a performance problem, and will demonstrate the effects of the optimization step.

5.3.1 Results on Unoptimized Configuration

In this early configuration, we had allocated the CPU counts listed in Table 1 for the 12 VMs of each Tile. The throughput of this run was 482 tpsV, which is 91 % of the single-phase throughput of the run in Sect. 5.2.2. This is a poor result since we want to showcase how well the virtualization platform can handle the cloud-like variations in load. To see the source of this performance drop, let us first consider the throughput curves in Fig. 8. We can see that the overall throughput stays over 500 tpsV until Phase 7, which starts at minute 72. At this point, when Groups numbered 1 in each Tile reach their peak demands, we have a slight drop in performance. The drop is more pronounced in Phase 8 when Groups numbered 2 reach their peak. We see in Table 1 that the CPU-heavy VM3 of Group 1 has 3 virtual CPUs. The CPU utilization graph of T1G1VM1 in

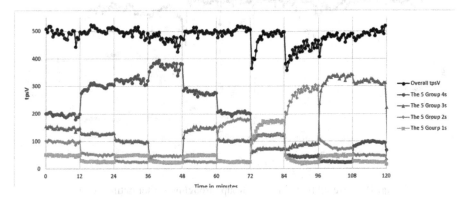

Fig. 8. Overall tpsV and per-Group throughputs

Fig. 9 (in yellow) shows an average utilization of over 200 % and even hitting 300 % during Phase 7. If there are any transient peaks, T1G1VM3 may not be able to satisfy the demand. The situation is more pronounced in Phase 8 for T1G2VM3 (in green) with 4 vCPUs and average utilizations that regularly approach 400 %.

Table 1. virtual CPU counts of VMs

Group	Group 1			Group 2			Group 3			Group 4		
VM	VM1	VM2	VM3	VM1	VM2	VM3	VM1	VM2	VM3	VM1	VM2	VM3
vCPUs	1	1	3	1	2	4	1	2	6	2	2	6

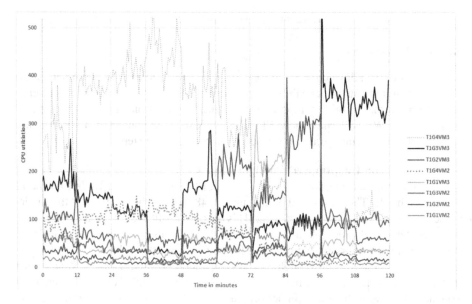

Fig. 9. CPU utilization of the 8 Tier B VMs of Tile 1 (Color figure online)

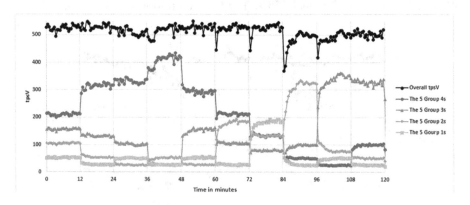

Fig. 10. Overall tpsV and per-Group throughputs after optimization

5.3.2   Optimized Results

We increased the virtual CPU count of VM3s in all Group 1s to 4 vCPUs, and VM3s in all Group 2s to 5 vCPUs, and repeated the experiment. Figure 11 shows that although there is a drop in throughput in Phases 8-10, it is not nearly as pronounced as in Fig. 9. In Fig. 11, we can see that T1G2VM3 can use more than 400 % of CPU time in Phase 8, so allocating 5 virtual CPUs to it ensured that it will always meet transient demand peaks, as did allocating 4 virtual CPUs to T1G1VM3.

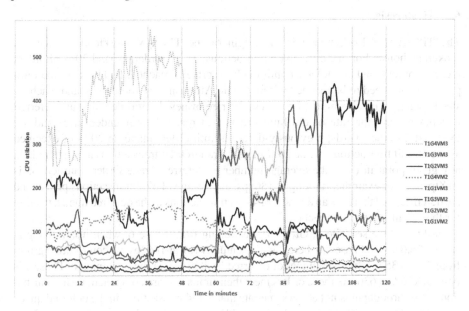

Fig. 11.   CPU utilization of the 8 Tier B VMs of Tile 1 after optimization

The throughput of this run was 512 tpsV, 6 % higher than the earlier run, and within 3 % of the run with no elasticity.

6   Performance Analysis of Results

6.1   Overcommitment and Elasticity

Optimizing a configuration for TPCx–V requires CPU *overcommitment*, a feature in wide usage in cloud environments. If we add up the CPU counts of all 60 VMs in the optimized case, we arrive at a total of 165. The server has only 80 hyperthreads. This is called overcommitment of CPU resources. We cannot expect to have all the VMs running at max utilization at once. However, allocating only enough virtual CPUs to handle the average load will leave the VM under-provisioned during its peak demand periods. So to optimize performance, we need to provision the virtual CPUs of each VM based on peak demand.

Overcommitment of virtual CPUs works well when the peak periods of one VM match up with the low periods of another VM (or the peak demand period of one tenant in a cloud server coincides with a low demand period of another). TPCx–V emulates this characteristic. We can see in Fig. 10 that the benchmark injects a nearly constant overall load, and as long as the virtualization platform is well-optimized, the server should be able to handle the load despite the wide variations of the load of each VM.

6.2   Hysteresis

The TPC-E workload, which is the origin of the TPCx–V workload, emulates a brokerage house. For one of its main transactions, Trade-Order, around 20 % of orders are *limit* orders, and are deferred until the limit price is reached. In TPCx–V, the limit price is guaranteed to be reached within 6 min. After running for a while and reaching steady state, an equilibrium exists where the rate of new limit orders that are deferred matches exactly the rate of old limit orders that reach their intended price and are executed. In other words, previously-deferred limit orders make up 20 % of executed Trade-Result transactions, while 20 % of new Trade-Order transactions are deferred. At any given point in time, the average number of deferred Trade-Order transactions is 24Xtps. So, for example, running at 186 tps, an average of 37.2 transactions per second are deferred; and there are an average of 4,464 transactions in the deferred queue, waiting for their limit price to be reached.

In Fig. 12 we see Tile 1, Group 1transitioning from Phase 6, when it is running at around 26.6 tps, to Phase 7, where it will eventually run at 186 tps. Its contribution grows from 5 % to 35 %. But the number of deferred limit orders at the beginning of Phase 7 is only 24X26.5 = 636. As these orders meet their limits and are completed, their contribution to the throughput is not at the same rate that 4,464 transactions in the deferred queue (corresponding to a 186 tps throughput) would have provided. Hence, we start at 122 tps, and it takes 6 min for all the limit orders from Phase 6 to be drained, before the Group runs at its steady state 186 tps for the next 6 min. The situation is reversed in the transition to Phase 8 where the Group wants to run at 26 tps again, but has a large backlog of 4,464 limit orders from Phase 7. It takes 6 min before throughput drops to the desired level.

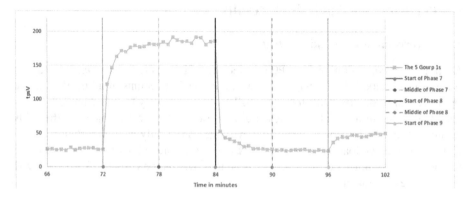

Fig. 12. Overall tpsV and per-Group throughputs after optimization

Although each Group has to deal with this hysteresis effect at every Phase transition, the too-high and too-low hysteresis effects of the various Groups should match up and cancel out, and the overall throughput should not be impacted if the SUT is well-optimized and the virtualization platform is efficient.

7 Future Work

Potential areas of future work with the TPCx-V benchmark involve expanding the database coverage of the benchmark and leveraging the workload and its characteristics to measure the performance of cloud and cloud infrastructure environments.

7.1 Database Coverage

Adding support to the TPCx-V kit for databases other than PostgreSQL would make the kit attractive to a wider audience. The use of the ODBC client API in the kit was a design choice to make it easier to add other databases. A logical next step would be to add support for the MySQL interface to the TPCx-V kit. Having this interface in the kit would immediately add support for many database environments such as MySQL, MariaDB, Percona, and others that support the MySQL interface. Having the ability to drive a TPCx-V load against these additional database environments would make the TPCx-V kit and benchmark interesting to individuals, academic institutions, and companies that are more familiar with these other database environments.

7.2 Cloud and Cloud Infrastructure

The TPCx-V workload and kit were designed to drive and measure the performance of multiple distinct database environments. The TPCx-V benchmark specification states that all these environments must be run on a single virtualized server. However, the usage of the TPCx-V kit could be expanded to measure the performance of environments where the Tiles/Groups/VMs can be placed on multiple servers, and the elasticity features of the benchmark can be used to measure the efficiency of the testbed in deploying and possibly migrating VMs and applications as the load changes and need arises. In other words, a better emulation of cloud data centers and cloud infrastructure. Also, since the TPCx-V kit does not inherently need to know the location or placement of the databases it is driving, the kit could be used to drive elastic database workloads in public cloud environments where the details of the underlying implementation are typically abstracted.

Acknowledgements. We thank Matt Emmerton, John Fowler, Karl Huppler, Matthew Lanken, Jamie Reding, Cecil Reames, Jignesh Shah, Wayne Smith, and Priya Sethuraman for contributing time and effort in the development of the TPCx-V benchmark. We are also grateful to the reviewers for their comments and corrections.

References

1. Bond, A., Kopczynski, G., Taheri, H.: Two firsts for the TPC: a benchmark to characterize databases virtualized in the cloud, and a publicly-available, complete end-to-end reference kit. In: Nambiar, R., Poess, M. (eds.) TPCTC 2012. LNCS, vol. 7755, pp. 34–50. Springer, Heidelberg (2013)

2. Bond, A., Johnson, D., Kopczynski, G., Taheri, H.: architecture and performance characteristics of a postgreSQL implementation of the TPC-E and TPC-V workloads. In: Nambiar, R., Poess, M. (eds.) TPCTC 2013. LNCS, vol. 8391, pp. 77–92. Springer, Heidelberg (2014)

3. Deehr, E., Fang, W.-Q., Reza Taheri, H., Yun, H.-F.: Performance analysis of database virtualization with the TPC-VMS benchmark. In: Nambiar, R., Poess, M. (eds.) TPCTC 2014. LNCS, vol. 8904, pp. 156–172. Springer, Heidelberg (2015)

4. Distributed Management Task Force: Open Virtualization Format Specification, Version 1.1.0, 01 December 2010

5. Figueiredo, R., Dinda, P.A., Fortes, J.A.B.: Guest editors' introduction: resource virtualization renaissance. Computer **38**(5), 28–31 (2005). http://www2.computer.org/portal/web/csdl/doi/10.1109/MC.2005.159

6. Nanda, S., Chiueh, T.-C.: A survey on virtualization technologies. Technical report ECSL-TR-179, SUNY at Stony Brook, February 2005. http://www.ecsl.cs.sunysb.edu/tr/TR179.pdf

7. Rosenblum, M., Garfinkel, T.: Virtual machine monitors: current technology and future trends. Computer **38**(5), 39–47 (2005)

8. Sethuraman, P., Reza Taheri, H.: TPC-V: a benchmark for evaluating the performance of database applications in virtual environments. In: Nambiar, R., Poess, M. (eds.) TPCTC 2010. LNCS, vol. 6417, pp. 121–135. Springer, Heidelberg (2011)

9. Smith, G.: PostgreSQL 9.0 High Performance. Packt Publishing, UK (2010)

10. SPECvirt_sc2010 benchmark info, SPEC Virtualization Committee. http://www.spec.org/virt_sc2010/

11. SPECvirt_sc2013 benchmark info, SPEC Virtualization Committee. http://www.spec.org/virt_sc2013/

12. VMware, Inc. http://www.vmware.com/products/vmmark/overview.html

13. IDC: Worldwide Virtual Machine 2013–2017 Forecast: Virtualization Buildout Continues Strong. http://www.idc.com/getdoc.jsp?containerId=242762

14. TPC: Detailed TPC-E Description. http://www.tpc.org/tpce/spec/TPCEDetailed.doc

15. TPC: TPC-VMS benchmark. http://www.tpc.org/tpcvms/default.asp

16. TPC: TPCx-HS benchmark. http://www.tpc.org/tpcx-hs/default.asp

17. VMware, Inc., PowerCLI documentation. https://www.vmware.com/support/developer/PowerCLI

18. VMware, Inc., VMmark 2.x. http://www.vmware.com/products/vmmark/overview.html

Author Index

Printed in the United States
By Bookmasters